Developing Integrated Programs

A Transdisciplinary Approach
for Early Intervention

Marcia Cain Coling, M.A.

Illustrations drawn under contract by
Charles Ortenblad III

**Therapy
Skill Builders™** ✱®
a division of
The Psychological Corporation
555 Academic Court
San Antonio, Texas 78204-2498
1-800-228-0752

Dedication

This book is dedicated to the memory of Timothy,
who didn't stay to see how it turned out, and to my two sons, Gene and Morgan,
who lobbied heavily to see their names in print and who also remind me constantly
what a remarkable adventure growing up can be.

About the Author

Marcia Cain Coling, M.A., received the degrees of master of arts and bachelor of science in special education from the University of Maryland. She also received a bachelor of arts in American studies from the University of Maryland. She is the author of *Psychological Assessment of Handicapped Children: A Guide for Parents* and has made several presentations in the eastern United States.

Ms. Coling is employed at the Child Development Center of Northern Virginia, where she is coordinator and infant educator for the homebound program for medically fragile infants, infant educator for two center-based parent-infant groups, and education specialist on an intake evaluation team for infant and preschool programs. She has held a number of positions in special education during the past 15 years, including classroom teacher for infants and children with a variety of developmental disabilities and infant educator and case manager with a home-based infant program.

Contents

Foreword

This book describes an approach to early intervention that represents an amalgam of ideas from a variety of fields, including occupational and physical therapy as well as education.

The ideas presented in this book are derived from my experiences working with several agencies in early intervention and other programs. I have also tried to incorporate some of the most promising approaches I have encountered in various workshops and through work with other professionals from various disciplines. What I present, I hope, is an outline for the core of an effective early intervention program. There are many components that could be added to this core program once it is working solidly.

An effective early intervention program could be based on many different models. In this book, I present one that I have participated in and found successful for a wide range of children. I hope that in sharing it, the lives of other children, their families, and the early interventionists who work with them will be similarly enriched.

Acknowledgments

I would like to thank coworker Jane Wolley for her critical and helpful comments on the speech-language sections and Deborah Falcigno for reviewing the manuscript from an administrative point of view.

I would also like to thank Cordelia H. Puttkammer, Angela Dusenbury, and Lorene Sherman for contributing significantly to the technical accuracy of the sections on neurodevelopmental treatment (NDT), sensory integration (SI), and speech-language therapy. Discussions with Suzanne Morris and Patricia Wilbarger helped clarify my presentation of their work, and I appreciate their generosity in sharing their time and ideas with me. My present coworkers have also contributed their ideas and support to this work, simply by being there and sharing the responsibilities of early intervention on a daily basis. Thanks also to the Technical Assistance Center #3, George Mason University, for the liberal use of their library facilities, expertise, and advice.

Finally, I want to thank my family and friends for putting up with me while I was writing this book.

Introduction

This book describes a sensorimotor approach to programming for infants and young children with developmental delays. It incorporates techniques based on the neurodevelopmental treatment approach (NDT) developed by Berta and Karel Bobath and techniques for the treatment of sensory integration dysfunction (SI) developed by A. Jean Ayres. It also incorporates an educational approach based on the work of Jean Piaget.

This approach is designed primarily for a center-based program, although the principles discussed are applicable to other models as well. The approach described constitutes a core developmental program. Once such a solid core has been established, other components may be added to enhance the quality of intervention provided by the program. Some of these components will be mentioned briefly in this book. However, it is essential that a solid core program be established first and that a program not undertake to incorporate too many changes or additions at any given time.

It is hoped that many of the concepts presented in this book will be helpful not only to the staff of center-based programs and the parents of the children there but also to other educators, therapists, and parents in providing intervention programs that facilitate development in infants and young children with handicapping conditions. This section will provide a brief introduction to the major theories on which the sensorimotor approach is based. Programming within the sensorimotor model will be discussed separately for speech, occupational, and physical therapies. Suggestions will also be pro-vided for blending these therapies with educational goals to provide a unified and comprehensive intervention plan for the classroom and the child.

The Sensorimotor Period

The period from birth to about two years has been described as the sensorimotor period not only by Piaget, but by others as well (for example, Bobath 1975). This is a good description because during this period almost all learning is based on what children process directly through the sensory and motor systems. Children are learning about the world by tasting, touching, smelling, listening to, and looking at everything they encounter. This is the sensory part of the sensorimotor period. At the same time children examine the world actively by shaking, hitting, throwing, banging, splashing, and otherwise manipulating various objects in it. Larger parts of the world can be explored through crawling, climbing, rolling, standing, walking, or other large motor movements. After mastering manipulation of individual parts of the world, children also combine different parts of the environment to learn more about them in relationship to each other. These actions are the motor part of the sensorimotor period. The sensorimotor period, then, is a time in which children are learning about the world primarily by using their sensory and motor systems to actively explore it. Learning during this period comes about primarily through doing things and observing the results. This kind of learning forms the foundation for all the rest of an individual's learning.

The process just described, of course, refers to normal development in typical children. But not all children are typical. Sometimes development proceeds differently. Children may be born blind or deaf or with a sensory integration dysfunction that makes processing certain kinds of sensory information difficult or impossible. Children may have conditions that limit the kinds of independent motor activities they can perform. Or development may follow the typical pathway, but at a much slower rate. Research has shown that young children who are developing differently from the norm still need to pass through the sensorimotor stage of development in order to establish a solid foundation for later learning (Connor, Williamson, and Siepp 1978; Dougherty and Moran 1983; Dunst and McWilliam, in preparation; Hupp, Able, and Conroy 1983a; Kahn 1983; Robinson and Robinson 1978). Early intervention, now mandated by an act of Congress (P.L. 99-457) for all children with developmental delays or who are at risk for developmental delays, must be designed to facilitate the child's active learning through the sensory and motor systems. That is what the sensorimotor approach to developmental programming is designed to do. An examination of the theories behind the three main program components—NDT, SI, and Piagetian theory—will help the interventionist understand why these components were selected, why the program works, and why these components are so important in any program for young children with developmental disabilities.

Neurodevelopmental Treatment Approach (NDT)

Neurodevelopmental treatment was originated by Dr. Karel Bobath, a physician, and his wife, Berta, a physiotherapist, in England in the 1940s (Campbell 1982). The approach was first developed to assist in the rehabilitation of adults with central nervous system damage resulting from head injury but was soon applied to the treatment of children with cerebral palsy (Bobath 1980; Bobath and Bobath 1952). The NDT approach, as it is now most commonly called, is a dynamic process that continues to be revised as its practitioners learn more about movement and the central nervous system. Practitioners are trained only by certified instructors in specialized courses. Therefore, relatively little current literature is available on the NDT approach (Campbell 1982).

While therapists, teachers, and parents can learn the fundamentals of this approach and can assist in a child's treatment under the direction of a qualified therapist, it is essential that a child with movement problems related to a central nervous system dysfunction be evaluated by a therapist familiar with NDT who will help plan and implement treatment goals and activities and who will be available to consult with the other members of the intervention team as needed.

The NDT approach is most useful for infants and children who have movement disorders as a result of damage to the central nervous system (Campbell 1982). Such disorders include cerebral palsy, various genetic syndromes such as Down syndrome, and a variety of other handicapping conditions, including encephalitis or psychomotor retardation, which result in multiple handicaps (Campbell 1982). Treatment is most effective before atypical movement patterns have become well established and before secondary complications such as contractures have developed, emphasizing again the importance of early intervention (Campbell 1982).

According to NDT theory, movement disorders are based on atypical postural tone, the inability to maintain normal postural stability against gravity, and the use of compensatory and atypical patterns of movement (Campbell 1982, 1984). The first step in intervention is an assessment of the posture and movement patterns used by the child and an analysis of the muscular components used to perform these patterns (Campbell 1984). The therapist should also evaluate the child's level of reflex development. Intervention is planned on the basis of each child's assessment results and consists of three components: preparation, facilitation, and inhibition. The following section will briefly discuss reflex development, postural tone, postural stability against gravity, and compensatory movement patterns. Some of the basic concepts involved in preparation, facilitation, and inhibition will then be presented.

REFLEX DEVELOPMENT

A reflex is a stereotyped movement or posture produced in response to a specific stimulus. A reflexive response is outside the individual's conscious control (Hanson and Harris 1986). Typical infants are born with certain reflexes, often referred to as "primitive reflexes," that are integrated into more mature, consciously controlled movement patterns over the course of the first few months of life. As the primitive reflexes become integrated, higher level reactions, such as equilibrium and head-righting reactions, begin to develop. These higher level reactions typically develop within the first two years (most emerge within the first year) and remain throughout life (Copeland and Kimmel 1989).

An assessment of a child's reflex development helps the therapist understand how mature the child's brain and central nervous system are. Babies who are born prematurely may not show some of the primitive reflexes because they are not mature enough to have developed them. In many such cases, the primitive reflexes may emerge later than would be expected with a baby born at full term. In other cases, the persistence of primitive reflexes after the time when they would typically have been integrated into more mature patterns may be an indication of damage to the central nervous system, as in children with cerebral palsy.

The persistence of primitive reflexes can contribute to a variety of movement problems. Reflexes are responses to specific stimuli, such as a head turn or touch to the cheek. Because the child cannot consciously control reflexes, the reflex may be activated each time the specific stimulus occurs. This can seriously interfere with normal, consciously controlled movement patterns. For example, the asymmetric tonic neck reflex (ATNR) is activated by a head turn to either side. The limbs on the side of the body to which the head turns extend (straighten) and the limbs on the other side of the body flex (bend). When a toddler who cannot consciously control the ATNR looks at a piece of banana placed to the child's right, the right arm automatically extends. The toddler may be able to pick up the banana in this way but will be unable to bring it to the mouth unless the child looks away from it, allowing the right arm to bend again.

There are many examples of how abnormal reflex development interferes with normal motor development. Each child's therapist will discuss the particular patterns that the child shows. NDT techniques discussed in the following sections and in chapter 2 may help the child accomplish movement tasks in spite of abnormal reflex development. For

more information on reflex development and testing and NDT and therapeutic activities that can be incorporated into the classroom, see the resource list in the appendix.

POSTURAL TONE

Postural tone has been defined as the amount of tension in the body's muscles (Campbell 1982). (Sometimes the term "muscle tone" is used similarly.) Tone will not be the same in all muscle groups at the same time, nor will it stay the same from one time to another. Tone changes in order to maintain body posture against gravity and to allow the performance of various motor activities (Campbell 1982).

In children with cerebral palsy and certain other conditions involving damage to the central nervous system, postural tone may be abnormal. There may be too much tension in the muscles to allow for free and easy movement, or there may be too little tension, so that movements are performed slowly and sluggishly. Sometimes the muscle tone may vary from too high to too low. Too much tension is referred to as high tone, or hypertonia. A group of NDT therapists in Switzerland who began to apply the Bobaths' techniques in their work with infants believe that most children with cerebral palsy begin with low tone and later develop high tone as a compensation for their underlying low tone (Campbell 1982; Kong 1966).

This idea illustrates that postural tone is not fixed but changes as a function of movement and activity. Postural tone is related to the contraction of muscles in response to sensory stimulation (Campbell 1982). All of those who work with children with cerebral palsy can attest to the fact that tone may change in response to temperature, excitement, distress, effort, and so on, as well as in response to specific movements that the child may be making (reaching, grasping, rolling, etc.) or experiencing (swinging, rocking, etc.).

One important part of an intervention program is to provide a graded level of sensory stimulation so that the child can produce as normal a movement response as possible (Campbell 1982). This means that the child is asked to perform only as much of a movement as can be performed using normal movement patterns. The therapist will assist with the rest of the movement using appropriate intervention techniques. As the child masters part of the movement, the therapist will gradually provide less assistance and ask the child to do more independently. But in each case, the situation is structured so that the child will be able to respond with an appropriate movement pattern. If the situation is too demanding, the child will resort to abnormal responses.

POSTURAL STABILITY AND COMPENSATORY MOVEMENT PATTERNS

All our movements (on Earth) occur against the influence of gravity (Ayres 1979; Campbell 1982). Normal newborn babies first learn to move primarily with the assistance of gravity, as when they turn their heads from midline to side when lying on their backs. Gradually, first through random efforts and then in more and more coordinated ways, infants learn to move against the influence of gravity. For example, they must work against gravity just to bring their hands together in front of them when they are lying on their backs. Once they can do this, they may reach up and bat at toys hanging over their heads. With increasingly better control, they begin to raise their heads, and later their upper bodies, off the ground when they are lying on their stomachs. Later, they learn to maintain a sitting posture and finally to stand and walk upright against the pull of gravity. These achievements come about as the child develops postural stability and balance (Ayres 1979; Campbell 1982).

Stability of the head, trunk, shoulders, hips, and pelvis allows for the coordinated movement of the limbs and head. Such stability comes about through the appropriate co-contraction of the muscle groups around the joint such that the joint is held stable while the other muscles remain free to move (Campbell 1982). For example, for the elbow to move freely, the shoulder must be stable. If, due to abnormal muscle tone, the child is unable to achieve such stability using normal patterns, the child frequently will use some sort of compensatory pattern instead. For example, to achieve stability in the shoulder girdle when there is inappropriate muscle co-contraction, the child may tip the head back to raise the shoulders (Campbell 1982).

Balance is maintained by changing muscle tone to adjust for changes in position (Campbell 1982). Balance and equilibrium reactions are automatic movement patterns that occur in response to changes in the relationship of the body's center of gravity to the force of gravity itself. Head-righting reactions are similar in that they are automatic responses to realign the body with the head when the body position is shifted (Campbell 1982). These automatic responses may occur in abnormal patterns when postural tone is abnormal or when there is other damage to the central nervous system.

COMPONENTS OF TREATMENT

Preparation. Preparation methods help to normalize tone and to establish appropriate cocontraction, joint alignment, and mobility. Preparation also includes attention to providing a stable and symmetrical base of support for further movement activities (Campbell 1982). Some specific guidelines will be provided in chapter 2 of this book, but again each child must be evaluated and a treatment plan developed by a therapist trained in these techniques.

Facilitation. Facilitation methods involve assisting the child in producing more normal patterns during active movement. It must be stressed that it is through the child's own active movements that new patterns can be learned. According to NDT theory, the child must experience what it is like to produce a normal or normalized movement pattern. (Normalized patterns are movement patterns that are facilitated to incorporate as many normal components as possible for the child.) Through repetition of these patterns during the child's own active movements, the child will come to internalize and use these patterns (Bobath 1975). Therefore facilitation does not involve passively "putting a child through" a movement pattern. Rather, it involves helping the child produce as normal as possible a pattern independently. More guidelines will be provided in chapter 2.

Inhibition. Inhibition methods decrease or prevent the use of atypical patterns of muscle contraction to produce postures or movements (Campbell 1982).

Positioning and Handling. Positioning and handling techniques are more static management approaches that all individuals working with children with cerebral palsy and other related movement disorders need to use. Positioning often requires the use of adaptive equipment to help the child maintain postures that facilitate more normal rather than atypical movement patterns. Handling techniques are methods for moving the child during regular daily activities. These methods help the child maintain more normal postures and movement patterns rather than reinforcing atypical ones (Campbell 1982). More guidelines on these methods will also be provided in chapter 2. Each child's NDT therapist is best equipped to provide specific suggestions to meet that individual child's needs.

SUMMARY

The NDT approach is based on the theory that movement disorders are based on atypical postural tone, the inability to maintain normal postural stability against gravity, and the use of compensatory and atypical patterns of movement. It is most useful for infants and children who have movement disorders as a result of damage to the central nervous system. Treatment is most effective when begun early, before the individual has developed a large repertoire of compensatory and abnormal postures and movement patterns. Treatment is based on facilitating the child's active movements through as normal a pattern as possible by providing a graded level of stimulation based on the child's abilities at any given time.

Sensory Integration (SI)

Sensory integration theory was originally developed by A. Jean Ayres, Ph.D., OTR, as an outgrowth of research she was conducting in southern California in the 1960s and 1970s. While working with school-aged children with learning disabilities, she observed behavioral patterns that she was able to relate to dysfunction within the neurological system. She continued to refine her ideas through much additional research, and numerous colleagues have elaborated on her work. Sensory integration theory is complex and requires specialized study to fully understand. Practitioners skilled in sensory integration theory and the evaluation and treatment of sensory integrative disorders are usually occupational therapists but sometimes may be physical therapists. The material presented in this book is not intended to provide the necessary background for full evaluation and treatment of a child with a sensory integration dysfunction. Rather, it is designed to give teachers, therapists, and parents a working knowledge of the most basic concepts behind sensory integration theory. In this way, interventionists may be better able to recognize a possible sensory integration dysfunction, make an appropriate referral for evaluation, and participate in a treatment plan under the supervision of a therapist trained in the evaluation and treatment of sensory integrative disorders.

Sensory integration is the ability of the brain to organize sensory input for use (Scardina 1986). In the earlier description of how children learn about the world through such sensations as taste, touch, sight, smell, and sound, two assumptions were made. The first assumption was that these sensations reached the central nervous system (CNS) through the sensory receptors and then through the spinal tracts. The second assumption was that the CNS organized and processed these incoming sensations appropriately. Treatment based on a sensory integration approach will not help the child's brain to receive sensory information if the sensory receptors are damaged. For example, if the child's eyes are not working properly, or the optic nerve that transmits visual sensations to the brain has been destroyed, the problem is not one of sensory integration dysfunction. A sensory integration dysfunction occurs when sensory receptors are working but the CNS is unable to organize and process sensory information in a functional way.

Before going further, it is important to define the kinds of sensory information we are talking about. In addition to the five senses of taste, touch, sight, smell, and sound, the brain also receives and processes sensory information about the body's position in space (sometimes called the vestibular sense), movement of the body and its various parts (kinesthetic and proprioceptive senses), temperature, pain, and pressure (Scardina 1986). Each of these sensations has its own special sensory organs that are responsive to that sensation and that transmit information about the sensation along specific nerve pathways to the brain. Some of these sensory systems develop prior to others and, like sensorimotor learning itself, form a foundation for the development and smooth functioning of other systems (Scardina 1986).

The vestibular, kinesthetic, proprioceptive, and tactile systems are the oldest of the body's sensory systems. Information processed through these systems affects learning and development in all other areas, including the learning of higher level skills such as language and social relationships (Ayres 1979; Scardina 1986; Wilbarger and Royeen 1987). Figure 1 (page 7) illustrates the sequence of skill development and the interrelationship of the various skills involved. Since an understanding of these systems is so basic to the theory of sensory integration, each will be discussed briefly.

VESTIBULAR SYSTEM

The receptors for the vestibular system are located in the inner ear. These receptors respond to sensory stimulation relating to gravity and to the movement of the body in space. The information obtained, when appropriately processed, is used to help maintain balance and normalize muscle tone. In addition, this sensory information plays a part in the development of control of eye movements, auditory processing skills, eye-hand coordination, visual-spatial skills, reading, and the ability to cope with stress and to control behavior. This information forms the basis for the individual's emotional development, social relationships, and sense of self (Ayres 1979; Scardina 1986).

Children whose nervous systems do not process information from the vestibular system adequately may develop a variety of different symptoms or behaviors, depending on the kind of processing dysfunction that is occurring. Some may have trouble balancing their bodies, which in very young children interferes with the development of motor and attention skills. Some may have difficulty coordinating eye and hand movements, which may result in a delay in the development of fine motor skills. Those who do not process information about gravity well may develop adequate motor skills but may also become very anxious and develop emotional problems as a result (Ayres 1979; Scardina 1986). Chapter 3 will discuss some behaviors that might indicate when a child is having difficulty processing vestibular information. Some suggestions for activities will also be provided, but any child suspected of having a sensory integration dysfunction should be evaluated by a therapist trained in the treatment of sensory integrative disorders, and all treatment activities should be carried out under the supervision of such a therapist.

KINESTHETIC/PROPRIOCEPTIVE SYSTEMS

The receptors for these systems are located in the muscles, joints, and tendons of the body. They respond to body movement and to the position of the body parts in relation to one another. The kinesthetic system is what helps a person be aware of body movements and be able to repeat them smoothly and without conscious effort. The kinesthetic system (with help from other systems, of course) enables the body to repeat the movements needed to throw a ball, skip, or hop or, on a more elementary level, walk or run without thinking the process through and learning each part of the movement each time. The proprioceptive system aids in this process by responding to pressure and movement in the joints so that the necessary adjustments can be made to lift a full cup of milk versus an empty cup, for example. Information from these systems is needed for the development of visual-spatial skills, body schema, motor planning skills, and overall motor development (Scardina 1986).

TACTILE SYSTEM

Touch receptors are located in the skin all over the body. The areas having the most touch receptors, which are therefore the most sensitive to tactile stimulation, are the lips and mouth, soles of the feet (especially the heels), face and head, genitals, and hands (especially fingertips). Touch receptors respond both to light touch and to deep touch or pressure. They respond in two different ways, for two different purposes. One response is protective, or defensive—one that sets off a fight-or-flight reaction in the body. This is the sort of response you might experience when you think you are walking alone down the street and suddenly someone puts a hand on your shoulder. The other response is used for learning—for tactile perception and discrimination. This is the sort of response you have when you are searching for a nickel in a pocket full of change.

Usually, the body switches off and on between these two kinds of tactile responses as the situation demands. Anyone in an unfamiliar or stressful situation will be more likely to have defensive responses to tactile stimulation. Almost everyone has had the experience of being alone in the house late at night and bumping into something in the dark. However familiar the object, the usual response is

FIGURE 1

A Hypothesized Sequence in Human Development Relating to Sensory Integration and Sensory Processing

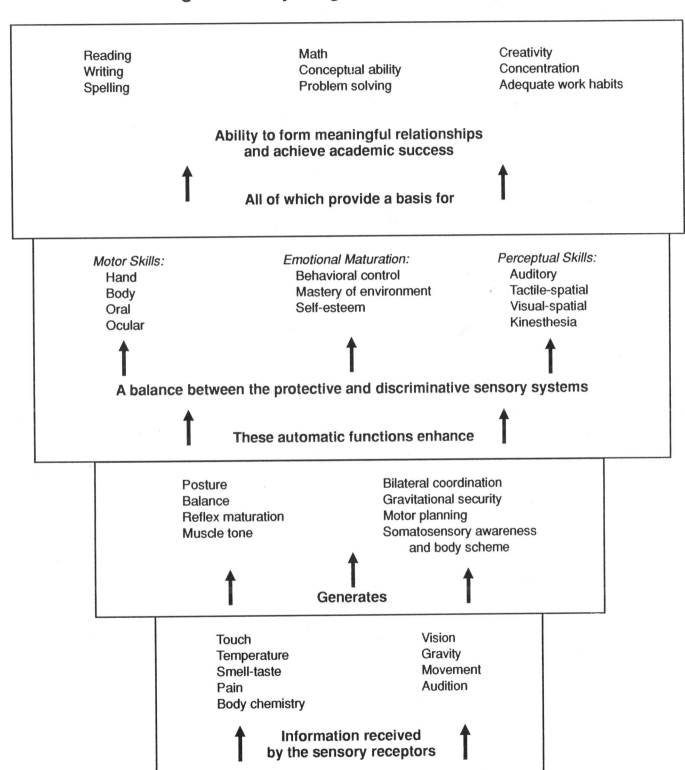

at least a startle, if not a muffled scream. Most people, too, have experienced how irritating the touch of bedclothes can be when they are sick and feverish. These are normal examples of increased defensive responses to tactile stimulation in stressful situations. Some children (and adults), however, seem to have increased defensive responses to tactile stimulation almost all of the time. This condition has often been called tactile defensiveness, although recently there has been a proposal to redefine it under the label of sensory affective disorder (Wilbarger and Royeen 1987).

Sensory affective disorders may have a variety of symptoms, depending on how severe the dysfunction is, whether it is combined with other sensory integrative dysfunctions, and if so, which ones. Because individuals with sensory affective disorders respond inappropriately to touch, they almost always have some impairment of social relationships and difficulties in emotional development. As infants, they may resist being held or cuddled. They may avoid contact with other people as they get older because such contact usually involves touch. They may appear to be unusually aggressive, hitting anyone who touches them, especially unexpectedly. Because there are so many touch receptors in the mouth, children with sensory affective disorders may develop feeding problems, avoiding certain tastes and textures. Children who are extremely sensitive may develop such severe feeding problems that they refuse to accept any solid food at all by mouth.

The ability to attend to a task is also affected by tactile hypersensitivity (Scardina 1986; Wilbarger and Royeen 1987). The child may be so irritated by the feel of clothing or the sensation of a chair pressing against the skin that it becomes impossible to focus on any other stimulus, such as the story the teacher is trying to read. A similar attention problem could result if a child is fearful of being touched by other children in the classroom. The list of possible behaviors and problems could go on and on. Chapter 3 will provide suggestions for activities to help children such as these respond more normally to tactile stimulation. Again, any child who is suspected of having a sensory affective disorder should be referred to a therapist trained in the evaluation and treatment of sensory integrative dysfunctions, and all treatment should be carried out under the supervision of such a therapist.

SUMMARY

Sensory integration, the ability of the brain to organize sensory input for use, turns sensation into perception and enables the individual to make sense of what is being experienced. Then the individual can make an adaptive response to the stimulation received. It is not enough simply to provide stimulation. As we have seen, the brain is not always able to organize such stimulation without some help. In an intervention program incorporating principles of sensory integration theory, stimulation should be controlled so that the individual has an opportunity to learn to make an adaptive response—a response that leads to learning, growth, and/or appropriate interactions. This means providing just the right experience at just the right time so that the child can respond appropriately. As the child masters the ability to respond at a particular level, more challenging experiences are presented. This technique of presenting what is often referred to as activities at graded levels of difficulty helps the child learn to produce similarly graded responses rather than the "all-or-nothing" responses a child with a sensory integration dysfunction typically produces. The child's appropriate responses guide the interventionist in deciding what activities to present to the child. As in the NDT approach, it is important that the child be an active participant in learning. The child's active responses enable the learning of new movement patterns and the strengthening of muscles. Passive movement will not accomplish these things.

Piagetian Theory

Jean Piaget was a Swiss psychologist who, from the 1930s to the 1970s, observed and worked with young children. His observations of how children's thinking develops have been very useful in planning appropriate educational programs and activities for children of all ages. Piaget was concerned mainly with the child's cognitive development—how children learn to think and how their thinking changes as they develop. Like the two theories already discussed, Piagetian theory is based on the idea of the child as an active learner. Piaget believed that individuals construct their own knowledge about the world based on their experiences in the world. He believed that individuals come to the same conclusions about basic concepts because those concepts are inherent in the experiences encountered (Gardner 1982).

Although the processes underlying cognitive learning aren't often discussed when talking about programming for young children with developmental delays, it is important to understand them and to keep them in mind when trying to understand where children are in their thinking. Piaget describes two related processes that he believed can explain how the child learns. The first of these is assimilation. When children first encounter something they will usually respond to the new thing in the same way that they have responded to other (similar) things in the past. The child is trying to relate the new experience to more familiar experiences. This process is assimilation. The second process Piaget describes is accommodation. Here children change their thinking (and behavior) to accommodate the new experience. For example, when a baby who has never been offered solid food is first given a spoonful of applesauce, the baby uses the process of assimilation to recognize that applesauce is something to be taken into the mouth and swallowed, just like milk. Most likely the baby will try to suck the applesauce off the spoon using the same kinds of mouth and tongue movements that have been used in the past for sucking milk from the breast or bottle. Soon, however, the baby accommodates to the applesauce experience by using different (and more effective) mouth and tongue movements to take the applesauce from the spoon.

Throughout the child's development, there will be phases during which assimilation is the primary developmental process. There will also be phases during which the primary developmental process is accommodation. When the two processes are equally balanced, Piaget would say that the child is in a phase of equilibrium. These three phases will alternate through various cycles of the child's development.

This book focuses on the developmental progression that would normally occur during the period from birth to about two years of age. Piaget (1952, 1954, 1962) has described six stages of development during this period. Brief descriptions of the characteristics of each stage follow. Intervention activities appropriate for each stage will be suggested in chapter 4.

STAGE 1:
USE OF REFLEXES

During this stage, the baby responds to experiences by using behavioral schemes that are already present at birth. These schemes include reflex activities such as rooting, grasping, and sucking; sensory capabilities such as visual fixation and auditory responsiveness; and motoric responses such as extension and flexion of the head, arms, legs, and trunk. At this stage, the baby's behaviors are made simply in response to something—a nipple, a bright light, a person's face. Without some type of stimulation, the baby does not use these inborn schemes. Piaget stresses that it is through frequent use that these schemes are developed so that they can be modified through the processes of assimilation and accommodation into the varied behaviors that children use to work and play in their world, and that in fact we all use to go about our daily lives.

STAGE 2:
PRIMARY CIRCULAR REACTIONS

During this stage, the infant develops the ability to coordinate two different schemes at the same time. Thus, it is now possible to look at mother while continuing to suck the milk or to listen to a voice while looking for the person speaking. The child is able to use schemes to bring about or to continue some events. For example, the sucking reflex, used at first only to get milk, can now be used to keep the thumb in the mouth. With primary circular reactions the infant is controlling its own body rather than objects or events in the larger world. Thumb sucking and hand watching are examples of primary circular reactions. These behaviors are called primary because they involve only the child.

STAGE 3:
SECONDARY CIRCULAR REACTIONS

When the child begins to use schemes to bring about or to continue actions from things or people in the larger world, the child is said to be using secondary circular reactions. Such behaviors are so named because they involve the child trying to get a second person to repeat a behavior or get an object to make the same movement or sound that the child has found interesting.

STAGE 4:
COORDINATION AND COMBINATION OF SECONDARY CIRCULAR REACTIONS

As the child's experience with the environment increases, the child begins to combine and coordinate secondary circular reactions to solve new problems. In most cases, one scheme is used as the means to get to the second scheme, which is the goal. For example, the child might use crawling as the means to get to a ball in order to roll it across the floor. Usually the child has planned to use one scheme as a means to get to the goal. This planning is referred to as intentionality. At Stage 3, the child did not plan ahead to shake the rattle in order to hear the noise but was able to repeat the action once it had occurred. At Stage 4, the child does plan goals before using behaviors to achieve them. Also at this stage the child develops the ability to use familiar schemes to try to solve problems in unfamiliar situations. A child who has been able to get toys that have been placed out of reach by pulling the support on which the toy has been placed (a tablecloth, for example, or perhaps the table itself) will use this means to try to reach a toy placed on a lazy Susan, rather than trying to spin the lazy Susan around to bring the toy within reach.

STAGE 5:
TERTIARY CIRCULAR REACTIONS

Behaviors at this stage have been described as actions modified by differentiated feedback (Uzgiris 1976). Piaget gave several different kinds of examples of Stage 5 behaviors. He described tertiary circular reactions as the child's repeated use of a particular scheme with variations. For example, the child who is playing with a ball by first dropping it from a height of four inches, then eight inches, then dropping it over the shoulder, then dropping it into a bowl, then dropping it onto a pillow is using a tertiary circular reaction. Piaget calls this kind of behavior an "experiment to see" (what happens). The Stage 5 child is fascinated by novelty for its own sake and will try out new behaviors to see what happens. At this stage the child will discover new means to accomplish familiar goals. The Stage 5 child will thus be able to solve the lazy Susan problem that baffled the Stage 4 child.

Research has also found that certain language and communication behaviors are related to Stage

5 development (see Coling 1979, for a review; also Bates et al. 1977; Ingram 1978; Morehead and Morehead 1974). While Piaget did not discuss these, they will be mentioned briefly here because they are so important to language development. Stage 5 is the stage when the child begins to interact with people and things at the same time (Trevarthen and Hubley 1978). Of course, parents have been playing with their children using toys for months, but it is only during Stage 5 that the children begin to be able to think about people as people and things as things at the same time. The child for the first time uses toys (or other objects) as a means to interact with people (by showing or giving the objects). In the same way, people are now used as the means for getting toys that are out of reach or for getting toys to work when the child cannot, as when the child looks at an adult and then points to a toy on a high shelf or hands a wind-up toy to an adult for winding.

STAGE 6:
SYMBOLIC REPRESENTATION

At this stage, the child begins to "think," or to represent ideas mentally, without needing to act in order to solve problems. The child is able to look at the toy placed out of reach on the shelf, look around the room for a stool to climb on, and get the toy without trying several other ways to reach the toy first. The child also starts to use words symbolically. This means that the child can now talk about a person or thing that is not there at the moment, without being reminded about the person or thing in some concrete way. For example, the child who is thirsty can simply say so, without first seeing a cup or hearing the sound of running water.

SUMMARY

More and more research is demonstrating the relationships between development in the cognitive, social, language, and motor areas. These relationships are easiest to see when they are grouped according to the stage of sensorimotor development they best represent. Examples of the most commonly cited representative behaviors from each stage of cognitive development are provided in figure 2 (page 12). For comparison, milestones that appear to correspond to these stages of cognitive development in the social-emotional area are included in figure 3 (page 13), while figure 4 (page 14) lists corresponding milestones from the language area. Although this work is still in the theoretical stages, it is useful to consider the possible relationships between development in the different domains when planning any type of early intervention program. The reader is referred to Coling (1987) for further discussion of the possible parallels between these developmental areas.

Both nonhandicapped and special needs children go through the stages of sensorimotor development outlined by Piaget (Connor, Williamson, and Siepp 1978; Dougherty and Moran 1983; Dunst and McWilliam, in preparation; Hupp, Able, and Conroy 1983a,b; Kahn 1983; Robinson and Robinson 1978). It is important to remember, though, that children with developmental delays may not pass through these stages within the same time frame as typical children. Also, no child, with or without a developmental delay or disability, would be expected to be functioning at the same stage of sensorimotor development for all categories of behaviors listed. Thus, a child might be functioning at Stage 4 for object permanence (the ability to remember and mentally represent an object when it is not in the child's sight) and at Stage 3 for vocal imitation. Such differences in performance are normal and to be expected. The reader is referred to Dunst (1980) for a more complete discussion of this phenomenon. It is important to remember that each child is different. No two children would be expected to have the exact same pattern of development. Nevertheless, Piagetian theory provides a useful description of the way in which a child's cognition develops during the first two years of life. Educators and parents can use this theory to better understand and explain why children do some of the things they do. Further, Piagetian theory helps educators predict which skills will develop next and plan activities that will facilitate such skill development.

The Three Theories in Summary

The three theories described here—NDT, SI, and Piagetian—are all applicable to the sensorimotor period of development. Further, they have a common fundamental thread—they all view learning as an active process in which children construct knowledge about their own bodies and about the world in which they live based on their direct actions and the responses received as a result of those actions. All three theories accept the premise that children's actions are based on the sensations they receive. All three also accept that the brain's organization and interpretation of these sensations (called perception) is an active process that can be modified by experience. Thus, any approach to intervention based on these three theories will be concerned with facilitating the child's active responses rather than with passively "putting the child through" activities.

Further, key to all three theories is the idea that providing appropriate stimuli that result in graded responses facilitates learning. The mere provision of stimuli without consideration of the child's level of ability to respond actively and appropriately is ineffective and may interfere with learning by facilitating or reinforcing inappropriate responses. Activities should be provided at the child's functioning level. The level of task difficulty should be gradually increased to facilitate the development of the next appropriate response level through the child's active participation in the activities. The child gradually learns new behavior patterns, cognitive or motor, through active participation and repetition over time. Careful assessment of the child's level of ability to respond appropriately to various stimuli and situations will indicate what activities to provide. The next chapter discusses some considerations for assessment within an intervention program for infants and young children.

FIGURE 2

Selected Characteristics of the Attainments of the Sensorimotor Period

Domains of Sensorimotor Development

Stages (Ages in Months)	Purposeful Problem Solving	Object Permanence	Spatial Relationships	Causality	Vocal Imitation	Gestural Imitation	Play
1 Use of Reflexes (0 - 1)	Shows only reflexive reactions to external stimuli.	No active search for objects vanishing from sight.	No signs of appreciation of spatial relationships between objects.	No signs of understanding causal relationships.	Vocal contagion: Cries upon hearing another infant cry.	No signs of imitation of movements.	No signs of intentional play behavior.
2 Primary Circular Reactions (1-4)	Adaptations first acquired: coordination of two behavioral schemes (for example, hand-mouth coordination).	Attempts to maintain visual contact with objects moving outside the visual field.	Reacts to external stimuli as representing independent spatial fields (visual, auditory, etc.) rather than as a spatial nexus.	Shows signs of pre-causal understanding (for example, places thumb in the mouth to suck on it).	Repeats sound just produced following adult imitation of the sound.	Repeats movements just made following adult imitation of the action.	Produces primary circular reactions repeatedly in an enjoyable manner.
3 Secondary Circular Reactions (4-8)	Procedures for making interesting sights last: repeats actions to maintain the reinforcing consequences produced by the action.	Reinstates visual contact with objects by (a) anticipating the terminal position of a moving object, and (b) removing a cloth placed over his/her face; retrieves a partially hidden object.	Shows signs of understanding relationships between self and external events (for example, follows trajectory of rapidly falling objects).	Uses "phenomenalistic procedures" (for example, generalized excitement) as a causal action to have an adult repeat an interesting spectacle.	Imitates sounds already in his/her repertoire.	Imitates simple gestures already in his/her repertoire, which are visible to him/her.	Repeats interesting actions applied to familiar objects.
4 Coordination of Secondary Circular Reactions (8-12)	Serializes two heretofore separate behaviors in goal-directed sequences.	Secures objects seen hidden under, behind, etc., a single barrier.	Rotates and examines objects with signs of appreciation of their three-dimensional attributes: size, shape, weight, etc.	Touches adult's hands to have that person instigate or continue an interesting game or action.	Imitates novel sounds but only ones similar to those he/she already produces.	Imitates (a) invisible movements made by self (for example, sticking out the tongue), and (b) novel movements composed of actions familiar to him/her.	During problemsolving sequences, abandons the terminus in favor of playing with the means. Ritualization: applies appropriate social actions to different objects.
5 Tertiary Circular Reactions (12-18)	Discovers "novel" means behavior needed to obtain a desired goal.	Secures objects hidden through a series of visible displacements.	Combines and relates objects in different spatial configurations (for example, places blocks into a cup).	Hands an object to an adult to have that person repeat or instigate a desired action.	Imitates novel sound patterns and words he/she has not previously heard.	Imitates novel movements he/she cannot see self perform (for example, invisible gestures) and has not previously performed.	Adaptive play: begins to use one object (for example, doll's cup) as a substitute for another (for example, adult-sized cup) during play with objects.
6 Representation and Foresight (18-24)	"Invents" means behavior, via internal thought processes, needed to obtain a desired goal.	Recreates sequence of displacements to secure objects: secures objects hidden through a sequence of invisible displacements.	Manifests the ability to "represent" the nature of spatial relationships existing between objects, and between objects and him/herself.	Shows capacity to (a) infer a cause, given only its effect, and (b) foresee an effect, given a cause.	Imitates complex verbalizations. Reproduces previously heard sounds and words from memory: deferred imitation.	Imitates complex motor movements. Reproduces previously observed actions from memory: deferred imitation.	Symbolic play: uses one object as a "signifier" for another (for example, a box for a doll bed). Symbolically enacts an event without having ordinarily used objects present.

Source: Dunst, C. J. 1981. *Infant learning: A cognitive-linguistic intervention strategy.* Allen, TX: DLM Teaching Resources. Reprinted by permission.

FIGURE 3

Selected Characteristics of the Attainments of the Sensorimotor Period

Domains of Social-Emotional Development

Stages (Ages in Months)	Attachment	Social Play	Affective/Emotional Development	Self-Recognition	Person Permanence	Reciprocity
1 Use of Reflexes (0-1)	Reflexive crying, rooting, sucking; postural adjustment for feeding; differential response to human voice, human face, eye contact.	Reflexive smiling; eye contact, visual fixation and following; differential response to human voice; early nondistress vocalizations; response to sound.	Generalized excitement in response to stimulation; reflexive smiling; startle response to pain; generalized distress response to discomfort or physical restraint.	Visual accommodations; response to tactile stimulation; response to sound.	Visual fixation; auditory accommodations.	Burst-pause cycle present during sucking; eye contact.
2 Primary Circular Reactions/Recognitory Assimilation (1-4)	Differential response to specific people (usually caregivers).	Differential response to familiar people; gaze-alternation cycle during dyadic interaction; visual regard of peers.	Disgust; delight; social smile (in response to familiar people); rage; obligatory attention to unfamiliar stimuli; wariness.	Sober staring at mirror, little sustained interest; differentiation of self from other; response to mirror image of mother.	Follows face through 180-degree arc; glance lingers at point where face disappeared.	Attention-withdrawal cycles during interactions both with people and with objects.
3 Secondary Circular Reactions (4-8)	Participates in contingency games with caregiver; shows preference for familiar versus unfamiliar people.	Participates in contingency games with caregiver; looks at and touches peer.	Active laughter in response to social games; interest; excitement; joy; anger; fear.	Responds to mirror image as if to another infant.	Attempts to regain visual contact with vanished person; touches barrier or exposed portion of partially hidden person.	Participates in contingency games; coordinated exchange of objects with caregiver.
4 Coordination of Secondary Circular Reactions/Intentionality (8-12)	Follows departing mother; greets returning mother; uses mother as a secure base from which to explore; uses primarily signaling to maintain proximity; other differential responses to mother.	Touches adult's hand to continue game; approaches and follows a peer; plays chase and peek-a-boo games with peer; shows socially appropriate play with objects; give-and-take games; "games with a script."	Fear; elation; anxiety.	Repetitive behavior while observing mirror image; reaches correctly for real object upon viewing mirror image.	Locates person seen hidden by a single barrier.	Participates in complex games, "games with a script"; initiates interactions; returns signs of affection; repeats performance in response to adult laughter; reciprocal exchanges involving objects; gives and takes on request.
5 Tertiary Circular Reactions/Behavior Modified by Differential Feedback (12-18)	Uses approach to maintain proximity.	Takes active-agent role in games; playful imitative games; triadic interactions.	Affection for others; practicing for mastery of environment; angry mood, petulance appear.	Coy behavior to mirror image; searches for mirror image; touches mark on own face in response to mirror image; turns in response to videotape of self approached from behind; differential response to photograph of self versus others.	Locates person seen hidden through a series of barriers; locates a person following a single invisible displacement.	Social imitation of peers; "conversations" with peers; emergence of reciprocal mode; rolls ball back and forth with partner; uses gestures to communicate; task-centered exchanges; triadic interaction.
6 Symbolic Representation (18-24)	Decline in proximity-seeking; ability to establish contact through "conceptual-symbolic" means.	Playful interactions with language; imitative games; use of one object to represent another.	Differential affection; shame; defiance; positive self-evaluation; jealousy; rudimentary guilt; self-representation.	Spontaneous use of own name or appropriate person pronoun in response to mirror image or photograph of self.	Locates person hidden through a series of invisible displacements.	Uses language to request interactions; engages in dialogue with adult using words and action.

FIGURE 4

Selected Characteristics of the Attainments of the Sensorimotor Period

Domains of Language Development

Stages (Age in Months)	Receptive Language	Vocal Expression	Nonvocal Expression
1 Use of Reflexes (0-1)	Shows reflexive response to sound; can differentiate among auditory stimuli; shows preference for human features.	Shows only reflexive crying, a few "comfort sounds," in response to bodily state.	Momentary gaze focused on adult or object. Individual sucking and rooting patterns.
2 Primary Circular Reactions (1-4)	Shows differential response to pleasant versus angry voices, familiar versus unfamiliar patterns of caretaking.	Develops differentiated crying; also cries in response to other than bodily state; laughs in response to pleasant stimuli; babbles (vocal play—makes sounds for the enjoyment of it).	Smiles in response to pleasant sensations, familiar stimuli; shows anticipatory behaviors such as adjustment of head/body when held in nursing position.
3 Secondary Circular Reactions (4-8)	Demonstrates recognition of familiar objects; attends selectively to familiar words/voices.	Repetitive syllable chains appear in babbling; intonations of adult speech added to babbling sounds; makes "call sounds" in attempting to obtain an object that is out of reach.	Generalized excitement (arm waving, bouncing, etc.) to cause continuation of a game; straining towards an object that is out of reach.
4 Coordination of Secondary Circular Reactions (8-12)	Shows comprehension of basic words ("no-no," name); responds appropriately in ritualized sequences ("wave bye-bye," "show me your belly button"); anticipates events (mother's putting on coat means mother is leaving).	Wordlike syllables (ma-ma, da-da) common; attempts to name familiar object on sight, with approximation of words; word forms appear in imitation of adult speech; echolalia added to babbling.	Manipulates adult's hand to cause continuation of a game; uses some form of locomotion to approach or withdraw from objects, persons; points to object without looking at person; tugs at person, holds up arms to be picked up.
5 Tertiary Circular Reactions (12-18)	Recognizes names of familiar people, objects present; follows simple commands ("give it to me").	First uses conventional words, refers to objects or people present; jargon used to communicate needs, wants, also for vocal play.	Uses objects to obtain adult attention (gives, shows); uses persons to obtain objects (points at object while looking back to person, pushes or pulls person to new location, hands toy to adult to have it activated).
6 Representation and Foresight (18-24)	Comprehends names of familiar objects, people in their absence.	Uses conventional words to obtain goals, in absence of referent; begins use of two-word sentences expressing relationships.	Symbolic play (uses one object to represent another); uses motor symbols (opens mouth to represent actions—opening box).

CHAPTER 1

Assessment

Assessment serves a number of different purposes—to identify the existence of a handicapping condition, to determine a child's eligibility for a particular program, to identify a child's strengths and needs in order to plan an appropriate educational program, to determine a child's rate of progress in an educational program, and to determine how well an intervention program is meeting the needs of the children and families it serves (Horowitz 1982). There are probably other reasons for assessment as well (see Fewell 1983a). This chapter will describe some approaches to each type of assessment listed above, but its main focus will be on assessment for program planning and evaluation of individual progress. Figure 5 (page 16) provides a flow chart of various steps in the assessment process. These will be discussed in order of occurrence, insofar as it is possible to do so. Before proceeding with that discussion, some further comments about evaluation to determine eligibility for services are in order.

Determination of Eligibility for Services

Where services for infants and young children are provided by state agencies under P.L. 93-142 or P.L. 99-457, an evaluation is used to determine whether the child is eligible for services under the guidelines of that state or jurisdiction. At present, criteria for eligibility vary widely, even among programs within a single jurisdiction (Hutinger 1988). The specific types of evaluations used depend on the criteria of the jurisdictions and agencies involved. They usually include some type of standardized assessment of the child's developmental functioning. If the program is following the guidelines established in P.L. 99-457, an evaluation of the family's needs in relation to the child will be included as well. Where services are provided by state agencies, the local jurisdiction usually determines an appropriate placement for the child, and the agency providing the services does not have to evaluate the child to determine whether its services are appropriate for that child. In other situations, the agencies themselves may have to evaluate the child to decide whether their services are appropriate and if not, to identify a more appropriate agency or intervention strategy.

Screening

Screening procedures are used to determine whether a child is at risk for a particular condition (Hutinger 1988). If the results of a screening test indicate that a child is at risk for, or may have, a particular condition, further evaluation is usually necessary to determine whether the child actually has the condition. Almost everyone is familiar with the screening test used to test newborn infants for phenylketonuria (PKU) (Bagnato and Neisworth 1987). The Apgar Scores (Apgar 1953) given at birth can be used as a screening test to indicate possible risk factors associated with disabilities that may show up as the baby gets older, as can the Dubowitz

FIGURE 5

A System of Identification Processes and Services
for Families of Handicapped and At-Risk Children under Three
Eligible for Early Intervention Services

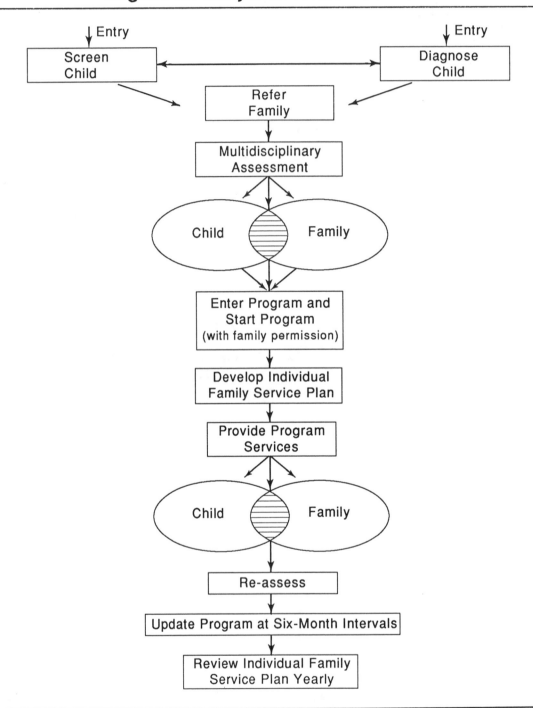

Source: Adapted from Hutinger, Patricia L. 1988. Linking screening, identification, and assessment with curriculum. In *Early childhood special education: Birth to three,* edited by J. B. Jordan, J. J. Gallagher, P. L. Hutinger, and M. B. Karnes. Reston, VA: Council for Exceptional Children. Used by permission.

Scale (Dubowitz, Dubowitz, and Goldberg 1970). The Denver Developmental Screening Test (Frankenburg 1978) has been widely used to screen for developmental disabilities in pediatricians' offices, clinics, and the like (Fewell 1983a; Horowitz 1982). In some ways, frequent well-baby visits to a pediatrician serve as a way of screening for possible developmental problems. Hutinger (1988) stresses that children with a diagnosed handicapping condition should not be screened but should move directly to the initial evaluation phase of the assessment process.

Diagnosis

Once a child has been identified as being at risk for some type of developmental disability, either through use of a screening test or, more usually, through the parents' concern about the child's progress, a more complete evaluation is needed to determine the degree of risk involved. For example, a child showing motor delays of two months at age six months is at risk for developmental disability. A diagnostic evaluation by a developmental pediatrician might reveal indications of cerebral palsy. At birth, a child might have signs of Down syndrome. This condition could be officially diagnosed only after a more thorough evaluation, including genetic testing. It must be emphasized that the diagnostic process relates to the child's medical condition and is carried out primarily by medical professionals (Hutinger 1988).

The diagnosis of a condition such as cerebral palsy or Down syndrome indicates the need for early intervention services. The degree of risk present in some factors identified through the screening process (for example, home environment factors) may not be evaluated more completely until the child is referred to an early intervention program and goes through the initial evaluation process.

Another function of a diagnostic evaluation can be to identify the presence of any medical conditions that would require special consideration in an early intervention program. Children with AIDS and ARC (AIDS-related complex) or who test positive for HIV without showing symptoms of disease may not be accepted into the usual early intervention programs because of concern about exposing staff and other highly vulnerable children

to the virus. Women of childbearing age are often reluctant to work with children testing positive for cytomegalic virus (CMV) or toxoplasmosis virus. Children with seizure disorders may require special handling, as do children with a variety of other medical conditions. It is important for the well-being of all children and the staff who serve them that medical conditions that might affect the children's program placement or intervention plan be identified as soon as possible, and that these children come into an early intervention program with clear instructions on managing their medical needs appropriately.

Screening and diagnosis are the initial steps in the assessment process. Before proceeding to a description of the more in-depth team evaluation, a discussion of issues relating to the evaluation of young children is in order.

Issues in the Evaluation of Young Children

Assessment instruments commonly used to evaluate the development of young children proceed from several different philosophical bases, and it is important that the instruments selected reflect, insofar as possible, the philosophical orientation of the intervention program (Fewell 1983a; Bagnato and Neisworth 1987).

There are four commonly used approaches to the overall evaluation of development (Fewell 1983a; Bagnato and Neisworth 1987). These include a developmental approach, such as seen in the Gesell Developmental Schedules (Knobloch and Pasamanick 1974) and the Bayley Scales of Infant Development (Bayley 1969). This approach, also referred to as norm-referenced assessment (Bagnato and Neisworth 1987), is based on a sample of behaviors that occur in the different domains of normal development, in the order in which they normally occur. There is no assumption that the skills assessed are necessarily linked or dependent on one another (Bagnato and Neisworth 1987). This type of evaluation compares the child's behaviors with the behaviors of groups of children with no identified disabilities.

Another approach is the developmental process approach (Bagnato and Neisworth 1987) or cognitive stages approach (Fewell 1983a), exemplified by Uzgiris and Hunt's (1975) Infant Psychological Development Scale based on the theories of Piaget. This approach assumes that the skills assessed in each domain develop ordinally. That is, the development of higher level skills is dependent on the emergence of the lower level skills. Because this approach is based on a theory that relates the various skills assessed to one another, it lends itself more readily to curriculum development and program planning than does the developmental approach described above.

An adaptive transactive (Fewell 1983a) or interactive (Bagnato and Neisworth 1987) approach may also be used, although this is less common. Examples of this type of approach include the Brazelton Neonatal Behavioral Assessment Scale (Brazelton 1973) and various experimental measures such as the Cicchetti and Sroufe (1978) procedures, the Infant Temperament Questionnaire (Carey and McDevitt 1977, 1978), or the Nursing Child Scales (Barnard 1979). Such an approach is based on the child's interactions with people and objects in the environment and focuses on how the child adapts behavior as well as on simply what behaviors the child has developed.

Finally, a behavioral, or criterion-referenced, approach may be used. Examples include the Brigance Diagnostic Inventory of Early Development (Brigance 1978) and the Uniform Performance Assessment System (White et al. 1981). These instruments compare children only with their own performance and are often used as the basis for planning intervention goals. Unlike the developmental process approach, however, there is no underlying theoretical basis for relating the various assessed behaviors to one another. Behaviors similar to those assessed using the developmental approach are selected and used to develop a curriculum, but the children are not compared to any normative group.

The evaluation of infants and young children is a controversial issue, particularly in the cognitive area. Tests of infant "intelligence" do not correlate well with tests of "intelligence" at later ages (Holden 1972). One explanation for this phenomenon is that infant intelligence is qualitatively different from what has been viewed as intelligence in older children and adults (McCall, Hogarty, and Hurlburt 1972). A related explanation is that infant intelli-

gence tests contain many items that require motor skill as well as problem-solving ability in order to pass successfully, thus penalizing the child with motor deficits (Copeland and Kimmell 1989; Fewell 1983a). Furthermore, since problem-solving abilities develop through the child's active manipulation of the environment, the child who is less able to actively manipulate the environment will be slower to develop problem-solving skills, even though the potential to do so may be adequate.

Evaluation results may be influenced by many factors, including the time of day, the child's state, rapport with members of the evaluation team, previous experiences, attitudes of the caregivers, and so on. Figure 6 identifies several categories of variables that can influence a child's performance during an evaluation. Thus, particularly in the cognitive, social, and language areas, results may indicate only the child's minimum skill level. For this reason it is important to get as clear a picture as possible of the child's typical behavior in a familiar environment. The child who is silent throughout the evaluation session but begins to chatter happily to a parent once they are out on the sidewalk has different needs from the child who uses no words in any situation.

Another danger in using standardized measures of developmental function is that the child's family and intervention team may adjust their expectations, sometimes inappropriately, around test results (Zelazo 1982). Thus, if test scores indicate that a two-year-old child is functioning like a one-year-old child in cognitive development, the adults involved may begin to treat the child too much like a one-year-old and fail to provide experiences that would help the child grow beyond the one-year functioning level. In the opposite situation, a two-and-a-half-year-old might show only a three-month delay in cognitive development on a standardized test, yet show many signs of processing problems and poorly developed play skills that would indicate more serious learning problems than the test results would seem to support. Yet because these problem areas were not represented in the standardized test, the child's parents could justify ignoring them.

The child with physical disabilities is most at risk for having cognitive and language skills underestimated. Because so many of the behaviors used to assess cognitive function in infants and young children are also based on motor performance,

FIGURE 6

Variables Affecting Evaluation Performance

Child Variables	Situational Variables
1. The child's state of hunger, fatigue, illness, stress level, and so on, affect overall performance.	1. The child's positioning affects task difficulty.
2. The child's attention span can affect overall performance, especially on repeat items or items toward the end of the session.	2. The position of test items or materials can affect task difficulty.
3. The child's temperament can influence responses during the evaluation. Such factors as distractibility, activity level, persistence, intensity level, and approach/withdrawal patterns are included with temperament.	3. The size of test materials can influence the child's responses. For example, the child may not see a small item or may not be able to grasp a large item.
4. The child's previous experiences with test materials or tasks, or with unfamiliar people and/or settings, may influence the child's performance.	4. The color of test items may influence results. Too many colors or colors that are too bright may distract the child from the task. Lack of contrast between items or between items and surfaces may prevent the child from seeing the materials.
5. The child's preference for certain types of items or interactions, sensory modalities, etc., can influence the child's performance.	5. The physical surroundings can affect the child's performance. Too much furniture, too many toys, novel equipment, noise, excess movement in the room, too hot or cold a temperature, and so on, can all distract the child from a task.
6. The child's ability to cope with unfamiliar situations can influence the child's performance. This sometimes includes the child's ability to organize and calm himself or herself after an upset.	6. The order in which test items are presented can affect the child's performance. Items that are too difficult or that the child finds unpleasant presented early in a session can result in negative behavior or refusal to cooperate with further testing. Gross motor activities often need to be presented later in the session when the child has become tired of sitting.
	7. The facility with which items are presented can influence the child's performance. Items need to be presented in rapid succession to maintain the child's interest. If the child has to wait with nothing to do between items, negative behavior is almost certain to occur.
	8. Lighting can be a critical factor, especially for a child with a visual impairment. Light shining in the child's eyes, dim lighting, or light that casts a lot of shadows can interfere with a child's ability to see test materials and/or to focus on them and/or visually attend to them for any length of time.

children with motor disabilities often have few ways to express their understanding, especially when their motor impairments affect their ability to speak. Often, their chief means of expression may be through difficult behavior. Such children may cry a lot, especially if left with strangers. They may be irritable and demanding as a way to get and maintain attention and alleviate boredom, since their motor impairments may severely limit their ability to play independently. They may also develop noncompliant behaviors as a way of controlling and manipulating their environment. Providing such children with a consistent means of communication may be the best first step in appropriate evaluation of their abilities. It may take years to develop such a communication system, however, so that behavioral observations become an important supplement to formal evaluation with such children. Through behavioral observations, it is possible to document responses that the child refuses to give during formal testing situations.

The use of clinical observations is also important in the evaluation of motor skills. While such evaluation may sometimes seem more straightforward than the evaluation of cognitive and language skills just discussed, the quality of movement is just as important to assess as the motor milestones. Knowing that the child can sit independently is one thing, but knowing that the child can sit independently only by spreading the legs apart for a wide base of support and fixing at the shoulders and pelvis to provide trunk support is quite another. Saying that a child can sit independently makes it sound as if the child has adequately mastered the task of sitting independently. A fuller description of the child's abilities makes it apparent that the child could use some help in improving the skills needed to support independent sitting.

The NDT approach cautions that it is a mistake to apply a developmental motor skills checklist approach to children with motor dysfunctions resulting from central nervous system damage (Bly 1983; Bobath 1975). As in the situation just described, the child is able to sit independently, but the underlying components of trunk stability and balance are weak. Thus, rather than helping the child develop the next higher skill on the checklist, an NDT approach would help the child improve the weak underlying skills so that both independent sitting and higher level skills could be built on a more solid basis.

Standardized tests for evaluating such qualities of movement are not available, and the evaluator must rely on clinical observations to assess this feature of motor development. The disadvantage of clinical observations is that they are not standardized, and therefore their reliability can be called into question. Nevertheless, such observations are being increasingly accepted as valid in both medical and educational settings.

Initial Evaluation

Once a child has been referred to an early intervention program, an evaluation should be conducted by a transdisciplinary team to determine the child's strengths and needs. These evaluations are conducted in an arena setting, with at least one motor therapist, an educator, and a speech-language clinician present. Ideally, both an occupational thera-

pist and a physical therapist would be available. Chapter 6 describes the makeup and functioning of the transdisciplinary team in more detail. When specialists from several disciplines are conducting an evaluation together, they can save time and energy for themselves, the child, and the child's family. In such a situation, the child has to adjust to interactions with only one or two unfamiliar people in one unfamiliar setting. The family has to schedule only one evaluation session. Further, many activities presented during an evaluation are relevant to several developmental areas. With specialists from all areas observing at the same time, these activities need only be presented once. Development in each area is closely related to development in all others, and specialists from each discipline can make important observations that relate to the child's functioning in other areas.

For example, the occupational therapist might observe that the child has poor shoulder stability, which affects the ability to control fine motor movements such as stacking blocks or putting objects into a cup. In consultation with the educator, they might decide that the child's poor performance on these tasks probably was related more to motor ability than to cognitive understanding of the task. This would indicate a different kind of intervention approach than if the child appeared to have the necessary motor skills but lacked cognitive understanding of the task. In another example, the occupational therapist might observe that the child appeared to be overly sensitive to tactile stimuli. The educator might observe that the child seemed to follow people and objects with the eyes and to stare at the place where an object or person was last seen. The team might conclude that the child's lack of object manipulation was a way to avoid touching things rather than a lack of understanding or interest in objects that might indicate a cognitive impairment. These kinds of hypotheses would need to be discussed with parents and tested during intervention activities but would help prevent the development of many inappropriate intervention plans.

The child's caregivers should be present during this evaluation, both to provide security and support for the child and to give information about the child's usual behavior at home. Depending on the program model, these team evaluations are conducted at the intervention program site or in the child's home. If the evaluation is conducted at the program site, a home visit should also be scheduled if at all possible to observe the child in familiar surroundings and to better determine the family's needs in relation to the child's care.

This type of evaluation should include the administration of a standardized assessment tool to determine the child's level of functioning in each developmental area. In addition, the evaluation should include a standardized format for determining the family's strengths and needs in relation to the child. The assessment tools used should, if possible, be related to the program's intervention philosophy. They should also provide enough information to assign the child to the appropriate classroom or intervention team and to begin to develop an intervention program for the child and the child's family. In addition to standardized assessments, clinical observations provide valuable information about the quality of the child's skills and interactions and can identify strengths and needs not evaluated by the standardized instruments presently available. A list of commonly used screening tests is in the appendix.

Figure 7 (page 22) summarizes the responsibilities of each evaluation team member for a sample team. Responsibilities may vary somewhat from team to team, but it is important that each team member's responsibilities be clearly agreed upon and written down for future reference prior to the team's first evaluation. An example of an initial evaluation form can be found in the appendix. The resource list in the appendix cites some instruments available for assessing child development and family strengths and needs in several domains.

The time before, during, and after a child's initial evaluation can be very stressful for the family. Meeting with the family as soon after the evaluation as possible to discuss the results can help alleviate at least one source of stress—waiting to know "how the child did." The family should be given a written report and the opportunity to discuss the team's findings with the team members. In addition, the family should be offered the opportunity for a second meeting or for telephone consultations to clarify explanations or answer questions that may come up after the interpretive meeting.

Evaluation for Program Planning

Once the child has been assigned to an intervention team, the members of that team will need to conduct their own evaluations to guide them in developing their individual treatment plans. This process can be frustrating to parents, but it seems to be an inevitable part of the intervention process. This is so in part because the law requires the use of standardized evaluation tools for an initial evaluation. These tools may not lend themselves easily to program planning, however. The interventionist must then reevaluate using a tool more suitable to guiding the development of an intervention plan. Bagnato and Neisworth (1981) have devoted an entire volume to a discussion of this problem and some possible solutions, and others discuss it as well (see Bricker 1982; Hutinger 1988).

Another reason for each interventionist to conduct an independent evaluation is to establish a rapport with the child and to observe not only what the child does but how the child accomplishes each activity. Also, observations made over time may provide much more information about the child's functioning than observations during a one- or two-session formal evaluation can do.

With P.L. 99-457, the family is brought much more closely into the intervention process. Individual family service plans (IFSPs) are developed based on the child's needs as the family sees them (National Early Childhood Technical Assistance System and Association for the Care of Children's Health 1989). Chapter 6 will provide a more in-depth discussion of IFSP development. But in discussing evaluation for program planning, it is important to keep the family's goals for the child in mind.

Evaluating the Child's Progress

Once the child's IEP (individualized education plan) or IFSP has been developed, intervention services can begin in earnest. In order to be sure that these services are effective and that the plan developed

FIGURE 7

Initial Evaluation Procedures
(for placement determination)

Responsibilities for assessment areas will be as follows:

Physical therapist,occupational therapist:

Fine motor (Early-Learning Accomplishment Profile)

Gross motor (E-LAP)

E-LAP self-help areas if appropriate: dressing, hand-to-mouth feeding, toileting and sleeping, reflexes, range of motion, muscle tone, movement quality, perceptual motor (evaluation), clinical observation.

Speech:

Language (E-LAP)

Oral motor section of self-help (E-LAP)

Oral motor exam to include clinical evaluation, reflexes, structure, and function

Teacher:

Cognitive (E-LAP)

Social-emotional (E-LAP), including representational play skills, parent-child interaction, child-to-task interaction, and child-to-test situation

The evaluation team will meet following the assessment to discuss their findings, recommendations, and text of the summary statement. The case manager will consult with the receiving teacher to show findings and determine if placement is appropriate.

Each team member will write the narrative summary for his or her assessment area and distribute copies to the rest of the team within three working days of the evaluation.

Completion of evaluation report face sheet will be done by the physical therapist or occupational therapist.

Speech-language clinician on team will complete summary statement of report following group discussion.

The complete written report shall be submitted to program coordinator for typing and distribution to team within 10 days of evaluation.

A case manager is assigned to child for intake and initial evaluation process.

Admission committee will meet to review case.

Case manager will contact and/or meet with parents to review evaluation placement recommendation.

Questions to ask parents during evaluation:

1. What do you perceive as the child's problem?
2. Have you been given a diagnosis? What does that mean to you?
3. What do you perceive as your child's strengths and weaknesses?
4. Describe your child's interaction patterns/play with other children.

When writing up evaluations, please:

1. Describe positioning used to assist with testing
2. Avoid quoting age ranges of sections
3. Provide a description of behavior within each section
4. Be positive; describe skills mastered or in progress rather than what the child can't do
5. Reports should be written in the past tense
6. All evaluation reports should be done legibly in ink before sent to typing
7. No abbreviations will be used (for example, ROM)
8. The summary statement should include a statement describing specific scores achieved

Summary should include:

1. Services child is currently receiving
2. Reason for referral
3. Strengths and weaknesses observed during testing
4. Areas of growth we can address

Source: Developed by Easter Seal Society staff, The Children's Center, 2800 13th St., N.W., Washington, DC 20009. Used by permission.

for the child is appropriate, progress on the plan should be evaluated at regular intervals. This is done informally each time the child participates in an activity and the intervention team says "That was great," or "That didn't work so well." The child's progress is also discussed, sometimes in general terms and sometimes in relationship to specific goals, during regular team meetings. Sometimes the child's progress toward a particular goal is charted or graphed each time the child participates in an activity designed to facilitate the development of that skill. Such progress charts are almost always used with children who are working on toileting skills, but they may also be helpful in other areas, especially with routines that need to be carried out every day. Range-of-motion or visual-training activities are two examples. A notebook that travels with the child between home and school can be used to keep a running anecdotal record of the child's accomplishments. On a daily basis it is hard to see changes, but a review of comments written over a period of months can provide a vivid picture of changes that the child has made.

At specified intervals, it is important to provide some type of formal evaluation of progress for parents and professionals who may not be a direct part of the child's early intervention program, such as the child's pediatrician. Unless local regulations specify otherwise, a quarterly review is generally appropriate. The midyear and end-of-year reports should be formal reports of the child's progress, including present levels of functioning in all developmental areas. The end-of-year report usually requires a formal team reevaluation. For infants (0-2 years of age) such a formal reevaluation is needed every six months. The first and third quarterly reports can be more anecdotal but do need to indicate how the child is progressing toward program goals. The IFSP may include other timetables for review, and these guidelines should be met and documented as appropriate to each situation.

Exit Evaluation

When the child leaves the early intervention program, a final evaluation is needed. The jurisdiction may determine the components of this evaluation, and the intervention program may or may not provide the evaluation. If the child leaves the program at the end of the intervention period, the end-of-year

evaluation may be appropriate as a final evaluation. A more thorough evaluation, similar to that done at the end of the year, may be necessary if the child leaves the program at some other point during the year.

If the child is entering another program, forwarding the child's records may be all the follow-up that is needed. If the child has progressed to the point where early intervention is no longer indicated, program staff may want to be sure the child is monitored in case problems arise in the future. The program may provide such monitoring services itself or refer the family to another source. The monitoring of children at risk for developmental delays but who are not showing signs of delay and/or of children who have shown delays that seem to have been resolved is another possible function of evaluation in an early intervention program.

Program Evaluation

An early intervention program should have a means of evaluating its own effectiveness at least once a year. Child progress is one measure of program effectiveness, but parent satisfaction is another important measure. Some standard format for eliciting family comments and suggestions needs to be incorporated into all early intervention programs, in addition to the informal means that will always be used to indicate family opinion. Progress toward IEP or IFSP goals or improvement of developmental test scores may not be the only relevant measure of the child's growth and development. The child's transition to a less restrictive environment and ability to better participate in community functions are also important variables, as are the child's self-esteem, independence, and social behavior and skills. These areas may or may not have been addressed on the IEP or IFSP, but they bear examination when evaluating an intervention program's effectiveness.

Family attitudes as well as family satisfaction may also provide a measure of program effectiveness. A program that has helped a family better act as advocates for their child's needs, negotiate social services systems more easily, or extend their support systems should be able to document these positive effects.

Staff satisfaction and development should also be included in a program's self-evaluation. An early intervention program cannot afford to provide quality services to families at the expense of its staff. Also, a staff that actively participates in developing the services it provides will be more effective and invested in the outcome of those services.

There are many issues in program evaluation (Johnson 1988; Korner et al. 1985), of which the ones mentioned above are but a few. Unfortunately this book cannot provide an in-depth discussion of these issues. Since appropriate program evaluation is such an important, and often neglected, part of any early intervention program, administrators and early interventionists are urged to explore this program component further. The resource list in appendix 1 provides some additional references on this topic.

CHAPTER 2

NDT Program Components

The introduction described the principles underlying the neurodevelopmental treatment (NDT) approach to motor therapy. This chapter will discuss how these principles can be incorporated into a comprehensive intervention program and who is responsible for carrying out the different components of this motor therapy. This chapter will also include guidelines and some suggested activities for each of these components. The references in appendix 1 provide further information about NDT theory and practice, including activities that can be incorporated into classroom and/or individual treatment sessions.

Remember that according to NDT theory, movement disorders are based on atypical postural tone, the inability to maintain normal postural stability against gravity, and the use of compensatory and atypical patterns of movement (Campbell 1982, 1984). NDT theory is also based on the idea that the child must actively participate in an experience in order to learn effectively from it (Bobath 1975). In the case of motor development, this means that the child must experience what it is like to actively produce a normal or normalized movement pattern. Then, through repetition of these patterns during active movement, the child will internalize and be able to use these patterns independently (Bobath 1975). The more opportunities the child has to experience normal or normalized movement patterns, the more likely it will be that the child will learn to repeat them independently or with less facilitation. Therefore it is important that as many people as possible who work with the child understand the child's

motor needs and can help to facilitate the child's use of more normal movement patterns during all activities (Campbell 1982).

Program Responsibilities

The introduction outlined several components of treatment. These included preparation, facilitation, inhibition, positioning, and handling. The first three of these are usually considered components of direct treatment by an NDT-trained therapist. Positioning and handling are components of treatment that parents and staff who interact with children who have motor impairments can learn and use all the time. In most intervention programs, the NDT-trained therapist is responsible for assessing each child's motor abilities and needs; planning a motor treatment program for each child; providing direct treatment to those children who need it; and training parents and staff in positioning, handling, and other techniques as indicated to reinforce treatment goals and facilitate the development of motor skills. The NDT-trained therapist is also usually responsible for evaluating the child's progress at regular intervals, assisting with the writing of motor-related IEP or IFSP goals, and providing ongoing consultation with parents and staff members as needed.

Other team members play a variety of roles in relation to NDT program components. While the primary NDT-trained therapist is usually the physical therapist, many occupational therapists have received NDT training or are familiar with the NDT approach. If the occupational therapist is not the primary NDT therapist in a program, the occupational therapy program will be planned to reinforce NDT therapy goals and to incorporate as many components of the NDT treatment program as possible into the occupational therapy activities planned. The occupational therapist may also provide supplemental training to parents and staff in positioning, handling, or other NDT techniques, and may be asked to supplement or at times to provide any of the services outlined for the primary NDT therapist above.

Like the occupational therapist, the speech-language pathologist may have NDT training or be familiar with the principles of NDT. Ideally, the speech-language pathologist will focus the NDT component of speech-language therapy on goals more specifically related to that domain but will reinforce the overall NDT goals whenever possible.

The teacher's role in an intervention program is usually broader than that of any of the therapists. The teacher, who may also have NDT training, is usually responsible for incorporating all of the individual therapy goals for all of the children in each class into appropriate individual and large- and small-group activities that are also designed to facilitate cognitive development and social interaction. The teacher is very often also the staff member who is in primary contact with the parents and so may need to answer parents' questions about NDT-based activities and even provide some training in positioning and handling in consultation with the primary NDT therapist. The teacher will plan the classroom activities to incorporate NDT principles and activities appropriate to the children's needs, based on the NDT therapist's suggestions. The teacher will also use appropriate positioning and handling techniques to facilitate normalized movement patterns and will help train the classroom assistants to use these techniques when necessary.

Because of the importance of positioning and handling techniques and because these techniques can be used by everyone who interacts with the child, some guidelines and suggestions for their use will be provided in detail, followed by briefer guidelines and suggestions for preparation, facilitation, and inhibition.

Positioning

Positioning involves providing the child with external postural supports to help compensate for the child's internal lack of postural stability (Campbell 1982). This often involves the use of adaptive equipment (Campbell 1982; Finnie 1975; High 1977; Wright and Nomura 1985). However, in many situations young children can be positioned most effectively when an adult's body is used in place of adaptive equipment to provide additional support (Jaeger 1981). Positioning is static rather than dynamic, and it is often used for the carryover and maintenance of NDT goals achieved through active treatment (Campbell 1982, 1984). Although not in itself an active form of treatment, positioning can still greatly influence the child's ability to perform in every developmental area (Campbell 1982; Finnie 1975).

Several general ideas relate to the specific positioning suggestions presented below. One is that the human body is designed for movement. However appropriate a particular position may be, the child cannot remain in it for long periods of time without becoming uncomfortable. Furthermore, the therapeutic benefits of the position will decrease as the child struggles to move into a different position. Ideally, a child should remain in one position for no more than 20 minutes before shifting to a different position or movement activity.

Second, positions selected need to be age appropriate (Campbell 1984). Young children often play while sitting or even lying on the floor, whereas older children do so much less often. Along with this idea goes the idea that the position that is selected should enable the child to participate in activities with the rest of the class. Thus a child might fit well in a group activity at the water table when placed in a stander but would not be able to interact as well in the stander during a circle activity when the other children were seated on the floor.

Third, positions need to be selected for function. For example, the NDT therapist might want a particular child to work on improving head control in sitting. Supportive seating adapted to allow for head movement while providing good trunk support might give the child an opportunity to work on head control during story time, when the child is expected primarily to sit and listen. During mealtime, working on head control and independent finger feeding might be too demanding for the child, and seating that provides additional head support might be needed. Standing might be an appropriate position for play at the sand table but not during mealtime, when it is generally considered inappropriate for people to stand and the position is too demanding to allow the child to fully concentrate on mealtime activities.

When children are placed in positions that are new to them, they are frequently asked to use movement patterns that are also new. In many cases these positions and patterns require more effort than the more familiar patterns. Young children can get tired very easily, and children who have heart problems, respiratory problems, or other health impairments may tire more quickly still. Parents and staff must always be alert to signals from the child that the position is too demanding or that the child has had enough for the time being.

Although this chapter cannot provide a complete guide to positioning of the child with motor dysfunctions, following are some basic suggestions designed to provide a place to start. Each child's therapy team will have specific suggestions for that child's positioning. In addition, the resources listed in appendix 1 may provide more in-depth information for those who need it. The following positioning suggestions are organized around floor activities, sitting, kneeling, and standing.

FLOOR ACTIVITIES

Supine. Most children with abnormal tone do poorly in terms of movement when placed flat on their backs. In this position, the force of gravity tends to pull them into the mattress or floor. Their movements also tend to be dominated by primitive reflexes if these have not yet been integrated. The asymmetric tonic neck reflex (ATNR), for example, tends to be activated in this position. Placing the child on a wedge to elevate the head and shoulders and to keep the head in midline, a roll under the knees to keep them bent, and toys suspended from a bar within reach of the child's hands can sometimes encourage the child to reach up and play without activating primitive reflexes or adversely affecting tone (figure 8). Elevating the child's hips

with a wedge can sometimes encourage exploration of the feet and may help reduce extensor tone in the hypertonic child. Suspending toys from a bar within reach of the feet may encourage kicking, especially if the toys also make noise when moved.

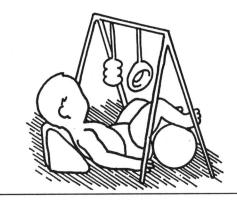

Figure 8

Sidelying. Children whose tone is more extreme will probably do better in sidelying. In this position, they do not have to work as much against gravity in order to move their arms to manipulate toys. Sidelyers, pillows, beanbag chairs, or other furniture can be used to help the child maintain the position. Figures 9-11 show some examples. It is

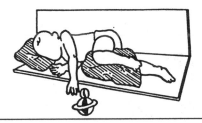

Figure 9

Figure 10

Figure 11

important that the child's neck remain flexed, especially if the child generally has high tone. This position of keeping the neck flexed is also referred to as using a "chin tuck." Position toys at about the level of the child's breastbone and a few inches away from the body to encourage the child to look down at the toy and maintain the chin tuck. When sitting or talking with the child, it is important to position yourself in about the same position recommended for the toy, again to encourage the child to maintain the chin tuck. If possible, separate the child's legs with a small pillow or roll. Ideally, the leg on the floor should be straight and the leg on top bent at the hip and knee to further reduce abnormally high tone and to provide the child with the feeling of the two legs being in separate positions (dissociation). Be sure that the child is allowed sidelying time on **each side.** If there is not time for the child to spend time on both sides during a single day, be sure to alternate sides from day to day, so that, for example, Mary is placed in sidelying on her left side on Monday, Wednesday, and Friday, and on her right side on Tuesday and Thursday. The following week, the sequence is reversed. An adult's body can also be used effectively to help a child maintain a sidelying position (figure 12).

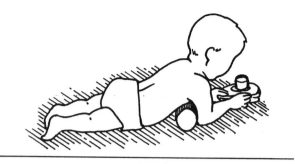

Figure 13

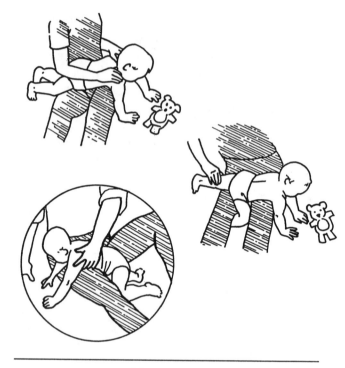

Figures 14-16

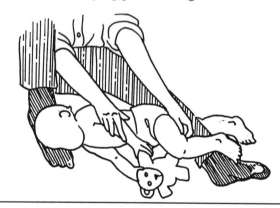

Figure 12

Prone. As in supine, most children with abnormal tone need assistance to maintain good positioning and movement when lying on their stomachs. Children with low tone tend to flop like a frog, with legs spread wide apart. Children with high tone tend either to collapse into total flexion or to arch into extension like a bow. A small roll or bolster under the chest just below the armpits can help the child lift the head against gravity and bear some weight on the arms (figure 13). An adult's leg can be used in the same way (figures 14-16). De-

pending on the child's motor skills, weight bearing will be done on the forearm (less advanced), as shown in figure 13, or on flat hands with extended arms (more advanced), as shown in figure 14. Many children will tend to keep their hands fisted in this position, either because of their high tone or because the touch of the rug or other surface is uncomfortable to them (see the sections on sensory integration in the introduction and on tactile defensiveness in chapter 3). The objective is weight bearing on flat hands if at all possible. Each child's therapist will be able to give specific suggestions on the exact position that will be appropriate for that child.

Sometimes a child may be positioned in prone on a wedge (figure 17), partially supported by a

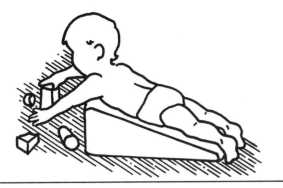

Figure 17

beanbag chair (figure 18), on a scooterboard (see figure 19), or using some other device. The basic position and principles described above apply to these prone positions as well. An adult can vary the prone position by using one leg in place of a bolster and using the hands to help the child flex at the hips so that the child is supporting some weight on one or both knees as well as on the open hands (figures 14-16). This is a more advanced task and should be done only with the recommendation of the child's therapist.

Figure 18

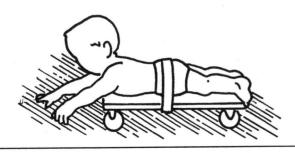

Figure 19

SITTING

Children can sit on the floor or in a chair. Floor sitting will be discussed in this section. A discussion of matching children to appropriate chairs will follow. Some options for children who cannot sit without support will be presented. Then possible positions for those who can sit independently will be discussed.

Floor sitting with support. Some children will require total support in order to sit at all. They may be held in an adult's lap or placed in an infant seat if they are still very young and very small. Otherwise, adaptive seats such as the Tumbleform seat with a base (figure 20), or sometimes a car seat (figure 21), can be used effectively.

Figures 20 & 21

For children who still need a lot of support but who are developing head control, a corner seat without legs or a base can sometimes be effective (figure 22). Floor seats with curved backs provide good trunk support for those children who don't

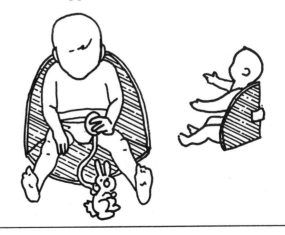

Figure 22

need quite as much support as the corner seat provides (figure 23). Sometimes a commercially available booster seat will provide all the support that a child needs. These booster seats are also useful for the child with low tone who tends to sit with the legs spread wide apart. For such a child, the booster seat will provide some added support while encouraging the child to keep the legs closer together, a more adaptive position for future motor development (figure 24).

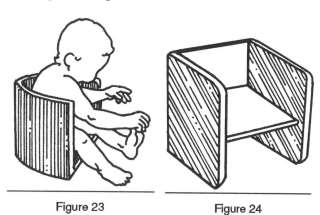

Figure 23   Figure 24

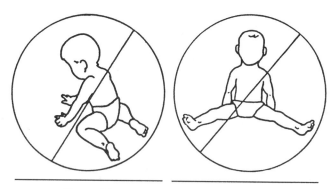

Figure 25   Figure 26

Floor sitting without support. Most children with abnormal muscle tone lack adequate trunk control. Their abdominal muscles tend to be weak. These children will sit in positions that avoid use of the abdominals. They also avoid use of trunk rotation in their movements because of inadequate trunk control and weak abdominals. Many children with motor dysfunctions also lack internal postural stability and will seek positions that provide them with external supports. In sitting, they will use positions that provide a wide base of support. Children with both high and low tone use W-sitting to help compensate for all of these problems (figure 25). The trouble with this compensation is that the child avoids working on the very skills that are needed for further motor development. In addition, W-sitting can stress the joints and ligaments that may already be stressed from the child's abnormal tone. W-sitting, then, is almost always to be discouraged and the child should be provided with more developmentally appropriate functional alternatives. Likewise, many children with low tone tend to sit with legs spread wide apart as if they were doing the "splits" (figure 26). This is another compensatory pattern that provides the child with a wide base of support but lets the child avoid developing better internal postural controls. Like W-sitting, this pat-

tern should be discouraged in favor of more developmentally functional alternatives.

Some alternatives for the child with low tone include long-leg sitting (figure 27) and side sitting (figure 28), as well as using the booster seat arrangement described in the section above. Children with high tone might benefit from ring sitting (figure 29) or "Indian" sitting as well. In long-leg sitting, the legs are straight out in front of the child with the back held straight. (Children with high tone usually cannot maintain a straight back in this position because

Figure 27

Figure 28   Figure 29

of the tightness of the muscles in the backs of their thighs [hamstrings]. In such cases, long-leg sitting is not recommended.) In ring sitting, the soles of the child's feet are touching each other in front of the child, and again the back is straight. "Indian" sitting is a variation on ring sitting in which the child's legs or ankles are crossed in front of the child. In side sitting, both knees are pointed in the same direction, either to the left or the right of midline. The child's weight is on the hip on the side of the body to which the knees are pointing. The child can take some weight (prop) on a forearm supported by a roll or bolster placed next to the weight-bearing side of the body (figure 30). If the child is able, the arm on the weight-bearing side of the body should be extended and the flat hand should support some of the child's weight. In this case, the extra support of the roll or bolster is not needed.

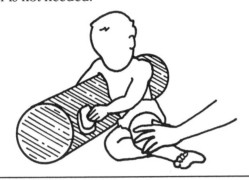

Figure 30

Chairs. While it is important that the whole body be positioned appropriately in a chair, checking the position of the child's hips, shoulders, and head will most likely indicate how well the child is positioned overall (Wood 1989) (figure 31). The hips should be well back in the chair. It is impossible to maintain any other body part in proper alignment if the hips are not positioned properly, so check the hips first if there is a problem with the child's positioning in the chair. A hip strap is often needed to keep the hips in proper weight-bearing position.

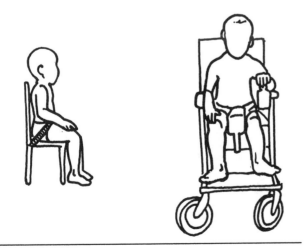

Figure 31

The shoulders should be relaxed and in a neutral position, neither rounded too far forward nor pulled back (retracted). Provide a higher tray for the arms to rest on and/or encourage the child to keep the elbow bent more if the shoulders are too far forward. Also check to be sure the hips are against the back of the seat. If the arms tend to be bent and the hands held up off the tray, the shoulders are probably also retracted. A small towel roll behind the shoulders may help (figure 32). The head should be upright and in midline.

Figure 32

In general, the body should be positioned at angles of about 90 degrees when the child is seated in the chair. This means that the feet are at a 90-degree angle from the legs, the lower legs are at a 90-degree angle from the thighs, and the thighs are at a 90-degree angle from the trunk (figure 31). (This general guideline may need to be modified some for individuals. Be sure to discuss each child's needs with the therapist.) Often, keeping the feet at a right angle from the legs can go a long way toward keeping the hips properly positioned in the seat.

Another concern in matching a chair to a child is seat depth and height. When seated in the chair, the child's back should rest straight against the back of the chair, with the hips all the way back in the seat. The knee should bend comfortably at the edge of the seat, but the whole thigh should be supported by the seat. The feet should rest either on the floor or on a foot rest. They should not dangle.

The chair selected should provide as much support as the child needs for function. This may vary depending on the task, so that it may be necessary to use more than one seating system for a given child during the course of a day. Some children will require total support and may need a custom-made chair with specialized modifications and adaptations. Others will be able to use regular classroom chairs with little or no modification. Still others will fall somewhere between these situations. A few general-purpose special chairs and adaptations will be discussed below. Children needing customized chairs will need to be fitted by a specialist in consultation with a physical therapist. The physical therapist will most likely make the initial adjustments and fittings for children needing special chairs or adaptations to regular chairs. Other staff and parents need to be aware of each child's seating requirements, however, in order to monitor the situation and make or recommend modifications as appropriate.

Corner chairs are similar to the corner floor sitter described above, except they have legs or wheel bases to bring them up to table height (figure 33). Commercially made corner chairs usually come with fitted trays. Barrel chairs are sometimes used with children who tend to keep their legs tightly crossed and extended in front of them (figure 34).

Figure 36

chairs may also be helpful in providing limits for children who find it difficult to sit in one place even for a very short time. The physical boundaries of the chair can often help children stay seated for a little bit longer than they could in a regular chair or on the floor.

Regular wooden children's chairs can often be modified easily by adding a lap belt (figure 37), being fitted with a footrest (figure 38), providing

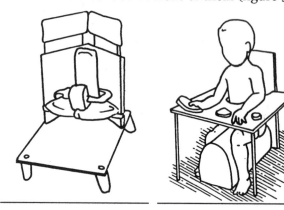

Figure 33   Figure 34

The child straddles a half-barrel shape while leaning against a backrest. These chairs sometimes have a fitted tray or can be used at a table. Wooden "cube chairs" have straight backs and sides, and some are fitted with a tray (figures 35, 36). These provide less support than a corner chair but more support than a classroom chair without arms or sides. These

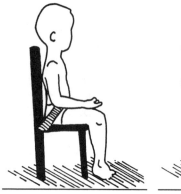

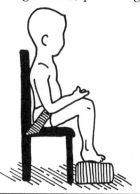

Figure 37   Figure 38

Figure 35

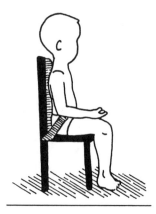

Figure 39

additional back support (figure 39), and so on. Many of the seating arrangements just described can also be provided in homemade wood versions or can even be made from heavy cardboard. Again, each child's therapist will make individual modifications as needed.

KNEELING

Kneeling provides a transition position between sitting and standing. It is a useful position in working with infants and young children, since it addresses the balance and trunk control issues in a more upright position and also provides weight bearing through the hips, while being less stressful for the child than standing. It is developmentally appropriate for this population, too, since many preschoolers play some of the time in a kneeling position. Children can be positioned in kneeling against a table, sofa, or other piece of furniture (figures 40-43). Some children may need the extra support of a kneel-stander (figure 44).

Figure 43

Figure 44

Figure 40

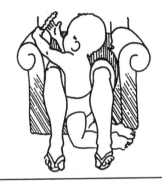

Figure 41

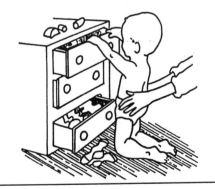

Figure 42

Many children have a tendency to sink into a W-sit from the kneeling position. Others may lean into the table or other surface and sink their bottoms onto their heels. Avoid letting children use these compensatory positions that do not further their motor development. Be sure to provide interesting activities for the children in this position, but do not expect them to be able to use their highest level of fine motor skills, especially if the position is relatively new for them.

The half-kneel (figures 45-47) is an important transition between sitting and standing, and between kneeling and standing. It is a position children need to learn in order to move from an all-fours position or from kneeling into standing. In addition, it facilitates weight shifting and trunk rotation and may give the child the experience of bearing more weight on the more involved side of the body.

Figure 45

Figure 46

Figure 47

The child will probably not maintain this position as long as the kneeling position, as the half-kneel is a more active, transitional position. However, it should be incorporated into activities as a transition whenever appropriate (figure 48). Children with

Figure 48

motor dysfunctions will often avoid using this transitional position by attempting to use their arms to pull straight up into a standing position from kneeling or crawling. Such a compensatory pattern should be avoided because by using it the child avoids appropriate weight shifting and weight bearing.

STANDING

There is some controversy over whether to place young children in a standing position when they are not developmentally standing on their own. Some therapists believe that children should not be placed in positions that they cannot assume for themselves. They believe that the child's sensory processing and thinking skills may be inhibited or may develop abnormally if the child is not developmentally ready for the position. On the other hand, children need to bear weight on their legs to facilitate appropriate long bone growth in the legs and in order for their hip joints to form properly. This is important to decrease the risk of hip dislocations as the child gets older (Saudek 1985). Children with cerebral palsy who are not walking are particularly at risk for this problem. Children beyond the age of one generally spend a good deal of time in standing, and parents of children with disabilities usually expect their children to be in more upright positions as they get older. Also, standing is the most appropriate position for a variety of play activities as children reach preschool age. For these reasons, most interventionists recommend that children be positioned in standing for at least a small portion of each day if at all possible. This will not be possible for all children, however. Always check with the physical therapist before positioning children in standing when they are not standing on their own.

There are two basic kinds of standers, with many variations of each. In the prone stander, the child's stomach leans against the stander (figure 49). In the supine stander, the child's back rests against the standing frame (figure 50). The physical therapist will have to determine which is the most appropriate type of stander for each child.

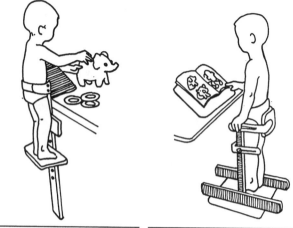

Figure 49

Figure 50

Figure 51

Some children can be positioned at standing tables (figure 51) or against ordinary furniture (figures 52-54). In many cases, the child will need the additional support of braces or inhibitive casts for the feet and ankles to be positioned properly. Again, the physical therapist will evaluate each child's situation and make appropriate recommendations.

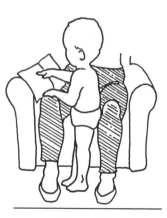

Figure 52

Figure 53

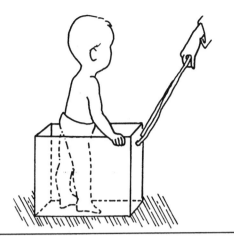

Figure 54

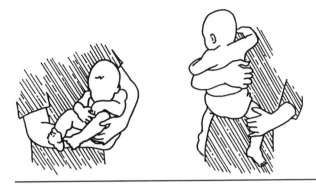

Figures 55 & 56

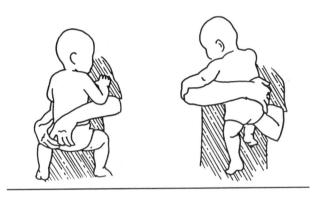

Figures 57 & 58

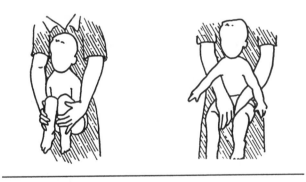

Figures 59 & 60

Handling

Handling techniques refer to therapeutic ways of moving children from one position or place to another during regular activities throughout the day (Campbell 1983). If used consistently, proper handling techniques can reinforce the goals of direct treatment and make a valuable contribution toward helping the child learn new movement patterns. The physical therapist will make specific recommendations for each child. These will need to be worked out with the parents and staff involved to make sure that the suggestions made are practical for the adults and situations involved.

According to Campbell (1982, 11), "the goal of handling is to insure that the child has the most opportunities per day to move with normal tone and with as normal patterns of stability and mobility as possible." The child may benefit more from appropriate handling techniques used consistently across people and situations than from direct NDT therapy provided for short periods in isolated settings (as is often the case in one-to-one therapy sessions) (Campbell 1982).

One general guideline in thinking about handling is to carry the child in a different position from what the child tends to assume independently. For example, if the child tends to lie stiff and extended, with both legs straight out, you will want to try to carry the child so that the hips and at least one knee are bent. Figures 55-62 provide several ideas. If a child tends to sit or lie with legs spread wide apart

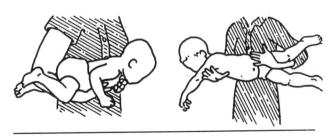

Figures 61 & 62

and turned out at the hips, you will want to carry the child with the legs close together and held in a neutral position at the hips (figures 63, 64).

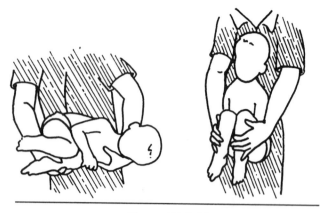

Figures 63 & 64

When you want to move a child, it is always best to give warning first. Tell the child what you are going to do and how you are going to do it, even if you think that the child does not understand what you are saying. The tone of your voice will at least give the child some warning, and you will be helping the child to learn the meaning of your words. Approach the child slowly, if possible, and pick up the child as smoothly as possible. If you can, avoid approaching the child from behind, at least until you have had a chance to explain what you are doing. For example, one-year-old Geoffrey is positioned in the sidelyer, playing with a roly-poly toy. It is time to bring him to the table for snack. You want to pick him up with his back supported against your trunk, flexed at the hips and knees, with legs turned out at the hips. You walk over to Geoffrey, sit on the floor near the toy, and say, "Geoffrey, it's time for snack now. I'm going to unfasten your safety belt and walk around behind you to pick you up and take you to your chair." This kind of approach helps prevent startles and the increase in high tone that can accompany them. It helps teach the child what to expect from the environment and helps teach understanding of language. It also shows your respect for the child by treating the child like a person who understands rather than like an object.

In making a transition from one position to another, you also want to use movements that are as natural and functional as possible (Campbell 1984). Thus, in shifting a child from sidelying on the right to sidelying on the left, you might want to try to bring the child up from the right into a sidesitting position, shift into a left sidesit, and from there move the child into the left sidelying position. Such a planned, functional transition will help give the child a better understanding of the relationship of the different movements and positions than if you simply pick the child up, turn the child around, and plop the child down again on the other side. The latter transition is disorganized and the components are functionally unrelated, reinforcing whatever internal disorganization the child may already have.

Preparation

Although preparation techniques are used in direct treatment, some of them can also be used by parents and staff to make positioning and handling easier and more effective (Campbell 1983). The purpose is to prepare the body for movement (Campbell 1982). Before movement is possible, the body must have a stable base of support. The phrase "stability is necessary for mobility" may help the interventionist keep that concept in mind. Therefore, the focus during the preparation phase of treatment is on normalizing tone and providing the child with a stable base of support from which movement will be possible (Campbell 1982).

NORMALIZING TONE

The first goal in a treatment session is usually to normalize tone. For children whose tone is usually high, slow, rhythmic movements may help to reduce tone. Joint approximation and traction and slow, shaking movements away from the joint are also techniques that may help reduce tone. Weight shifting using patterns of dissociation may also help to reduce tone, as may weight bearing (Campbell 1984). Environmental and sensory influences may also affect tone. These influences are discussed in more detail in the sections dealing with sensory integration (see introduction and chapter 3), but the ideas presented should be incorporated into an NDT treatment session to maximize its effectiveness. Music with a 60-beat-per-minute tempo, such as is used in many baroque classical pieces, has been found to have a calming, centering effect that can help to normalize high muscle tone and increase the effectiveness of a treatment session (Morris

1985). See the resource section in the appendix for more information about the appropriate selection and use of music during movement therapy.

Brisk movements such as quick bouncing or tapping can help to increase tone in children who are generally hypotonic. Resistance, as in activities that require a child to push or pull a heavy object, can also help increase tone (Campbell 1984). Vestibular stimulation, discussed in the section on sensory integration (see chapter 3), can help increase tone in the child whose tone is usually low. As with hypertonic children, other environmental and sensory influences may also have an effect. The sections on sensory integration in the introduction and chapter 3 provide more discussion of these influences. Folk music with a brisk, clear, rhythmic beat has also been found to increase muscle tone and facilitate therapeutic activities such as have just been described (Morris 1985).

Facilitation/Inhibition

As with preparation, facilitation and inhibition techniques are used in direct treatment. Parents and interventionists can also use many of these techniques effectively in their daily interactions with children. Facilitation involves helping the child produce a response. Inhibition involves helping the child not produce a response. It is useful to talk about the two together, since they complement each other and are used together in treatment.

FACILITATING MOVEMENT

A stable base of support is necessary for movement. The person must be well balanced in the position. The base should be wide enough to provide stability but not so wide as to inhibit free movements. Once the base of support is established, a person must shift weight before movement is possible. For example, a baby lying on its stomach must shift its weight to the left side, and especially onto the left forearm, in order to reach for a toy with its right hand. A child must shift all its weight onto the right foot to take a step with the left foot. (Try experimenting with various movements, especially transition movements from one position to another—sit to stand, lying to sitting, and so on—if this is difficult to picture. Figures 65-73 on this page and page 38

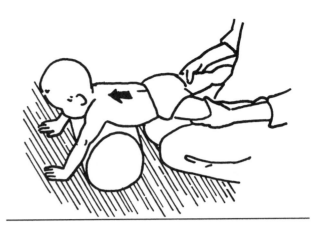

Figure 65

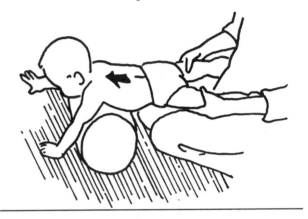

Figure 66

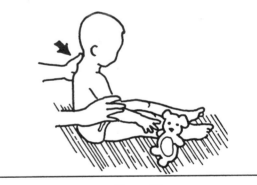

Figure 67

Figure 68

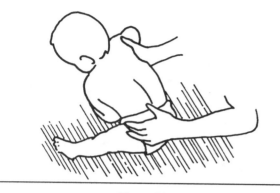

Figure 69

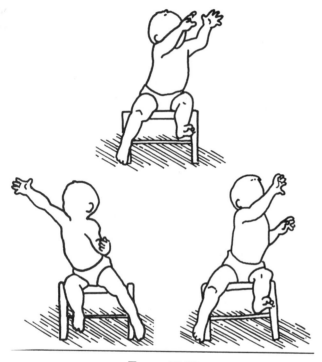

Figures 70-72

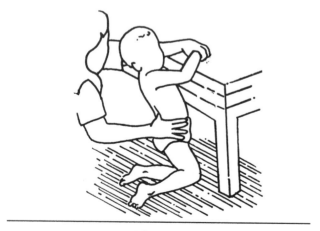

Figure 73

show some examples of weight shifting in various positions.) During treatment, the therapist can often facilitate new movement patterns by helping the child shift weight appropriately. This requires hands-on guidance of the relevant muscle groups but does not require force. The therapist's hands very gently guide the child's body rather than pushing or pulling. The therapist does as little as possible, letting the child experience as much control over the movement as possible.

The position of the therapist's hands also determines how much control the therapist has over the movement being facilitated. Supporting the child closer to the trunk gives the therapist more control over the child's movements. For example, holding the child's hips to facilitate walking gives the therapist more control than holding the child's hands. Likewise, supporting the child high up on the trunk gives the therapist more control than holding the child lower down on the body. Supporting a child at the waist positioned in sitting on a therapy ball gives the therapist more control over the movement than supporting the child at the hips. The hips and shoulders are often key points of control in facilitating more normalized movement patterns. In rolling, the therapist will facilitate the movement from the child's hip (and shoulder if necessary) rather than from the knee or waist. As the child gains better control over a particular movement pattern, the therapist may facilitate from a position that provides less control or may reduce the amount of facilitation in other ways. (Try some of the various possibilities with a coworker, experimenting with hand positions that provide more or less control of the other person's movements. Let a coworker facilitate your movements and experience hand positions in which you felt the facilitator had more or less control.)

Inhibition techniques involve the use of positions and movements that help to prevent certain responses or movements. These techniques are used in combination with facilitation techniques when facilitation techniques alone are not effective (Campbell 1984). For example, the ATNR is triggered when a child turns the head to one side. Keeping the head in midline inhibits the ATNR. Keeping the neck flexed inhibits the total extensor pattern seen in children with very high tone.

Summary

The child's NDT therapist will have the final say on which NDT-related techniques are appropriate and when. The NDT therapist will also be sure that parents and staff are using the techniques appropriately. The therapist will help all others interacting with the child incorporate NDT techniques into the child's daily activities as much as possible. Special motor activities might be suggested, and individual guidelines for positioning and handling the child might also be provided. The resource list in appendix 1 includes sources of suggestions for activities as well as sources of more information on the NDT approach.

CHAPTER 3

Sensory Integration Program Components

The introduction described the concepts behind sensory integration in some detail. This chapter will discuss the responsibilities of the various program staff members in regard to sensory integration program components. It will also provide general guidelines for tactile, vestibular, and proprioceptive activities, as well as suggestions for some activities that have been used successfully in a variety of infant and preschool programs.

Program Responsibilities

As the introduction pointed out, specialized training is required to understand, evaluate, and treat sensory integration disorders. Certified practitioners must complete a course of study and a practicum and pass a specialized exam. Training is offered through a private organization and is in addition to training leading to a university degree. Most SI certified practitioners are occupational therapists, although some may be physical therapists. In this book, we will assume that the primary SI therapist is the occupational therapist.

The SI-certified occupational therapist's usual responsibilities in an early intervention program include the following:

- evaluating the child's sensory integrative status

- evaluating fine motor skills and evaluating self-help skills in consultation with the classroom staff

- planning a treatment program to address sensory integration, fine motor, and self-help needs (in consultation with family and other team members)

- providing direct treatment to children as indicated

- training parents and staff in appropriate activities and techniques to enhance the child's sensory integrative functioning

- suggesting classroom activities to address occupational therapy goals

- assisting with the writing of sensory, fine motor, and self-help related IEP or IFSP goals

- evaluating the child's progress in these areas at regular intervals

- providing ongoing consultation with parents and staff as needed

Other team members will incorporate an understanding of each child's sensory integrative status and needs into daily activities and interactions whenever possible. The physical therapist, for example, may use SI techniques to help normalize muscle tone and to help facilitate normalized movement patterns. The speech-language pathologist may incorporate similar techniques in therapy and may plan language activities that also address sensory integration goals. For example, a language activity for a child who was learning to touch different textures with the hands might involve having the child name the different textures, describe their colors, follow directions with the textures (for example, "give me the soft one," "put the fuzzy one in," etc.), depending on the child's goals in each area.

Likewise, the teacher would plan class activities to reinforce various occupational therapy goals, including goals for sensory integration. In addition, the classroom staff needs to be particularly sensitive to each child's sensory integrative status and to the impact of the environment on each child. For example, a visitor to the classroom might need to be warned not to try to pat Tyrone on the head because he is very defensive and that action would most likely upset him. In another situation, the teacher might need to be aware that Barbara has been unable to sit still today because she is wearing a new outfit and the touch of the fabric is uncomfortable and distracting to her. As with the NDT program component, the teacher is also most likely to be in contact with the family and therefore may be called on to explain some of a child's SI needs and/or teach the family techniques for managing the child's SI needs at home.

Goals and activities for addressing the child's sensory integration needs fall into the general categories of tactile, vestibular, and proprioceptive activities. The rest of this chapter will present some general guidelines and suggested activities for each of these categories. As with other therapies, it is important to remember that each child's situation is unique, and specific recommendations for any individual must come from that child's therapist.

General rules for intervention stipulate that the child will direct treatment. This means that the therapist will not push the child to perform activities if the child is actively resisting. Activities will be graded so that the child will be completely successful with the first activities tried during a session. New and more challenging activities will be introduced gradually, as the child demonstrates readiness for them. The activities should be designed for fun. Also, a key to effective SI programming lies in discovering what calms and what excites each individual. Knowing these things, the interventionist can control the child's environment to help the child gain better self-control.

One clue to understanding the child's sensory needs is to take careful note of the activities the child approaches and the activities the child avoids. By analyzing the sensory components of these activities, the interventionist can figure out which kinds of stimuli to increase in the child's environment and for which kinds of stimuli the child will need extra support to process appropriately. For example, the child who is always pushing classmates, gripping objects too tightly, and running into walls may need more proprioceptive input than the child presently receives. Providing the child with more appropriate ways to get such stimulation will help the child improve sensory processing, become better organized, and eliminate some of the less appropriate behaviors.

Figure 74 (pages 43-44) is a commonly used checklist of a child's sensorimotor history. It is designed to give an indication of problem areas in the child's ability to integrate sensory information from different modalities. One or two indicators checked in any given area does not mean that the child has a sensory integration dysfunction in that area. Several indicators checked in a single area would indicate that the child might be experiencing difficulty integrating sensory information from that modality.

Tactile Activities

Tactile defensiveness, or sensory affective disorder, was discussed in the introduction. It results when the body is overly responsive to touch. The nervous system responds in a defensive rather than a discriminatory way to most touch stimuli. A sensory affective disorder can influence social and emotional functioning as well as motor performance. It can affect the child's ability to attend, interfering with learning in all other areas (Ayres 1979; Wilbarger and Royeen 1987). The first step in intervention is understanding the disorder and its effects on the child's behavior (Scardina 1986; Wilbarger and Royeen

FIGURE 74

Sensorimotor History

Place a check in the appropriate column. Items marked "yes" may indicate sensorimotor problems.

Questions	No	Yes	Comments
Tactile Sensation			
Does the child:			
1. Object to being touched?	___	___	
2. Dislike being cuddled?	___	___	
3. Seem irritable when held?	___	___	
4. Prefer to touch rather than be touched?	___	___	
5. React negatively to the feel of new clothes?	___	___	
6. Dislike having hair and/or face washed?	___	___	
7. Prefer certain textures of clothing?	___	___	
8. Avoid certain textures of food?	___	___	
9. Isolate self from other children?	___	___	
10. Frequently bump and push other children?	___	___	
Auditory Sensation			
Does the child:			
1. Seem overly sensitive to sound?	___	___	
2. Miss some sounds?	___	___	
3. Seem confused about the direction of sounds?	___	___	
4. Like to make loud noises?	___	___	
5. Have a diagnosed hearing loss?	___	___	
Olfactory Sensation			
Does the child:			
1. Explore the environment with smell?	___	___	
2. Discriminate odors?	___	___	
3. React defensively to smell?	___	___	
4. Ignore noxious odors?	___	___	
Visual Sensation			
Does the child:			
1. Have a diagnosed visual defect?	___	___	
2. Have difficulty eye tracking?	___	___	
3. Make reversals when copying?	___	___	
4. Have difficulty discriminating colors, shapes?	___	___	
5. Appear sensitive to light?	___	___	
6. Resist having vision occluded?	___	___	
7. Become excited when confronted with a variety of visual stimuli?	___	___	
Gustatory Sensation			
Does the child:			
1. Act as though all food tastes the same?	___	___	
2. Explore by tasting?	___	___	
3. Dislike foods of a certain texture?	___	___	

FIGURE 74 (continued)

Place a check in the appropriate column. Items marked "yes" may indicate sensorimotor problems.

Questions	No	Yes	Comments

Vestibular Sensation

Does the child:

1. Dislike being tossed in the air?
2. Seem fearful in space
   (e.g., going up and down stairs, riding teeter-totter)?
3. Appear clumsy, often bumping into things and/or falling down?
4. Prefer fast-moving, spinning carnival rides?
5. Avoid balance activities?

Muscle Tone

Does the child:

1. Have any diagnosed muscle pathology
   (e.g., spasticity, flaccidity, rigidity, etc.)?
2. Seem weaker or stronger than normal?
3. Frequently grasp objects too tightly?
4. Have a weak grasp?
5. Tire easily?

Coordination

Does the child:

1. Manipulate small objects easily?
2. Seem accident prone (i.e., have frequent scrapes and bruises)?
3. Eat in a sloppy manner?
4. Have difficulty with pencil activities?
5. Have difficulty dressing and/or fastening clothes?
6. Have a consistent hand dominance?
7. Neglect one side of the body, or seem unaware of it?

Reflex Integration and Development

1. Was the child slow to reach the usual developmental milestones
   (e.g., sitting, walking, talking)?
2. Was the child irritable in infancy, particularly when held?
3. Does the child have difficulty isolating head movements?
4. Does the child lack adequate protective reactions when falling?

Source: Copyright © 1977 by Western Psychological Services. Adapted from Pat Wilbarger, OTR, Special Education Workshop, St. Paul Public Schools, St. Paul, Minnesota, August 1973. Reprinted from Montgomery, P., and E. Richter, *Sensorimotor integration for developmentally disabled children: A handbook,* by permission of the publisher, Western Psychological Services, 12031 Wilshire Boulevard, Los Angeles, CA 90025.

1987). Once a mother understands that her son squirms in her arms instead of relaxing and cuddling not because he does not love her, but because his nervous system does not know how to interpret touch sensations appropriately, she will be able to carry out specific intervention activities more effectively. Understanding can also help to prevent secondary problems from developing, such as the disturbed relationship that would result from the mother's misinterpretation of her child's behavior in the preceding example.

BRUSHING

Wilbarger and Royeen (1987) have described a brushing program that they have found effective with a wide variety of infants, children, and adults. The treatment consists of brushing selected areas of the child's skin using deep pressure with a soft, multiple-bristle, nonscratching brush (such as a surgical scrub brush), followed by joint compression to selected areas. This procedure is repeated several times a day for a trial period of one to two weeks. Wilbarger (1989) has recently published a manual that provides more information about the approach.

The theory behind this program is complex. The following description is adapted from Wilbarger and Royeen (1987). Think of the system for processing touch sensations as regulated by a thermostat. Above a certain setting, touch is processed in the defensive mode. Below that setting, touch is processed in the discriminative mode. (See the introduction for a more detailed discussion of these two modes.) Ordinarily, the threshold setting for defensive processing is high. In children with a sensory affective disorder, the threshold setting is unusually low. The brushing and joint compression work together to overwhelm the thermostat and reset it at a higher level. However, the body tends to reset the thermostat after about an hour. Therefore, frequent treatments are necessary initially to keep the thermostat at a higher setting. After a few days of keeping the thermostat at a different setting, the body will begin to accept that setting as the "normal" one to return to. At that point, the child's behavior can determine the best frequency of treatment.

Although the program has reportedly been very successful when used as described (Wilbarger and Royeen 1987; Wilbarger and Wilbarger 1988;

Wilbarger 1989), it has sparked controversy because it imposes a treatment on individuals who may resist, especially initially. As was stated in the introduction and again in the general guidelines at the beginning of this chapter, children learn most effectively when they are allowed to direct their own learning. Children should not be forced into activities if they actively do not want to participate, for on some level they are indicating that they are not ready for the activity. In all other situations described in this book these guidelines apply. However, in the case of the child with a sensory affective disorder, Wilbarger and her colleagues believe the rules must change (Wilbarger and Royeen 1987; Wilbarger and Wilbarger 1988). In order to help the child's nervous system readjust to a more appropriate response to tactile stimuli, they believe it is necessary to go against the child's perceptions of readiness for the activity. Intensive treatment over a short time could possibly produce a major, long-term change in the child's response to touch, preventing many disabling symptoms from forming (Wilbarger and Royeen 1987).

Many interventionists have expressed concern about the conflict between the need to treat tactile defensiveness and the invasive nature of the brushing program just described. Suzanne Evans Morris (1989) is presently investigating the use of hemi-sync music (music that promotes learning by activating the information processing capabilities of both hemispheres of the brain) to develop an alternative treatment approach that is effective in resolving tactile defensiveness but less invasive to the individual. Her approach involves helping the child achieve a calm, centered, organized state through the use of specialized music, and then gradually exposing the child to tactile stimuli. As the child is exposed to the tactile stimuli, the music helps the child maintain the central nervous system in a discriminatory rather than a defensive mode. This approach has promise both theoretically and practically, and interventionists may want to experiment with these ideas as well in treating tactile defensiveness.

Before incorporating techniques for tactile desensitization into a child's intervention program, it is essential that their appropriateness be evaluated carefully. Such a program should be carried out under the supervision of a therapist trained in the specific techniques to be used. The therapist will then be able to monitor the program and add other activities as indicated for each individual child to increase the effectiveness of the treatment. It is also essential that the child's parents/caregivers and other staff members be well informed of the program philosophy and its theoretical basis and that they be in agreement with the treatment approach. An intensive brushing program should be considered only for carefully selected individuals and only after less invasive techniques have been ruled out. Because of the severity of problems that can develop secondary to tactile defensiveness, however, the dysfunction must be treated when it is discovered.

ORAL DEFENSIVENESS

Because touch sensations are processed along one neural pathway for the body and along another for the mouth and head, a brushing program may not be an effective treatment for tactile defensiveness of the mouth and face (Wilbarger and Wilbarger 1988). Wilbarger and Wilbarger (1988) have found that firm pressure on the roof of the child's mouth, followed by pressing down through the lower jaw, is helpful in alleviating this problem. This treatment can accompany the usual programs of oral motor stimulation and may help the child to better accept other oral motor activities.

GENERAL TACTILE ACTIVITIES

Even after successfully completing a brushing program or other desensitization program, children with sensory affective disorders continue to need structured exposure to tactile experiences to help them process these sensations and integrate them into overall learning schemes. Children with no tactile processing deficits usually greatly enjoy a variety of activities and need these experiences to form an integrated model of their experience in the world. Children with low tone often need a stronger stimulus and/or a longer response time in order to experience and process sensory information, including tactile stimuli. For all these reasons, an early intervention program should provide many activities with a high tactile component. Some specific suggestions are provided in figure 75 (page 48). The activities suggested are not listed in any particular

sequence and are appropriate, with adaptations, for a wide range of ages from infancy through the elementary grades. (This is true for the activities listed in the other figures in this chapter as well.) Some general guidelines for increasing the tactile component in activities may also spark new ideas.

Be aware of the child's tactile environment. Think about the surface areas in the room. How could these be modified to increase the variety of tactile sensation? (Plan also for areas that are rather neutral in sensory stimulation, including tactile stimulation, to provide "time out" space for children who have become overstimulated. Such neutral areas might be painted neutral colors such as beige. Surfaces should be fairly smooth. If possible, such areas should be fairly well enclosed—perhaps covered on three sides by sheets—and provided with indirect lighting. If the room is noisy, have quiet, centering music playing, provided that such music is appropriate for the children who would be using the neutral area.) Be aware of the tactile stimulation provided by toys. Are they mostly smooth, shiny plastic? Could some toy surfaces be covered with textured materials to increase their tactile value? On the other hand, do some children avoid certain toys or activities because of their tactile components? Are children uncomfortable in their chairs because of the vinyl surface or the itchy carpet roll used to give them more back support? (These are not necessarily indications of tactile defensiveness. Everyone has probably had the experience of trying to sit still on a hot day on a chair or couch covered with old, scratchy upholstery.) Plan to maximize variety and comfort.

Also consider the touch sensations associated with social interaction. Are some children avoiding group activities because too much touching is involved? Do some children resist any physical help with activities? It is useful to remember that children with sensory affective disorders can usually accept firm touch better than light touch. It is also useful to remember that at certain developmental stages, children are very focused on independence. Thus, resistance to physical help or being held on a lap may indicate resistance to restraint rather than tactile defensiveness.

Vestibular Activities

The vestibular system processes information relating to gravity and to the position of the body in space. Vestibular processing impairments may affect a child's balance and muscle tone and secondarily may affect control of eye movements, auditory processing skills, eye-hand coordination, visual-spatial skills, behavioral control, and the ability to cope with stress (Ayres 1979; Scardina 1986). Children with significant impairments in motor development may experience ineffective vestibular processing in part because they are unable to move freely and to experience the wide range of movement necessary for adequate vestibular functioning. Other children are born with vestibular processing impairments or develop them early in life. While they may have many of the necessary motor skills to move freely in the environment, their inadequate vestibular processing may prevent them from doing so (Ayres 1979). For both types of children, providing appropriate vestibular activities can help improve vestibular processing and may also improve functioning in related skills.

It is important that vestibular activities be monitored by a therapist knowledgeable in sensory integration techniques. Too much vestibular stimulation or the wrong kind of vestibular stimulation could cause nausea, seizures, or other serious side effects. This caution applies in particular to spinning a child in circles. Even though children who need this type of stimulation often crave it and will spin themselves for long periods of time if given an opportunity, this activity must be supervised by a trained therapist or by someone especially trained by the therapist to monitor such activities. Activities involving movements in more of a straight line can usually be supervised by the classroom staff at school and by parents at home.

It is the variety of movements that aids in vestibular processing. Therefore, in planning vestibular activities, try to incorporate several different kinds of movements; for example, climbing up a hill and then rolling down. Starting, stopping, and changing direction are all important components in vestibular processing. Therefore, if you are planning activities on a swing, plan to stop and start, change direction and speed, and so on. Vestibular information is processed differently depending on the position of the head and body. A child may be comfortable swinging in a supportive wooden seat but not lying in prone on a platform. Therefore, in planning vestibular activities, try to incorporate a number of different body positions in repetitions of the same activity. Figure 76 (page 49) provides some suggestions for activities involving vestibular input.

Proprioceptive Activities

The proprioceptive system responds to deep pressure and movement in the joints. Proprioceptive activities can help normalize tone for children with high tone as well as children with low tone. Children with low tone especially need stronger stimuli in order to process proprioceptive information adequately. Proprioceptive activities can help calm and desensitize the child with tactile defensiveness. Such activities are useful in increasing the child's own body awareness and improving the body image. Proprioceptive activities are easily incorporated into classroom activities.

In thinking about proprioception, think about deep pressure. Think about pushing and pulling. Think about lifting heavy objects. Think about the feeling of jumping from a chair and landing with both feet on the floor. Think about bear hugs. Also think about the comforting feeling of wrapping yourself up tightly in a blanket on a cold winter's night or perhaps when you just aren't feeling well. Think about what opportunities the children in your program might have to experience some of these feelings. Figure 77 (page 50) provides some suggestions for activities that offer a lot of proprioceptive input.

FIGURE 75

Tactile Activities

Activity	Content Areas	Comments
1. Obstacle course (use lots of textured items—carpet squares; sand, rice, beans on the floor; sticky tape or contact paper to walk or crawl over; "egg-crate" mattress; fake fur; plastic foam chips to crawl through, etc.)	Gross motor; language and cognition if movements, surfaces, relationships, and so on are described (e.g., climb over the sticky tape, Leslie's in the chips, etc.); social interaction; following directions	
2. Finger paint (can be modified by using edibles such as pudding, gelatin, or whipped cream for young children to encourage hand-to-mouth behavior; can be modified by adding textures such as glitter, sand, oatmeal, and so on to the finger-paint media for variety; can use other media such as shaving cream, crazy foam, or soap flakes; can be modified by having children use other body parts to paint with, such as feet, elbows, and so on; temperature of the finger-paint media can also be varied, using warm and cold pudding, for example)	Gross motor (control of arms, legs); fine motor (control of fingers and hands, eye-hand coordination, using two hands together, hand-to-mouth activities); language (colors, descriptions, following directions); social skills (if the activity is done in a group)	Be sure none of the children are allergic to media used. Glitter and similar substances can be dangerous if they get in the eyes.
3. Gluing textures—have the children glue rice, beans, a variety of fabrics, any textured substance onto paper. (This activity can be varied by using colored sand, rice, macaroni, etc. Fabric or paper can be cut into shapes to reinforce a theme—hearts for Valentine's Day, for example. At a higher level, shapes could be drawn on the paper and the children expected to glue within the shape or on the line.)	Fine motor (control of hands and fingers; eye-hand coordination; use of one hand as a support and the other hand for function, crossing midline); language (same as activity 2); cognitive (reinforce concepts of shapes, colors, holidays, field trips, etc.); social skills (if done as a group activity)	Many children will try to eat the beans, rice, and so on.
4. Hidden object hunt—have the children look for objects hidden in a box of plastic foam chips, cellophane "Easter grass," or other textured substance. (At a higher level, ask them to guess what they've found without looking first.)	Cognitive (object permanence, following directions, memory, matching skills); language (following directions, naming, describing); fine motor (hand and arm control, reaching in, grasp and release, crossing midline); gross motor (balance, other skills depending on positioning)	It is easy to confuse tactile defensiveness or lack of interest for lack of object permanence.
5. Play-Doh® (objects can be hidden in Play-Doh®, too, as another variation on activity 4. Play-Doh® can be rolled by hand or with a rolling pin, shaped in various ways, pressed through a garlic press, made into "cookies," used to make handprints or footprints, etc.)	Gross motor (arm extension, proprioception, balance, other skills depending on position); fine motor (hand and finger movements, increased strength, using two hands together, crossing midline); cognitive (pretend play, reinforcing concepts as in activity 3); social skills, including turn taking; language (naming, describing, concept development)	Theraputty®, available from therapy supply companies, can be used in similar ways, but it offers more resistance.
6. Cooking	Cognitive (sequencing, problem solving, conservation, tool use); language (naming, describing, questioning and responding to questions); gross motor (mixing, stirring); fine motor (mixing, pouring, using two hands together, crossing midline); sensory (organization of tastes and smells, which is often neglected in other activities)	The ultimate activity for combining goals from all developmental areas. Be sure to check for allergies and food prohibitions for medical or religious reasons.
7. Rub hand lotion or oil on hands, other body parts. Variations on this activity include using face paints or makeup, drawing on various body parts with markers, soap crayons, and so on.	Gross motor (control of arms, legs); fine motor (control of fingers and hands, eye-hand coordination); body awareness; language; pretend play	
8. Textures box (box filled with various fabrics, sandpaper, loofahs, scrubbies, sponges, and so on; various textures mounted on a wall or suspended from the ceiling within the child's reach are variations on this idea)	Gross motor (reaching for items); fine motor manipulation; cognitive and language (matching, describing, problem solving, variety of manipulations with objects)	
9. Match textures instead of colors in board games	Language; social skills (turn taking, game skills); cognitive (matching, following directions); fine motor	

FIGURE 76

Vestibular Activities

Activity	Content Areas	Comments
1. General playground activities, especially swinging and merry-go-round activities, rolling down hills, and so on	Gross motor; cognitive (problem solving, concept development [up, down, in, out, etc.] spatial relations, pretend play); language (naming, describing, use of action words); social interaction	See precautions described under general guidelines for vestibular activities. Use safety precautions on the playground to avoid accidents.
2. Rolling (variations include in a barrel, up and down inclines, along a path, etc.)	Gross motor; language (following directions, use of action words); social skills (turn taking)	
3. Blanket games—children can be swung in a blanket or pulled across the floor while sitting or lying on a blanket.	Gross motor (in the blanket pull—balance); language (using action words); cognitive (pretend play); social (if several children are pulled on the blanket in a group)	Following the blanket swing or pull activity, the blanket can be incorporated into other activities such as making a tent, filling the blanket with balloons and bouncing them up and down, or using it for a picnic.
4. Scooterboard activities (Children who cannot move themselves on the scooterboard can be positioned on the board and gently moved in different directions. Others can propel themselves, scoot down low inclines, have races, crash into padded walls, and so on. Scooterboards can also be tied together to make trains.)	Gross motor (weight bearing on arms, weight shifting, reciprocal arm movements); cognitive (pretend play, problem solving, concept development, spatial relations); language (describing, using action words)	Be especially careful that children don't run over fingers with the scooterboards. Some of these activities can be used with riding toys or tricycles if they are carefully supervised.
5. Roughhouse—rocking or swinging a child in your arms, bouncing on your lap, carrying a child piggyback or riding on your shoulders, tossing up in the air, playing "airplane" with the child resting on your legs or in prone over your outstretched arms	Gross motor; social skills; pretend play	

FIGURE 77

Proprioceptive Activities

Activity	Content Areas	Comments
1. Sandwich games (roll the child up in a blanket, squash the child between two mats, etc.) or steamroller games (roll a large therapy ball or bolster over the child's body). Both can be done as group activities.	Language (following directions, using action words); cognitive (sequencing, recall, pretend play); social (if done as a group activity); sensory (also a strong tactile component)	Add pretend play to the activity by having the child imagine ketchup and mustard being poured on the sandwich as you apply gentle pressure, imagine being a butterfly in a cocoon, and so on.
2. Pushing and pulling heavy objects in carts or wagons, large balls, boxes, or furniture. Push and pull other children on the swing or other equipment—especially good if they can use a rope to avoid getting hit by the swing. One child can hold onto a rope while the other pulls.	Gross motor (balance, strength, coordination, developmental milestones); social skills; cognitive (problem solving, concept development, spatial relations, pretend play); language (naming, describing, using action words)	Theraband®, a stretchy material like a large rubber band, can be used to provide more resistance where appropriate. It is available from therapy supply companies. Bicycle inner tubes can also be used effectively.
3. Wheelbarrow walking (walking on the hands with the legs supported by another person)	Gross motor (reciprocal movements, weight shifting); fine motor (strengthens the shoulder girdle to provide more stability for fine motor skills); sensory (helps to desensitize the palms of the hands)	
4. Jumping, kicking (these can be adapted for some children with significant motor involvement by helping the child complete the movement, letting the child kick from a seated position, and so on.	Gross motor (see activity 3); language (following directions, using action words, turn taking); social skills	
5. Beanbag games (throwing and catching, throwing into a container, etc.)	Gross motor (see activity 3); language (see activity 4); social skills; cognitive (spatial relations, possibly object permanence, concept development)	
6. Massage	Body awareness; language (identifying/naming body parts); social interaction; sensory/tactile normalization; normalization of body tone	
7. Elastic-bandage wrap	Body awareness; sensory normalization; normalization of body tone; gross motor	Monitor the child to be sure circulation is not impaired by the wrap.

CHAPTER 4

Piagetian
Program Components

Piaget's theory of cognitive development fits well with the NDT and sensory integration approaches because it also is based on the idea that the child is and must be an active participant in learning. Furthermore, like NDT and SI, Piaget's theory is based on the notion that the infant's first channel of learning is through active physical manipulation of the environment. While it has been demonstrated that children whose physical disabilities severely limit their ability to physically manipulate their environment do form many of the concepts identified in Piaget's sequence of sensorimotor development, the qualitative aspects of concepts so developed is still questionable (Gratch 1982; McDonough 1984; Robinson 1982). Whether the children have formed concepts through active manipulation or through observation of others' manipulations, the concepts formed and the sequence of their development appears in most cases to follow the sequence Piaget identified (Dunst and Rheingrover 1981; Hupp, Able, and Conroy 1983a,b).

Another advantage of using Piagetian theory as a basis for cognitive intervention is that it can help teachers avoid the common pitfall of teaching test items. Most assessments of infant cognitive function are based on developmental milestones with strong motor and/or language components. The tendency is then to provide activities designed to teach the items failed. This is understandable enough, espe-cially since for the most part the infant assessments do not help with program planning by breaking down cognitive functioning into its component parts. Piaget's theory provides an analysis of seven components of cognitive functioning in the sensorimotor period, making it easier to think and plan in terms of skill areas and generalization activities rather than specific and sometimes isolated skills.

Analyzing the component parts of cognitive function also makes it easier to identify a child's strengths and weaknesses in this area. The child's overall cognitive function as assessed on a standard infant test may be adequate but could mask a specific deficit in one area that could interfere with development later on. Dunst (1980, 1981) and others (Uzgiris 1976) have shown that there are relationships between development in different cognitive skill areas, between certain cognitive components and different aspects of language development (Bates et al. 1977, 1979; Bricker and Dennison 1978; Edwards 1973; Morehead and Morehead 1974), and between certain cognitive components and certain aspects of social and emotional development (Bell 1970; Bertenthal and Fischer 1978; Brossard 1974; Decarie 1978; Dunst 1978; Lewis and Brooks-Gunn 1979). Fewell (1986) has developed a Play Assessment Scale that incorporates many of the components of cognitive development identified in Piagetian theory.

The introduction outlined the Piagetian theory of cognitive development during the sensorimotor period. This outline presented the stages of development and discussed the process by which the child moves from one stage to the next. This chapter will discuss the different components of cognitive development at each stage and provide charts with some suggestions for activities at each level. Before doing that, it is important to discuss how cognitive intervention can be most effectively carried out and to define the roles and responsibilities of the different team members in the cognitive component of early intervention.

Play and Intervention

Babies and young children learn through play. The statement "a child's work is play" has become a cliche in early intervention circles. Nevertheless, it is useful to keep reminding ourselves of this idea in our work with young children who have developmental delays and disabilities. With this population it is very easy to focus on "what's wrong" and to want to try to "fix it"—a deficit model of intervention. In our efforts to help the child achieve the maximum potential, we may want to work very hard. We push activities on the child because they are what the child is "supposed" to be learning. Or we may push the child to move ahead faster, starting to work on the next skill as soon as the child demonstrates the skill we have focused on. We may insist on a level of obedience and cooperation from children with disabilities of which no other population of like-aged children would be capable. For these reasons, we need to remind ourselves of how typical children behave in mainstream nurseries, day-care centers, and preschools. We need to provide environments that allow children with disabilities to be children first. We need to focus our interventions on play.

There is a lot of learning taking place while a child is playing. By structuring the environment to provide certain kinds of problems, the child will be in a natural situation to try to solve them. The problem, and its solution, will have meaning for the child because it will have arisen out of the child's own interests and activities. Likewise, by providing selected objects and activities, the interventionist can encourage the child to play in ways that will help develop new skills. Paying attention to the

activities that the child chooses then gives the interventionist additional information about the child's strengths, interests, motivation, and readiness for learning new skills.

Allowing the child to direct the learning activity is an important step in developing feelings of independence and self-esteem (Hohmann, Banet, and Weikart 1979). Likewise, giving the child choices whenever possible can help the child develop skills that will be useful throughout life. For young children, these choices have to be carefully structured ("Would you like apple juice or grape juice?" rather than "What would you like to drink?" or "We can use the blocks or the garage right now," rather than "What do you want to play with now?"). These skills need to be fostered as early as possible in order to help the child with a disability develop and maintain a positive self-image and allow the child to be appropriately assertive in the world.

Activities selected should be interesting, fun, and appropriate for the child's age. They should be conducted in a playful, flexible manner. The children should direct the activity and the adults should follow their lead, at the same time keeping in mind a set of relevant goals for each child that can be introduced into the activity as it unfolds. Whenever possible, the children should be given choices about what will happen next.

Program Responsibilities

The teacher is the team member generally responsible for evaluating cognitive functioning and planning activities designed to facilitate cognitive development. Along with these responsibilities, the teacher will usually be responsible for training other staff members, including the teaching assistants, in techniques to facilitate cognitive development. The teacher will provide suggestions for incorporating appropriate cognitive activities for each child into other therapeutic activities. In consultation with the parents and other relevant staff members, the teacher will help develop IEP or IFSP goals related to cognitive development and will provide suggestions for appropriate home activities based on the interests and needs of the family and child.

The teacher is also responsible for running the classroom on a daily basis. This involves planning and carrying out developmentally appropriate activities, coordinating the educational and therapeutic programs, incorporating special events, and so on, as well as general care of the children (monitoring health, changing diapers, supervising behavior, etc.).

The teaching assistants are often primarily responsible for implementing individual activities in the classroom. Like the teacher, the assistants need to have a good understanding of each child's goals and be able to incorporate these goals in playful, child-directed activities.

Often the speech-language pathologist's goals and activities will overlap significantly with cognitive goals and activities. It is therefore important that these goals and activities be coordinated so that they complement and reinforce each other rather than repeating or distracting from one another.

While the teacher frequently plans classroom activities to reinforce SI and NDT goals for each child, the therapists primarily responsible for these program components are also in the classroom a good deal of the time. Therefore it is important for the SI and NDT therapists to have a good understanding of classroom activities in all domains. These therapists also need to have a flexible and playful approach if they are to fit successfully into classroom activities.

Cognitive Content and Activities

Piagetian theory has identified seven domains of cognitive development during the sensorimotor period. They are means-ends, object permanence, spatial relationships, cause-effect, vocal imitation, gestural imitation, and schemes for relating to objects (Uzgiris and Hunt 1975). In addition, Fewell (1986) has developed a Play Assessment Scale that incorporates many components of Piagetian theory. The following section will discuss each of these domains, including play, briefly. The charts (figures 78-84) provide some suggestions for activities for each developmental stage and domain.

OBJECT PERMANENCE

Object permanence involves the ability to remember an object when it is out of sight and to remember or mentally reconstruct where it might be hidden. It is probably the cognitive skill most people think of when they think of Piaget's ideas about how infant thinking develops. Many people assume that knowing the child's stage of understanding for object permanence will tell them where the child is functioning in other cognitive domains as well, but this is not necessarily the case (Dunst 1981). Very often, the child moves into a new stage of sensorimotor development in the domain of object permanence before reaching that level of understanding in the other areas (Dunst 1981). Also, while object permanence is related to "people permanence," the two skills are not identical. People permanence usually develops somewhat ahead of object permanence (Bell 1970; Brossard 1974). In assessing a child's understanding of object permanence, it is critical to take the child's interest in the hidden object into account, since children will not persist in searching for objects that they don't really want. Watching where the child's gaze is directed may provide clues as to the level of understanding the child has, even when the child is unable to reach for an object that has been hidden. Figure 78 (page 54) shows activites related to object permanence.

MEANS-ENDS AND CAUSE-EFFECT

One way to explain the difference between means-ends and cause-effect behaviors is to say that means-ends behaviors involve an understanding of how to achieve a desired goal while cause and effect involves an understanding of what makes things happen. Also, except at the earliest levels, mean-ends behaviors focus around more mechanical problem solving with objects, while cause-effect behaviors tend to center on interactions with adults as causal agents. Thus, an understanding of cause-effect relationships in particular would appear to be directly related to an understanding of the process involved in communication through the use of language (Dunst 1981). Means-ends behaviors, on the other hand, involve an understanding of the use of tools and thus are related to a number of self-help skills (for example, eating with utensils or combing hair) and pre-academic skills (for example, using writing or drawing instruments). See figures 79 (pages 55-56) and 80 (page 57) for activites related to means-end and cause-effect behaviors.

FIGURE 78

Object Permanence Activities

Developmental Stage and Characteristics	Activity
1—**Reflexive responses** need to be exercised and the coordination of two responses encouraged.	1. *Visual fixation.* Hold objects in the position where the infant seems to focus best. Use objects that make noise and/or have moving parts to better attract the infant's attention. 2. *Visual fixation.* Encourage the infant to focus on an adult's face. Talk softly and/or move your face slightly to increase the time the infant will focus. 3. *Visual fixation.* Repeat activity 2 using a black-and-white schematic drawing of a face. You can also try other bold black-and-white patterns.
2—**Primary circular reactions**—two responses are coordinated; encourage use of responses to continue interesting activities outside the child's own body.	1. *Horizontal tracking.* Slowly move objects in a horizontal arc, and encourage child to follow. (The young baby may turn the whole head.) Again, use objects that make noise or contain moving parts. 2. *Horizonal tracking.* Repeat activity 1 using your face as the moving object. Talk to the child if this helps. 3. *Disappearing object.* When the child can follow the object or face successfully, let the target disappear to one side of the arc and reappear on the other. Encourage the child to keep looking for the target. 4. *Visual following.* Encourage the child to visually follow adults as they move around the room. Talk to the child from different parts of the room. Speak to the child before coming into the child's line of sight to help develop the idea that you are still there even when you are out of sight.
3—**Secondary circular reactions**—the child uses a response to cause another behavior outside the child's own body to continue; encourage the child to combine such responses.	1. *Continue stage 2, activity 3.* 2. *Peek-a-boo.* Cover your face, uncover, and say "peek-a-boo." As the child learns the game, wait for some response from the child, such as a coo or sigh, before uncovering. Alternate and cover the child's face. Again, wait for some response from the child before uncovering. 3. *Partially hidden objects.* Hide objects so that part of them shows, for example, a pen sticking out of a shirt pocket or a toy hanging over the edge of a toy basket. Encourage the child to find the toy. A scarf stuffed part way into an empty toilet paper roll is a variation of this activity.
4—**Coordination and combination of secondary circular reactions**; encourage the use of behaviors modified by different environmental responses.	1. *Anticipating an object's return.* Continue stage 2, activity 3. Encourage the child to anticipate where the object will reappear. This can be more fun if you use some activity such as a train running on a circular track with a tunnel. The child will then anticipate where the train will come out of the tunnel. Wind-up toys can also be set to walk behind obstacles such as blocks, toy houses or trees, and so on. 2. *Hidden objects.* Continue stage 3, activity 3, but gradually hide more and more of the object until it is completely hidden. 3. *Hidden objects.* Begin to keep certain common items (toys, clothing, foods, etc.) in specific places. Take the child with you to get these items. 4. *Which hand?* Begin to play hidden objects with two hiding places. For example, which hand did I hide the keys in? Which pocket has the toy mouse hiding in it? 5. *Disappearing objects.* Select some toys where the child drops an object into a hole or slot and the object disappears either to come back out another hole or until you open the container and remove it. Homemade favorites include a can with a slot in the top for dropping in buttons or poker chips or the "milk bottle drop" using a container that the child can't see through. 6. *Water play.* Objects can disappear in a container of soapy water. This activity can be varied by hiding objects in containers of sand, rice, beans, and so on.
5—**Tertiary circular reactions**—behavior changes in response to different feedback from the environment; encourage the use of symbols and representations of things and ideas.	1. *Continue with stage 4, activities 3, 5, and 6.* With activity 5, emphasize the toys in which the disappearing object reappears in another place. 2. *Continue with stage 4, activity 4,* but include more hiding places. 3. *Getting needed items.* During family activities, begin to request that the child get needed familiar items. For example, during a cooking project, the child could find the pot or mixing bowl. When getting dressed to go out, the child could get his or her own shoes, and so on. Similar activities could be used in school. 4. *Garage.* Toy cars could drive into a homemade garage with several doors. The child would then have to find where the car was parked. A similar activity could be used with animals and a barn.
6—**Symbolic representation**—the child can solve some problems mentally and is beginning to use representations of things and ideas.	1. *Continue with stage 5 activities* but add more complexity to the possible hiding places. For example, the horse might arrive at the barn in a van and be unloaded while the child could not see which stall it might go into. In sand play, objects could first be hidden in the hand and then the hand buried before the child could look for the object. 2. *Object hunt.* Include many variations on the theme "find all the blocks in the room and put them in the box." This is especially fun with a theme such as a pumpkin hunt at Halloween. 3. *Water play.* Have the children throw objects into a container of soapy water. They have to find the objects before they can repeat the activity.

FIGURE 79

Means-Ends Activities

Developmental Stage and Characteristics	Activity
1—Reflexive responses need to be exercised and the coordination of two responses encouraged.	1. *Response to objects.* Hold objects where the child seems to see them best. Move them around to encourage the child to look. Encourage the child to respond by movement, vocalization, or other means of showing excitement. (Sometimes if the child is already active, quieting can be a response to the object or activity.) 2. *Response to objects.* Especially for a child with visual impairment, repeat stage 1, activity 1, but emphasize the sound and/or the feel of the object. Look for similar responses.
2—Primary circular reactions—two responses are coordinated; encourage use of responses to continue interesting activities outside the child's own body.	1. *Hand watching.* Put brightly colored mittens or socks on the child's hands to attract the child's attention to them. Bracelets or soft elastic bands with jingle bells attached may also draw the child's attention to the hands. Commercially made "wrist rattles" are another variation. Be sure that whatever you use is safe for the child to mouth. 2. *Printed sheets.* Placing the child in prone on sheets with colorful designs or on brightly colored blankets will often help the child to notice the hands. This position may need to be modified or may be inappropriate for some children with severely abnormal muscle tone. 3. *Mobiles.* Hang mobiles within reach of the child's hands so that random swiping motions will activate the mobile. Be sure to use mobiles that are safe should the child knock them down or mouth them.
3—Secondary circular reactions—the child uses a response to cause another behavior outside the child's own body to continue; encourage the child to combine such responses.	1. *Mobiles.* Continue stage 2, activity 3. When the child seems to understand batting the mobile to make it move, try moving the mobile further away and tying a soft ribbon from the child's wrist or ankle to the mobile so that kicking or arm waving will make the mobile move. Be sure to alternate where you tie the ribbon so that all four extremities are used equally. 2. *Roly-poly toys.* Introduce roly-poly toys that rock back and forth and chime when the child swipes them. 3. *Crib gym and toy bars.* Suspend toys from a rod over the child's crib or when the child is in a stroller, infant seat, or swing, or even on the floor. Encourage the child to reach for and bat at the toys. 4. *Reaching for toys.* Begin to offer the child toys to hold. Encourage the child to reach for the toy and grasp it as you hold it. Then give the child an opportunity to play with the toy before repeating the activity. Be sure to encourage the child to look at the toy when reaching for it.
4—Coordination and combination of secondary circular reactions; encourage the use of behaviors modified by different environmental responses.	1. *More than one object.* Once the child can reach for and hold single objects for a reasonable period of time, begin offering two objects at a time—two spoons, two rattles, and so on. When the child can hold and manipulate two objects, try offering a third. To make the game fun, use a third object that is different from and more interesting than the ones the child is already holding. Let the child try to solve the problem of what to do to get the third object. 2. *Detour reaching.* Encourage the child to reach around or over barriers to get objects. The child should be able to see the desired objects. Examples of naturally occurring barrier problems include reaching around a plate or glass to get a cracker or cookie at mealtime, reaching into a toy box to remove a toy, reaching into a shape sorter box or similar toy to retrieve pieces dropped inside, reaching over someone's leg to get a toy that has dropped there, reaching into a container of water to retrieve a toy, and so on. 3. *Blanket pull.* Place toys slightly out of reach when the child is lying or sitting on a blanket. Encourage the child to pull the blanket to bring the toy close enough to reach. 4. *More barriers.* Use cardboard boxes, blocks, or other obstacles to build walls for the child to knock down in order to get the objects behind them. Balls or balloons can be used as barriers in the same way.

FIGURE 79 (continued)

Developmental Stage and Characteristics	Activity
5—Tertiary circular reactions—behavior changes in response to different feedback from the environment; encourage the use of symbols and representations of things and ideas.	1. *Pull toys.* Introduce some pull toys. (Start with fairly short strings. It is also helpful sometimes to tie a large bead to the end of the string to make it easier for the child to grasp and pull.) When the child can get toys by pulling strings along a horizontal surface like the floor, try tying some toys to the high-chair tray or stroller. (Again, start with short strings.) Vary this activity by tying a helium balloon to the child's chair or stroller. 2. *Sticks and spoons.* These activities help the child to develop an understanding of simple tool use. Musical instruments such as a drum, xylophone, or triangle that require the use of a stick are good activities to offer. Catching floating objects in the bathtub or pool with a large wooden or plastic spoon is another enjoyable activity, as is digging in the sand or dirt. All kinds of ball games can be used to develop tool use. Any games using a stick to hit a ball (tee-ball, golf, hockey, etc.) qualify. A child can bat at a ball suspended from the ceiling or a tree or simply chase a ball around and hit it with a stick. Self-help activities such as spoon feeding, tooth brushing and hair combing are everyday opportunities to practice using tools. These activities can be incorporated into doll play for further reinforcement and to develop representational play skills as well. Art activities using crayons, markers, paintbrushes, or other tools provide another way to reinforce this concept. Wall painting with water is a popular variation on this theme.
6—Symbolic representation—the child can solve some problems mentally and is beginning to use representations of things and ideas.	1. *Mismatched parts.* In play, use some toys with parts that don't fit. For example, with a toy garage, provide some cars that are too big to go down the ramp, along with cars that are the right size. Or, give the child a puzzle piece that doesn't belong, along with all the correct pieces. With these activities, be sure to use toys that the child is very familiar with and has previously mastered the ordinary use of. 2. *Choices.* Give the child a choice between an item that will solve a problem and one that will not. For example, with a yogurt snack offer the child a choice of a fork or spoon. To carry water to the sand box, offer a bucket or a sieve, and so on.

FIGURE 80

Cause-Effect Activities

Developmental Stage and Characteristics	Activity
1—Reflexive responses need to be exercised and the coordination of two responses encouraged.	*Response to voice.* See vocal imitation (figure 82), stage 1, activity 1. Encourage the child to vocalize and/or smile in response to an adult talking to the child.
2—Primary circular reactions— two responses are coordinated; encourage use of responses to continue interesting activities outside the child's own body.	*Hand watching.* See means-ends (figure 79), stage 2, activities 1, 2, and 3.
3—Secondary circular reactions—the child uses a response to cause another behavior outside the child's own body to continue; encourage the child to combine such responses.	1. *Keeping a toy going.* See means-ends (figure 79), stage 3, activities 1, 2, and 3. 2. *Using procedures.* See gestural imitation (figure 81), stage 2, activity 1. Here the focus is on the child's use of a consistent behavior (procedure) in order to get the adult to repeat the behavior. Toys that produce a repetitious action, such as a pinwheel or "jumping jack" activated by pulling a string are often effective. During games such as pat-a-cake or tickle, the adult can stop after one turn and wait for the child to respond in some consistent way before taking another turn. The adult can also perform such interesting activities as "beeping" the nose, snapping the fingers, or blowing into a pop bead to create a whistling noise. It is a good idea to use a variety of different kinds of these games so that the child generalizes the idea of using a procedure in order to cause an adult to continue a behavior.
4—Coordination and combination of secondary circular reactions; encourage the use of behaviors modified by different environmental responses.	*Continue stage 3, activity 2.* Encourage the child to use some socially meaningful gestures in order to cause the adult to continue or initiate an activity. For example, the child could manipulate the adult's hands to continue a game of pat-a-cake or reach up to the adult to signal "pick me up."
5—Tertiary circular reactions— behavior changes in response to different feedback from the environment; encourage the use of symbols and representations of things and ideas.	1. *Showing off to get attention.* Children usually don't have to be taught to do this. However, they do have to perform some behavior that gets laughter or some other strong response from an adult in order to have an opportunity to repeat it. Be sure to provide such opportunities frequently. 2. *Giving and/or showing objects to initiate interactions.* Provide children models for this type of behavior by showing them objects to initiate interactions with them. As much as possible, respond to such initiations from the child, especially when they represent a new behavior. 3. *Using gestures, eye gaze, and vocalizations in combination to communicate.* The child at this stage begins to look at the adult, look at the desired object, point to it, and vocalize. It is important that adults respond to the child's requests. Often this kind of communication can be facilitated by putting highly desirable objects in sight but out of the child's reach. Having some but not all of the materials needed for an activity can also elicit requests for the missing items.
6—Symbolic representation— the child can solve some problems mentally and is beginning to use representations of things and ideas.	1. *Wind-up toys.* Introduce mechanical wind-up toys. Encourage the child to figure out how to activate them. 2. *Gum-ball machines.* Toys (or real gum-ball machines) that require two different actions to activate can be introduced at this time. A cash register that requires the child to put in a coin and push a button before the drawer opens, or a key-operated toy in which a key unlocks a door that then needs to be opened with a handle are two examples.

GESTURAL AND VOCAL IMITATION

The ability to imitate is extremely important in facilitating learning. It is much easier to learn new behaviors, especially motor behaviors, through imitation than by any other means. Once the child develops the concept of communication, vocal imitation makes the expressive use of new words possible. Despite the fact that both skills are based on the basic skill of imitation, gestural and vocal imitation appear to develop independently of one another (Dunst 1980). Therefore it is important to assess the two skills separately. An ability to imitate in one domain but not in the other might point to a motor problem in the lesser developed area, or it might indicate a lack of exposure to appropriate models in that area. Poor vocal imitation with good gestural imitation might also indicate a hearing loss or a lack of understanding of the significance of speech and language in the environment.

Repetitive vocalizations such as occur in babbling are often associated with repetitive motor movements. For example, a baby might be banging a rattle on the table and vocalizing "dadada." Or a baby might utter "gagagaga" when bouncing on the father's lap. Therefore, pairing such motor movements with sounds that you make may facilitate the baby's imitation. An awareness of the developmental sequence of both gestural and vocal imitations will also help keep the interventionist's expectations reasonable, so that the child is not asked to imitate developmentally more difficult behaviors before learning to imitate easier ones. Figures 81 (page 59) and 82 (page 60) explain activities related to gestural and vocal imitation.

SPATIAL RELATIONSHIPS AND SCHEMES FOR RELATING TO OBJECTS

Like means-ends and cause-effect behaviors, spatial relationships and schemes for relating to objects are sometimes difficult domains to differentiate. It is sometimes helpful to think about the domains as representing the two kinds of knowledge that babies have to gain about things in their environment. One is an understanding of the physical properties of objects—their size, shape, color, what material they are made of, and so on. Objects have other properties that children need to explore. For example, some bounce and some break. Some stack and some don't. Some fit inside others; some are good for putting things in. Some are the same all over and some have different sides that look and feel different and can be used differently. All these qualities relate to the understanding of spatial relationships—how objects relate to each other and to their environment in space.

The other kind of understanding children need to develop is the social properties of objects—what people in their environment generally do and don't do with certain objects. This is the kind of understanding that the schemes for relating to objects describes. Some of the social properties of objects are related to their physical properties. For example, people generally throw balls but not teacups. In other cases, socially accepted uses must simply be learned from observation and/or teaching. For example, at some point children learn to differentiate a hairbrush, a toothbrush, and a scrub brush, although initially they may seem interchangeable. During the early stages of development, the child's schemes for relating to objects will seem more reflective of the object's physical than its social properties. Yet the child is continuing to develop increasingly more differentiated and complex actions that will evolve into socially directed behaviors as the child matures. See figures 83 (page 61) and 84 (page 62) for activities related to these two areas of development.

PLAY

Fewell (1986) has developed a Play Assessment Scale that examines a child's spontaneous play behaviors in some detail. Although many behaviors included here are also included in the schemes for relating to objects or spatial relations domains just described, the focus is sufficiently different that Fewell's analysis should be considered along with the more standard Piagetian domains. One significant difference in organization is that, especially after the first year, Fewell focuses on how the child combines objects and behaviors and how the child sequences behaviors. Her analysis is more detailed, and the relationships examined appear to be significant to the development of certain language forms (see Carter 1978; Greenfield 1978; Morehead and Morehead 1974; Sinclair 1971).

During the 1988-89 school year, the author used both a standard cognitive assessment (Hawaii Early Learning Profile) (Furuno et al. 1985) and

Fewell's (1986) Play Assessment Scale to evaluate the development of a class of two- and three-year-olds with developmental disabilities. Several children's age equivalents for cognitive development, while delayed compared to their chronological ages, were still advanced as much as a year over the spontaneous play skills shown in the classroom. This situation indicates how early intervention can fail to provide young children with important life skills, for here was a group of children who were successfully developing pre-academic skills but who did not know how to play. These children are in danger of remaining too dependent on others to provide their learning for them because they have not developed the skills to explore and manipulate their environment constructively. They are also in danger of remaining socially isolated because they lack the skills necessary to interact effectively with other children their own age. By structuring cognitive intervention around the development of play skills, the teacher can help to alleviate this situation while still incorporating the Piagetian cognitive domains.

FIGURE 81
Gestural Imitation Activities

Developmental Stage and Characteristics	Activity
1—Reflexive responses need to be exercised and the coordination of two responses encouraged.	*Attending.* Encourage the child to watch you perform different actions using toys or just your hands. With toys, some gestures might include shaking a rattle, banging a spoon on the table, or making a stuffed toy hop up and down on the table. Just using your hands, you might play peek-a-boo, clap, or wave.
2—Primary circular reactions—two responses are coordinated; encourage use of responses to continue interesting activities outside the child's own body.	*Continue stage 1, activity 1.* Encourage the child to use some gesture or consistent action in response to your actions. Wait for the child's response before repeating your action.
3—Secondary circular reactions—the child uses a response to cause another behavior outside the child's own body to continue; encourage the child to combine such responses.	1. *Simple gestures.* The child can now be expected to begin to imitate familiar simple gestures such as shaking or waving an object, banging an object on the table, patting the table, or waving "bye-bye." (Simple gestures usually involve the use of only one hand in an up-and-down motion. Familiar gestures are gestures that the child performs spontaneously in a nonimitative situation.) 2. *Complex gestures.* After the child begins to perform stage 3, activity 1, try using more complex gestures with familiar components. These usually involve some type of midline skill and may require the use of both hands. Some examples include banging two objects together, sliding an object on the table, or playing pat-a-cake.
4—Coordination and combination of secondary circular reactions; encourage the use of behaviors modified by different environmental responses.	1. *Continue stage 3, activity 2.* 2. *Unfamiliar visible gestures.* Visible gestures mean gestures that the child can see itself perform. Many simple baby games and finger plays are appropriate at this point. Be sure the child has the motor skills needed to imitate the gesture. Gross motor action may be easier to imitate than smaller movements. Doing "silly" things with objects can also elicit this level of imitation. For example, make a car fly or drive upside down instead of driving in the usual way. Or have the wagon pull the horse instead of the other way around.
5—Tertiary circular reactions— behavior changes in response to different feed-back from the environment; encourage the use of symbols and representations of things and ideas.	1. *Invisible gestures with objects.* Invisible gestures are actions that the child cannot see itself perform. These are usually easier for the child when they involve the use of an object. Examples include putting a toy on the head or behind the ear. 2. *Invisible gestures without objects.* Examples might include patting the head or blinking the eyes. At this stage, the child may attempt to imitate invisible gestures but will not be able to do so accurately or easily.
6—Symbolic representation— the child can solve some problems mentally and is beginning to use representations of things and ideas.	*Continue stage 5, activities 1 and 2.* At this stage, the child will begin to be able to imitate unfamiliar invisible gestures more accurately and easily without trial and error.

FIGURE 82

Vocal Imitation Activities

Developmental Stage and Characteristics	Activity
1—**Reflexive responses** need to be exercised and the coordination of two responses encouraged.	1. *Response to voice.* Talk to the child as much as possible. Experiment with different tones of voice and with how loudly or softly you speak to see if the child responds differently. 2. *Imitating the child.* Whenever you can, imitate the child's vocalizations. Even if you can't get all the "baby sounds" just right, try at least to make some vocal response to the child's vocalizations. This will help increase the child's awareness of the child's own vocalizations and will establish a good beginning for communication.
2—**Primary circular reactions**—two responses are coordinated; encourage use of responses to continue interesting activities outside the child's own body.	1. *Continue stage 1, activities 1 and 2.* 2. *For infants who are not making many sounds,* oral stimulation such as rubbing the gums may help elicit more vocalizations. 3. *Tickling and other gentle games* involving touch and motion may also help to elicit more vocalizations.
3—**Secondary circular reactions**—the child uses a response to cause another behavior outside the child's own body to continue; encourage the child to combine such responses.	1. *Beginning imitation.* Continue stage 1, activity 2. Encourage the child to repeat the vocalization you have just imitated. 2. *More imitation.* Sometimes when the child is attending but not vocalizing, make a sound you have heard the child make and see if the child will imitate it. 3. *Imitating words.* Continue stage 1, activity 1. Emphasize certain familiar words. See if the child will vocalize in response to those words. Encourage the child to use vocalizations similar to the words themselves, such as "baba" for bottle or baby.
4—**Coordination and combination of secondary circular reactions;** encourage the use of behaviors modified by different environmental responses.	1. *Continue stage 3 activities.* Expect more consistent, exact imitations at this point. 2. *Unfamiliar sounds.* In play, make noises to go along with actions. For example, say "vroom-vroom" as you run a toy car along the floor. Encourage the child's attempts to imitate these sounds. 3. *Unfamiliar words.* Introduce less familiar words to the child in play or conversation. Encourage the child's attempts to imitate these words by repeating the word after each of the child's attempts to imitate it.
5—**Tertiary circular reactions**—behavior changes in response to different feedback from the environment; encourage the use of symbols and representations of things and ideas.	*Continue with stage 4, activities 2 and 3.* Expect the child's imitations to be more exact.
6—**Symbolic representation**—the child can solve some problems mentally and is beginning to use representations of things and ideas.	*Continue stage 4, activity 3.* The child should begin to repeat unfamiliar words with a minimum of trial and error. Very often this becomes a game in which the child will try to repeat every new word heard.

FIGURE 83

Spatial Relations Activities

Developmental Stage and Characteristics	Activity
1—**Reflexive responses** need to be exercised and the coordination of two responses encouraged.	1. *Response to voice.* See vocal imitation (figure 82), stage 1, activity 1. 2. *Response to sounds.* Use different noisemakers (rattle, squeak toy, bell, etc.) to see if the child will look in the direction of the sound.
2—**Primary circular reactions**—two responses are coordinated; encourage use of responses to continue interesting activities outside the child's own body.	1. *Localizing sounds.* See object permanence (figure 78), stage 2, activity 4. Encourage the child to turn to the place where the voice or sound is coming from. Also continue stage 1, activity 2, but hold the noisemakers further from the child so that the child really has to turn to the sound. 2. *Two objects.* Hold two very different looking objects up for the child to see (one in each hand). Notice if the child looks from one to the other. Try moving first one and then the other to encourage the child to look back and forth. Repeat using objects that make different sounds.
3—**Secondary circular reactions**—the child uses a response to cause another behavior outside the child's own body to continue; encourage the child to combine such responses.	1. *Grasping objects.* See means-ends (figure 79), stage 3, activity 4. 2. *Tracking dropped objects.* While the child is watching, drop an object so that it falls on the tray or floor in front of the child. It is important the child be able to see the dropped object without needing to change body position. At first, you may want to use objects that will make a noise when they fall. Later, experiment with quiet objects such as a yarn pompom.
4—**Coordination and combination of secondary circular reactions**; encourage the use of behaviors modified by different environmental responses.	1. *Dropped objects.* Continue with stage 3, activity 2, but allow the object to fall so that the child must shift body position to see where it landed. 2. *Reversed objects.* Give the child opportunities to play with objects that have an "interesting" side and a blank side, such as a mirror, a picture postcard, or a busy box. After the child has had several opportunities to explore these objects, experiment with handing the child the object with the blank side up. See if the child will turn the object over to look at the functional side. Be sure to use objects small enough for the child to manipulate easily. 3. *Combining objects.* Let the child have a container and small objects to put in and dump out. Pots and pans from the kitchen are big favorites for this activity. Also give the child opportunities to bang on one object with another. See mean-ends (figure 79), stage 5, activity 2, for some ideas. Encourage the child to bang two similar objects such as blocks or spoons together, too. 4. *Dumping out.* Drop bits of cereal or other treats into jars or bottles and encourage the child to get them out. Single-serving cereal boxes are also good to use for this activity; they encourage the child to use both hands together and solve the problem of opening the box as well.
5—**Tertiary circular reactions**—behavior changes in response to different feedback from the environment; encourage the use of symbols and representations of things and ideas.	1. *Building blocks.* At this stage, the child may be ready to begin stacking objects on top of one another. Many children enjoy stacking canned goods in the kitchen, and this activity is particularly good for children with low muscle tone. Provide a variety of different stackable materials such as pillows or cardboard boxes. 2. *Stacking rings.* The child may also begin putting rings on stacking pegs, although not necessarily in the correct order. Putting bracelets on themselves and others incorporates the same idea. 3. *Inclines.* Let the child roll toy cars down a garage ramp or a ramp built from blocks. A bowling activity in which the child rolls a ball down a ramp to knock over cardboard boxes or blocks also helps develop the idea of letting things roll downhill by themselves. 4. *Detours.* In play, let an object such as a ball or toy car roll behind a piece of furniture so that the child has to go around the furniture to retrieve the object.
6—**Symbolic representation**—the child can solve some problems mentally and is beginning to use representations of things and ideas.	1. *Detours.* At this stage, the child can be introduced to complex detour problems, such as from a cul-de-sac, to retrieve an object that has rolled or bounced away during play. 2. *Missing persons.* At school, during roll call or circle time, ask who is missing. Encourage children to name all their classmates, including ones who are not in the room. Talk with them about where their family members are when they are at school. Use similar activities at home to encourage the child to remember missing people and imagine where they might be.

FIGURE 84

Schemes for Relating to Objects Activities

Developmental Stage and Characteristics	Activity
1—**Reflexive responses** need to be exercised and the coordination of two responses encouraged.	*Grasping finger.* Encourage the child to grasp your finger as you play with and talk to the child.
2—**Primary circular reactions**—two responses are coordinated; encourage use of responses to continue interesting activities outside the child's own body.	1. *Grasping objects.* Offer the child objects that are easy to grasp (clothespin size usually works well). If the child has difficulty grasping, wrap the child's hand around the object and wiggle or pull on the object. Offer a variety of different textures, shapes, sizes, and weights. 2. *Mouthing objects.* Once the child can hold an object well, the child will most likely bring the object to the mouth for further exploration. A child with motor dysfunction may need help to do this. For young children, exploration with the mouth is a bridge to exploration with the eyes. Some children with tactile defensiveness may avoid holding and mouthing objects. See the sections on SI for suggestions in such cases. 3. *Looking at objects.* Encourage the child to look at the objects as the child is holding them. Toys that make sounds, such as rattles, may facilitate this behavior.
3—**Secondary circular reactions**—the child uses a response to cause another behavior outside the child's own body to continue; encourage the child to combine such responses.	1. *Shaking, banging.* Demonstrate these actions for the child and provide appropriate objects. A variety of rattles and large spoons are usually successful. 2. *Examining.* Encourage the child to examine objects on all sides. Talk to the child about all the different features of the object as you demonstrate how to examine all its sides. Be sure to offer objects that have different features on different sides—for example, a rotating busy box with a different activity featured on each side. 3. *Dropping.* Release may still be difficult for the child to control. The child usually releases objects suddenly, with no attention to what happens to them. Provide the child with lots of small objects that are easily grasped and released.
4—**Coordination and combination of secondary circular reactions**; encourage the use of behaviors modified by different environmental responses.	1. *Complex actions.* Introduce objects that elicit more complex behaviors than simple shaking or banging. Paper, old necklaces, toy cars, balls, etc., are all useful objects for this purpose. 2. *Dropping/throwing.* At this point, the child may be better able to release objects with control. Provide containers for the child to put small objects in. Encourage the child to throw objects into a wading pool or tub of water, throw beanbags into a basket, or play a modified game of basketball. Encourage the child to watch where the thrown object goes. Many children also enjoy the game of "drop" at this point. This game involves dropping objects from the high chair, crib, or other high place, usually while the parent is busy with some other task. The child then screams for the parent to retrieve the objects and immediately drops them again. Try to indulge in this game when you can, and tie some toys onto the furniture so the child can retrieve them when you are too busy. 3. *Functional use of objects.* At this point the child may begin to show understanding of how people usually use the objects in the environment. One of the first signs of this understanding is the child's offering an adult bites of food. Please accept, or at least pretend to. Other behaviors may include showing how to use a hairbrush, telephone, spoon, or shoe. The child will direct these actions toward other people or toward itself. Provide the child with lots of opportunities to play with functional items, and take turns with the child in demonstrating their use.
5—**Tertiary circular reactions**—behavior changes in response to different feedback from the environment; encourage the use of symbols and representations of things and ideas.	1. *Giving and/or showing objects to initiate interactions.* See cause-effect (figure 80), stage 5, activity 2. 2. *Functional use of objects.* See stage 4, activity 3. At this stage, the child will begin to direct these behaviors toward a doll or stuffed toy. Be sure to provide a wide variety of functional objects, as well as a variety of dolls or other stuffed toys. Many children, especially boys, will not play with baby dolls but will pretend to feed and groom a teddy bear or stuffed characters from TV programs.

FIGURE 84 (continued)

Developmental Stage and Characteristics	Activity
6—**Symbolic representation**—the child can solve some problems mentally and is beginning to use representations of things and ideas.	1. *Representational play.* Here the child begins to use objects to represent other objects. For example, blocks can be used to represent food when pretending to cook or a peg can represent a doll's bottle. To facilitate the development of this kind of play, set up scenarios in which some necessary items are missing. Provide items nearby that could be used as substitutes. During play, make comments such as, "Oh, we need some money for the cash register. We don't have any. What could we use instead?" Provide lots of these experiences. 2. *Naming.* Encourage the child to name people, objects, and actions in the present environment. Songs and games that include all the children's names ("Sally's Got the Hat," "Hello Song," etc.) are useful. If the child is ready, requiring the child to name the object before getting it can facilitate naming. Sometimes an adult can facilitate naming with "planned stupidity"—not being able to figure out what the child wants until the child names the item. Snack time is wonderful for facilitating naming behavior. See also gross motor and sensory integration activities for more activities to facilitate naming, especially of actions. It is important that the child really be ready for these activities before requiring naming in order to get a snack or objects. If the child really cannot perform the task, the frustration may only serve to further block communication and result in the child's refusal to try to participate.

CHAPTER 5

Speech-Language Components

The discussion of NDT, SI, and Piagetian theories thus far has assigned responsibility for overseeing implementation of each to a particular therapeutic discipline. In most cases, the physical therapist will be responsible for overseeing NDT program components. The occupational therapist will oversee SI program components, and the educator will oversee Piagetian components. What then is the speech-language therapist's role in such a program?

Like members of the other disciplines, the speech-language clinician must have a working knowledge of NDT, SI, and Piagetian approaches in order to effectively participate in the type of program outlined in this book. NDT positioning and handling techniques, as well some facilitation and inhibition techniques, are important in order for the speech-language clinician to facilitate the appropriate motor components of speech production. Oral-motor skills are important for speech as well as for feeding. Both NDT and SI approaches are important in the evaluation and treatment of oral-motor dysfunctions. An understanding of the relationship between cognitive and social skills and language development is critical to facilitating the development of a child's communication skills. Thus, the speech-language clinician's skills overlap with those of each of the other team members in addressing different aspects of speech and language development. A discussion of the speech-language therapist's specific responsibilities and suggested activities that will tie speechlanguage therapy into other program components follows. The resource list in the appendix provides sources for additional ideas for activities that emphasize the speech and language components of learning.

Program Responsibilities

The speech-language clinician's responsibilities in an early intervention program usually include evaluation of the child's speech and language skills and oral-motor function. In consultation with the child's family and other team members, the speech-language clinician plans treatment goals to address the child's needs in these areas. The speech-language clinician also may provide direct treatment to those children who need it and will suggest activities that can be used in the classroom, during other therapy sessions, and/or at home to enhance the child's speech, language, and oral-motor development. In addition, the speech-language clinician will assist in writing IEP or IFSP goals related to speech, language, and oral-motor development and will evaluate the child's progress in these areas at regular intervals. The speech-language clinician will also provide ongoing consultation with parents and other staff members as needed and will help to train staff and parents in any techniques they need to learn to better carry out speech, language, and oral-motor program goals. The speech-language clinician will most often be in the classroom participating in daily activities and using such activities as an opportunity to increase the speech and language skills of each child. Other staff members will also be responsible for reinforcing speech and language goals in their activities whenever possible.

Program Components

While there are many ways to analyze how children develop language, most early intervention programs address three main areas. These are feeding skills, the understanding of communication, and speech production. In some cases, the speech-language clinician will also need to address the child's response to auditory stimuli. This section will discuss some of the major considerations in each of these areas and will suggest some appropriate activities for each.

FEEDING

Speech therapy addresses feeding issues for two reasons. One is that many of the same muscles and motor movements that are needed for efficient feeding are used for speech production. Therefore, the development of good oral-motor skills is believed to be one of the precursors of good speech articulation. Problems in muscle tone, position, coordination of breathing, and so on, that affect a child's feeding abilities will also affect that child's speech production (Foltz and Lewis 1985). Oral-motor issues aside, the feeding situation is very powerful in the communicative possibilities that it encompasses (Morris 1987). During feeding, the child is likely to be highly motivated to communicate on a variety of topics, either positively or negatively. "More," "no more," "I like it," "I don't like it," "faster," "slower," "I'm finished," "I want something else instead" are among the possible ideas that even an infant may try to convey during feeding. These messages are likely to be strong ones. Thus, the feeding situation offers an excellent starting point for helping the child begin to understand the process of communication (Morris 1987). The oral-motor aspects of feeding will be addressed here. The communicative aspects of feeding will be discussed under the communication heading below.

Preparation for feeding. Preparation for feeding involves the same components as preparation for other movement activities—normalization of muscle tone and the establishment of a stable base of support. (See the section on NDT in the introduction and chapter 2 for a more complete discussion of these treatment components.) In addition, preparation for feeding may also involve the normalization of oral hypersensitivity. The chapter on sensory integration described one technique to

help normalize the child's responses to touch around the face and mouth. Other techniques that also might be used include rubbing the face and gums with the hands and/or a dry washcloth, rubbing the gums with a child's toothbrush or rubber Nuk® toothbrush, tapping the cheeks and chin gently, and shaking the cheeks gently. Imagine dividing the face into quadrants for these procedures, as shown in figure 85. Begin at the hairline and work toward the lips. Move from quadrant I to II to III to IV. In general, the firm rubbing may help to reduce tone that is too high, while shaking and tapping may help to increase tone that is too low. The speech-language clinician will recommend which specific techniques are appropriate for each individual child.

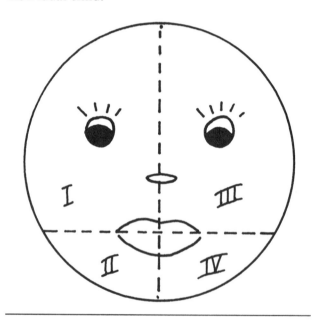

Figure 85

Position for feeding. The child's position for feeding should be socially and developmentally appropriate as well as comfortable for both the child and the feeder, and it should facilitate the normalization of muscle tone and motor movements as much as possible. The guidelines discussed in the NDT section on positioning apply as well. If at all possible, the feeder should be positioned with the face a little below the child's eye level in order to facilitate neck flexion ("chin tuck") rather than the hyperextended pattern frequently seen in children with abnormal tone. This position will open the child's airway, encourage active use of the lips, cheeks, and tongue, and help to prevent food from leaking into the pharynx prematurely. Unless there is some special reason not to do so, the spoon should be presented at the child's midline. In addition to positions discussed in the NDT chapter that might be appropriate for feeding, consider the following positions:

Child on a wedge or pillow that is supported partially by the table edge and partially by the feeder's lap (figure 86). An extra pillow behind the child's head can keep the child's head forward if necessary. This position can be adapted by simply holding the child in this position on the feeder's lap. The feeder's knees are bent to raise the child's head and bring it forward. Be sure the feeder has good back support for both these positions.

Figure 86

Child held in the feeder's arms (figure 87). Be sure the child is held relatively upright, since the

Figure 87

tendency with this position is to hold the child in a horizontal position and pour the food in. Keep the child's hips bent to encourage more normalized muscle tone and better body alignment and to help control any "pushing back" that the child may do. A stool under one of the feeder's feet may help to control the child's position, too. Again, the feeder needs good back support.

Chin tuck. In these and most other positions the feeder can help the child maintain head and neck flexion, or a "chin tuck," by applying deep pressure downward on the chest below the chin

Figure 88

(figure 88). This technique will also help the child keep the jaw in a neutral position. The chin tuck position facilitates appropriate lip, mouth, and tongue movements for sucking, biting, chewing, and swallowing, as well as contributing to appropriate breathing patterns. This position also helps to prevent choking.

Jaw control. Jaw control techniques provide external support for the child and help facilitate more normal movement patterns than the child is able to make independently. Some children also have such unstable joints that their jaws may become subluxed during feeding. Jaw control can also help to prevent this from happening.

Jaw control techniques require that the adult's hand be placed on the child's face, lips, and/or chin. Because of sensitivity to touch or a dislike of restraint, many young children may resist the use of these techniques. Therefore their use depends on establishing a trust between the child and the feeder as well as on the normalization of oral hypersensitivity. In some cases, you will have to modify the amount or type of control you can use or not use it at all. Figures 89 and 90 show two types of jaw control. The speech-language clinician will teach you how and when to use these techniques appropriately.

Figures 89 & 90

Types of foods. Because of problems with oral-motor control and/or because of a sensitivity to food tastes, textures, temperatures, and so on, the child may be eating a very limited diet. However, the child who never attempts more challenging foods will not have the opportunity to improve oral-motor control or reduce oral hypersensitivity. The situation becomes a "vicious circle," frustrating to everyone involved. Part of any feeding program, then, involves stimulating the child to try more challenging foods. The continuum of solid foods, from easiest to most difficult to manage, is pureed, ground or junior, mashed table foods, coarsely chopped table foods, easily chewed meats, and more difficult meats (Morris 1977). Thick liquids are easier to manage than thin liquids. Figure 91 provides some examples of common foods in each category. Again, the speech-language clinician will make specific recommendations for each child.

FIGURE 91

Food Categories
(in order of difficulty)

Smooth with Slightly Lumpy Texture
Easier
Cake
Oatmeal
Soft boiled eggs
Mashed potatoes
Junior vegetables
Noodles or spaghetti

Granular Texture
Cookies
Tapioca pudding
Junior meats
Melba toast or rusks
Granola

Lumpy
Fried eggs
Hamburger meat
Scrambled eggs
Mashed, cooked vegetables
Cottage cheese

Crisp
Raw carrots, lettuce, fruits
Fried bacon
Cheese twists
Potato chips
Crackers

Easy Fibers Requiring Minimal Chewing
Raisins
Chicken
Skinless wieners
Fish
Luncheon meat
Cheddar cheese
Steamed vegetables

Very Chewy— Tough and Firm
Roast beef
Pork and lamb chops
Steak
Ham
Raw celery
More Difficult Chewy bacon

Liquids
Easier
Heavier milky liquids
ice cream
milk shakes
yogurt
custard or pudding

Thin milky liquids
milk
cream soups

Heavier clear liquids
apricot juice
tomato juice
pineapple juice

Thin, clear liquids
water
bouillon soup or broth
carbonated beverages
apple juice

Very Smooth Semisolids
Finely mashed fresh banana
Gelatin
More Difficult Strained fruits
Applesauce

In considering foods to add to a child's diet, allergies, medical conditions requiring special dietary considerations, and religious, ethnic, and other social considerations need to be taken into account. Children with swallowing disorders also require special considerations, and changes in their diet should be made only in consultation with their physicians. Sugary drinks and foods tend to increase saliva production and should be avoided with children who drool a great deal (Wilson, n.d.). Milk and milk products tend to increase mucus production and should be avoided with children who tend to be congested. There has also been some concern that very cold temperatures in certain parts of the mouth or throat could trigger seizures in a child with a seizure disorder, so foods such as frozen juice bars should be used cautiously (Farber, n.d.).

Coordination of functions for feeding. Some children have difficulties with feeding because they have difficulty coordinating breathing, sucking, and swallowing. If a baby inhales and swallows at the same time, for example, he or she may choke or aspirate food or liquid into the lungs. Children who have difficulty coordinating these functions often resist feeding because it is so uncomfortable or frightening for them. Some of the techniques described in this section, such as appropriate positioning, jaw control, and attention to the consistency of foods, may help them to better coordinate breathing, swallowing, and related functions. The use of structured, 60-beat-per-minute music, such as baroque music, has sometimes been helpful in improving such a situation by providing an appropriate steady rhythm that organizes and structures the child's responses (Morris 1985). Such background music can also help the feeder coordinate actions with the child's breathing and feeding patterns (Morris 1985). More information on the appropriate selection and use of music to facilitate therapeutic interventions is provided in appendix 4.

General techniques. In spoon feeding, present the spoon in the center of the child's mouth with the child's head in midline. Applying gentle, downward pressure on the tongue with the bowl of the spoon may facilitate the child's closing the lips to help remove the food from the spoon. Try to encourage the child to do as much as possible independently. Avoid scraping the spoon against the child's upper teeth or gums to remove the food, and avoid cleaning the chin too often as this can increase the child's tone and sensitivity.

To encourage chewing, place small pieces of soft foods such as banana on the child's gums or molars. Be sure to alternate sides equally. Sometimes the feeder can use a strip of dried fruit or similar food to facilitate chewing by placing one end on the child's molar area and keeping hold of the other end for control. Children with low tone or who have decreased sensation in their mouths may need heavier, crunchy foods to facilitate chewing. In all cases, be sure to use types and sizes of foods that the child could not accidentally choke on.

Normally, infants begin experimenting with drinking from a cup at around six months. By one year they are usually able to hold a cup in both hands and drink with only some spilling (Copeland and Kimmel 1989). It is even more important to introduce drinking from a cup early on to children with developmental disabilities, since they may take longer to develop the necessary skills (Foltz and Lewis 1985). An early introduction to drinking from a cup may also help prevent the development of some abnormal compensations that may result if the child uses only a bottle for too long (Copeland and Kimmel 1989).

A cut-out cup (figures 92, 93) is useful with many children who have feeding dysfunctions. Such a cup helps the child maintain a chin tuck while drinking rather than tilting the head back into hyperextension to get the liquid out of the cup. The therapist or classroom staff usually can make such cups from regular soft plastic cups. Children often bite pieces from paper and especially from styrofoam cups; introducing a danger of choking on these small pieces.

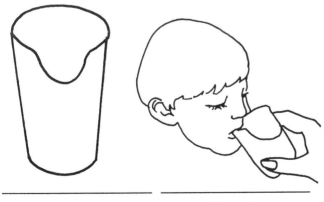

Figure 92

Figure 93

Many therapists use the Infa-trainer® (figure 94) as a first cup because it has a top to prevent excess spilling and to control the flow of liquid into the child's mouth. Unlike the covered cups with a spout, however, the Infa-trainer® top has a lip like a glass. This lip promotes the more mature muscle movements

Figure 94

needed for drinking from a cup while the use of the spouted cup continues to reinforce the same sucking patterns used with a bottle. For this reason, therapists often discourage the use of the cups with spouted tops (Copeland and Kimmel 1989), although for some children they may be appropriate (Morris 1987). The child's therapist may also recommend one of a variety of other special cups, depending on the child's needs and abilities. Morris (1987) provides a useful guide to adaptive cups and other feeding implements.

Jaw control, described above, is often needed in helping a child with drinking from a cup. Be sure that the rim of the cup is placed on the child's lower lip but not between the teeth. Otherwise, the child may develop the habit of biting on the cup for stability.

Group activities. Snacks or meals seem to encourage children to try new foods simply because there are other children eating them. Plan meals to reinforce feeding skills that individual children are working on while at the same time reinforcing cognitive and language concepts.

Cooking activities add further incentive for children to taste new things. For example, in a class where several children need to improve their chewing skills, the class could make fruit salad using mostly softer fruits such as bananas, peaches, and melons. Children could be learning to name the fruits while putting pieces into a container. (This involves cognitive, fine motor, and language skills, in addition to sensory awareness and normalization of sensory responses.) During the eating, they would be working to improve their chewing skills.

"Tasting parties" are a variation on this theme. "Color food" is another variation in which the children are given a variety of different foods that are the same color. For example, during green food day, the snack might consist of green beans, slices of green pepper, and lime gelatin. The resource list in appendix 1 provides references with more suggestions for cooking and snack ideas for young children.

SPEECH PRODUCTION

Normally, infants make cooing sounds consisting primarily of vowels during the first month or two of life. Gradually, as they gain control over their vocal mechanisms, they begin to produce some consonant sounds and to combine consonants and vowels in babbling. The section on vocal imitation in chapter 4 offers suggestions for increasing vocalizations when the child is not making many sounds.

Generally if the child has the necessary motor control to make speech sounds and understands the idea of turn taking and communication, speech will develop through imitation of the sounds the child hears. Improving the child's feeding skills, as just discussed, may also help improve the child's oral-motor control for speech production. The activities discussed in the section on communication will help the child develop the understanding of communication necessary for meaningful use of language.

It is also important to be sure the child is able to hear adequately, since the child who does not hear speech sounds will not be able to reproduce them. All children in an early intervention program should have regular audiological screenings to rule out the possibility of hearing loss. Ear infections are common in young children and are even more common among the population of children with developmental disabilities (Rossetti 1986). Ear infections can cause temporary hearing loss. A child with frequent ear infections may be unable to hear adequately for a significant portion of the time, and this intermittent hearing loss needs to be identified and addressed before that child can be expected to develop appropriate speech.

Another important aspect of speech production is breath support and respiration. Often children with abnormal muscle tone lack adequate breath support to produce more than a word or two or in some cases even a word. Or they may be unable to speak loudly enough to be heard. In other cases, coordination of breathing itself may be difficult, so that the child is not able to successfully coordinate breathing with other activities such as feeding or speech (Foltz and Lewis 1985; Golbin 1977). While this problem may be addressed as a part of the child's therapeutic feeding program, it may also arise as a separate issue in the child's speech production. Activities that encourage trunk rotation (lots of twisting and turning) and activities that require the child to raise the hands above the head help to activate the muscles in the rib cage, which helps to increase breath capacity and lengthen exhalations. Activities that require the child to push or pull while speaking also help develop increased breath support, as do such activities as singing, playing a kazoo, blowing bubbles, or blowing through a straw. There are other specific NDT techniques that may apply in individual cases. The child's therapist will recommend these as appropriate.

AUDITORY RESPONSIVENESS

Once the child's hearing status has been determined, the speech-language clinician may need to help the child improve auditory responsiveness or discrimination. Chapter 4 described some activities for beginning auditory awareness and sound localization. Beyond these initial activities, all kinds of sound matching games can help the child increase auditory skills. For example, matching animal sounds to the animals that make them (using pictures, stories, songs such as "Old MacDonald," field trips, etc.) or matching common household sounds such as the ringing of a telephone or the hum of a vacuum cleaner to their sources are higher level activities that increase the child's awareness and discrimination of sounds. Many activities and games involving following directions (put it in the cup, put it on the cup; go in the box, go on the box, etc.; Simon Says) also serve this purpose.

General listening activities can help to increase the child's auditory awareness. Story time, music time, quiet time, and so on all reinforce the need to listen. Sound matching activities could also be included here, where the children hear a bell and a dog barking and have to decide whether the sounds are the same or different. Obviously, all these activities incorporate many other skills and require prerequisite understandings for the child to be successful.

COMMUNICATION

Central to the functional use of language is an understanding of the idea of communication (Dunst 1981; Mahoney 1982; Mahoney and Powell 1984). Communication is fundamentally a social act, for it requires at least two people. Even written communication usually requires that the writer have in mind some other who will read and understand what has been put down on paper. Some children who lack a good understanding of communication may develop speech, but their speech is often used inappropriately and does not serve to communicate. The "cocktail speech" sometimes seen in children with spina bifida is one example. Echolalic speech, in which children parrot back whatever they have heard said, is another example.

In order for language to be used functionally, the child must understand that words can be used to make things happen (Anisfeld 1984). Underlying this idea is the concept of cause and effect. Activities for developing an understanding of cause and effect are presented in chapter 4. There is a close relationship between representational play and the functional use of language. An understanding of the use of representation, using one thing to stand for another, underlies an understanding of using words to do things (Anisfeld 1984). Many of the activities presented in the section on developing schemes for relating to objects, also in chapter 4, serve to help the child develop this concept.

An understanding of turn taking is also essential to the child's ability to use language appropriately (Mahoney and Powell 1984). Turn taking is fundamental to conversation, but its foundation is established in the earliest interactions between the caregiver and the child (Kaye 1977). Early exchanges of eye contact, cycles of attention alternating with cycles of withdrawal, and participation in contingency games in which the adult performs an action and waits for the child to give a response before repeating the action are all early examples of turn taking, or reciprocity. Any activities that encourage the development of turn taking will also facilitate this aspect of language development. At first, activities will most likely involve only two participants. Later, others may be added.

Figure 3 in the introduction gives examples of turn taking at different stages of sensorimotor development. Handing objects back and forth is one early turn-taking activity that typically occurs during Stage 3 of sensorimotor development. Games with a "script" ("I'm gonna get you," peek-a-boo, and "so big") and a variety of individually developed activities occur during Stage 4. During Stage 5, more structured turn taking occurs, with the child more actively aware of the structure involved. Rolling a ball or car back and forth is one such activity. Triadic interactions begin to occur during this stage.

Triadic interactions are the interactions involving a child, an object, and an adult that were described in the section in the introduction on Stage 5 development in Piagetian theory. The development of these interactions is critical to the development of functional language, as research has established a strong relationship between triadic interactions and the onset of first words (Anisfeld 1984; Bates, Camaioni, and Volterra 1975; Dunst 1981; Zachry 1979). For activities to facilitate the development of triadic interactions, see chapter 4, cause-effect activities for Stage 5.

Returning to the discussion of turn taking, Mahoney and others (MacDonald and Gillette 1985; Mahoney and Powell 1986; Sandall, n.d.) have presented guidelines for enhancing reciprocal communications between adults and young children. These include following the child's lead, balancing the number of turns taken, and extending the interaction. Following the child's lead is a principle common to all of the components (NDT, SI, and Piaget) that have been incorporated in this model of early intervention. In the turn-taking situation, following the child's lead involves imitating the child's actions or vocalizations, waiting for the child to initiate or respond, attending to what the child is interested in (blocks versus doll, pegs versus puzzles, etc.), and as much as possible positioning yourself at eye level with the child.

In many turn-taking interactions with children, and especially with children with disabilities, adults tend to take far more than their fair share of the turns. This is because adults are more skilled in interacting and can respond faster. They may also have an agenda for the interaction that the child does not share. However, it is important to try to balance the turns taken by each partner equally in order to facilitate the child's developing competence. Therefore, adults need to take a turn and wait for the child to respond. The child's response may not always fit the adult's expectations, but it still counts as a turn.

For example, the adult may hand the child a block and say "Let's build." The child may respond by throwing the block. The turns in this situation are equally balanced, and the adult may want to follow the child's lead by changing the topic of interaction, possibly to throwing balls or beanbags.

Some children have very delayed response times, and it is important to differentiate between delayed responses and no responses. One child sometimes took up to a full minute to imitate a simple gesture. By the time she responded, her partner had usually forgotten what the topic of their interaction had been. In situations like this, the goal is to recognize the response and then work on decreasing the child's response time to something approximating a reasonable interval. If the adult has waited for a reasonable time and the child has not responded with a gesture, vocalization, or other action, the adult can cue the child to take a turn. It may be necessary to shape the child's response or to provide physical guidance. For example, in a ball-rolling activity, the child who is just holding the ball can be cued verbally ("Tonya, give me the ball now"), shaped by touching her arm to indicate the appropriate response, or physically guided through the entire response.

The length of turn-taking interactions can be extended through the principle of "one more turn." One more turn means encouraging the child to stay with the interaction for one more turn after that child has signaled that it is time to stop. This technique helps increase the child's ability to attend to an activity for longer periods without being too frustrating to either partner. It also assures that the adult's expectations for length of interaction are reasonable, since they will be only one turn longer than what the child had in mind, rather than fixing on some arbitrary length of time such as five minutes to attend to an activity. Over time, the child's ability to stay with an activity will increase (Mahoney and Powell 1984).

The content of turn-taking interactions can be expanded by adding or changing one thing at a time. For example, if the child is building towers with blocks, the adult could expand the activity by modeling a train running next to the tower. If the child is consistently imitating the sound "ma" in one interaction and "ba" in another, the adult might switch from "ma" to "ba" in an exchange to see if the child will follow. In other situations, new behav-

iors could be modeled along with familiar behaviors. For example, after the children became familiar with a dress-up activity of exchanging hats, shoes, and purses, putting on makeup from the purse could be added. In a ball-throwing game, kicking could be introduced in the same way (Sandall, n.d.).

The feeding situation is also a very powerful one for facilitating communication, particularly with children who may be relatively uncommunicative at other times. Mealtime is often a good place to begin a communication program with a child whose attempts to communicate may be inconsistent or difficult to interpret (Morris 1981). At this time, the child is usually highly motivated to communicate such ideas as "I want that," "I don't want that," "I want more," "I want a drink first," "I don't like that," and so on. Because of the high degree of motivation to communicate, concepts underlying communication, such as initiation and response and the use of a common signal system, can be developed at this time and later applied in other contexts (Morris 1981).

Morris (1981, 1985) has developed an "Observation of Communication at Mealtimes" form for recording behavioral observations that may help a child's feeders become more aware of the specific communicative behaviors the child uses at mealtimes. Feeders check off different behaviors they observe the child using over a period of about a month. These behaviors are analyzed according to their modality, complexity, clarity, and intensity. Strengths and weaknesses can be identified and a more consistent signal system can be established. The child's repertoire of communicative behaviors can then be expanded, laying the groundwork for the use of a more formalized system of augmentative communication if necessary (Morris 1981).

This idea can be applied to other situations, if appropriate. For example, a child's parent or teacher could use a similar observational format to learn more about how the child communicates during a play situation. The child's communication system during play could then be expanded just as during the mealtime situation. Mealtime is often the best place to begin such a communicative intervention, however, because of the high degree of motivation involved in the child's communicative attempts.

Children must also understand the content of language in order to be able to use it meaningfully.

Through play, children come to understand the meaning of behaviors observed in the environment. They imitate cooking, cleaning, child care, therapy, and a variety of other activities that they have seen adults engaged in. In so doing, the meaning of these acts becomes clearer. Further, children experiment with various behavioral relationships that can later be expressed by language—agent, action, object combinations and words describing location, attribute, recurrence, nonexistence, and so on. They experience these concepts physically, through play and body movements, before being able to express them linguistically (Dunst 1981). While the child is playing, adults can provide a stronger language experience by using words to describe the activity for the child.

Children need to have real-life experiences before being able to play them out or communicate about them. Children who have never been to the grocery store, for example, could hardly be expected to relate meaningfully to a play store activity set up in the classroom. Therefore it is important for children to participate in a variety of community activities from an early age. Their understanding of these activities and events grows with repeated experience and exposure. Again, adults model language during these activities in order to guide the children's developing language.

In addition to understanding the concept of communication (pragmatics) and the content of language, the child must also develop an understanding of the structure of language (syntax). Children begin using syntax when they begin combining words (Anisfeld 1984). As their use of language grows, they use increasingly more complex rules to express increasingly more complex ideas. Such concepts as agent, action, and object are developed. Early language is used to express such concepts as attribution (descriptions of things, for example, "big green ball"), possession ("Mommy keys"), recurrence ("more dog"), and negation ("all gone juice") (Anisfeld 1984). Children need exposure to syntactical language in order to structure their expressions according to the rules of the language they are learning. In other words, they need to hear others speaking the language so that they can learn the rules of its structure. Research also indicates that children need to incorporate these structures in their play on a nonverbal level in order to be able to express them through the structure of their lan-

guage. In other words, children enact agent-action-object relationships, for example, in their play before expressing these same relationships through their spoken language. Anisfeld (1984) has provided a good review of this research. These findings underscore again the importance of play in facilitating growth in all developmental areas. They stress again the need for children with developmental disabilities to develop play skills. Through their play, they will develop the concepts that underlie other major goals, such as the development of syntax in language.

AUGMENTATIVE COMMUNICATION

No discussion of speech-language intervention for children with developmental disabilities would be complete without mention of augmentative communication. Augmentative communication basically refers to a variety of approaches and devices to facilitate communication when the intent to communicate is present but the development of spoken language is impaired. Sign language, picture communication boards, and synthesized speech are all forms of augmentative communication that have been used effectively even with very young children (Burkhart 1987). Eye gaze, gestures of the head or other body parts, facial expressions, and pointing have all been used by nonverbal people to indicate responses and for more elaborate communication as well. Research has shown that the use of augmentative communication does not interfere with the development of speech if speech is going to develop (Burkhart 1987; Vanderheiden and Grilley 1975). Rather, augmentative communication often enhances the use of spoken language because it ensures that the child develops the ability to communicate and reduces frustration until the child's oral-motor coordination is adequate to produce speech (Burkhart 1987). If speech is not going to develop, the use of an augmentative communication system in the early years gives the individual a head start in learning the communication system that may serve for a lifetime.

For those children whose disabilities prevent them from using speech as their primary means of expression, augmentative communication can mean the difference between communication and no communication. It can mean the ability to control their lives and to interact in socially appropriate ways with both adults and peers. It can mean the difference between high and low self-esteem, between "retarded" and "normal" intelligence, between dependence and independence (Burkhart 1987; Butler 1988). A complete discussion of augmentative and other forms of technological intervention is beyond the scope of this book, but a few possibilities will be mentioned here. The resources listed in appendix 1 will provide further information on this important topic.

Sign language. In addition to its use with the hearing impaired population, sign language has been effectively used for children with Down syndrome for several years. It is also appropriate for other children who have the motor and cognitive abilities to imitate gestures (Kent-Udolf 1984). Limited signing is possible with those children who may not be able to imitate but can reproduce the gestures after physical shaping. Sign language used as part of a total communication program in the classroom can often enhance language learning for children with processing problems as well. The resource list in appendix 1 includes references to help develop a signing or total communication component to an early intervention program.

Picture communication boards. Pictures are symbolic representations of objects, and picture communication boards often include symbolic representations of actions, feelings, and other more abstract concepts. Therefore, young children must be taught how to use such augmentative communication devices in a step-by-step manner that takes a variety of factors into account. Children can be taught a specific association between a picture/symbol and a concept such as *yes* or *no* by repeatedly pairing the picture/symbol and concept during activities. The child must also have some means of selecting the appropriate picture/symbol from a set of at least two in order for the communication to be meaningful. Eye gaze, pointing, and use of a head pointer are some methods that have been successful even for children with very limited motor control. Switch-activated scanning devices have also frequently been used. Behrmann, Jones, and Wilds (1989) have presented an overview of the skills young children need in order to use such technology. Burkhart (1987) has provided a thorough discussion of techniques for teaching many of these skills. It should be noted that picture communication systems appear to be most effective with young children when paired with some type of voice response (Burkhart 1987).

Synthesized speech. Augmentative communication devices incorporating synthesized speech basically work in the same way as the communication boards described above, except that they add a voice to the response. Thus, when the child touches or shines a light from a head pointer on a picture of a cup, the speech synthesizer may state "I want a drink." Very simple devices can be constructed using a pressure-plate-type switch and a tape recorder to give the nonverbal child a "voice" for simple requests such as "come here" (Burkhart 1987). These devices are limited to repetition of a single phrase, however. While they serve as a good introduction to augmentative communication devices, in most cases they will quickly need to be replaced with an approach that provides for more variety in the choices offered. Again, the reader is referred to Burkhart (1987) and to the resources list in appendix 1 for a more complete discussion of augmentative communication possibilities.

CHAPTER 6

Tying It All Together

So far, this book has discussed the theoretical background of NDT, SI, and Piagetian approaches to early intervention. It has also discussed how these approaches may be applied separately and provided suggestions for activities that lend themselves to the development of skills in a number of different developmental areas. This chapter will focus on the transdisciplinary team and how its members can work together to reinforce skills in all developmental areas.

Team Model

Three main types of team model are commonly described in the literature relating to early intervention services. These are the multidisciplinary team, the interdisciplinary team, and the transdisciplinary team (Fewell 1983b; Woodruff and McGonigel 1988). Before proceeding further, it will be helpful to distinguish among these models and to identify the advantages of the transdisciplinary model for the program described in this book.

Figure 95 (page 76) illustrates the lines of interaction with the child and/or family and the lines of communication among team members for each of the three models. In the multidisciplinary model, each team member functions almost independently, both in terms of interactions with the child, the child's family, and other members of the intervention team (Woodruff and McGonigel 1988). The interdisciplinary model is similar, except that the team members do interact in an organized way to share their findings, opinions, and treatment plans

with one another (Woodruff and McGonigel 1988). Finally, in the transdisciplinary model, all team members participate together in assessment and intervention planning. A designated team member or members, usually the educator and the parents, carry out the actual intervention activities, with support services provided by other team members as necessary (Woodruff and McGonigel 1988). This means that if the team feels a child needs the direct services of a physical therapist, the teacher would not be expected to provide that therapy. Rather, direct physical therapy services would be provided by the physical therapist as a support service to the primary interventionists (teacher and parents) (Woodruff and McGonigel 1988). The provision of support services is often omitted when discussing the transdisciplinary model, thus rendering it far more controversial than need be! Figure 96 (page 77) summarizes the similarities and differences among these three models relative to several important early intervention program components.

The transdisciplinary model is best suited to the service delivery model outlined in this book for several reasons. Without transdisciplinary communication and sharing of knowledge and ideas among team members, it is impossible to address several developmental components in a single activity. In an intervention program for infants and young children, such an approach is doubly necessary because of the interrelated nature of developmental domains and because of the complexity of developmental problems that occur within this age group. P.L. 99-457 mandates that the child's family be involved

FIGURE 95

Team Interaction

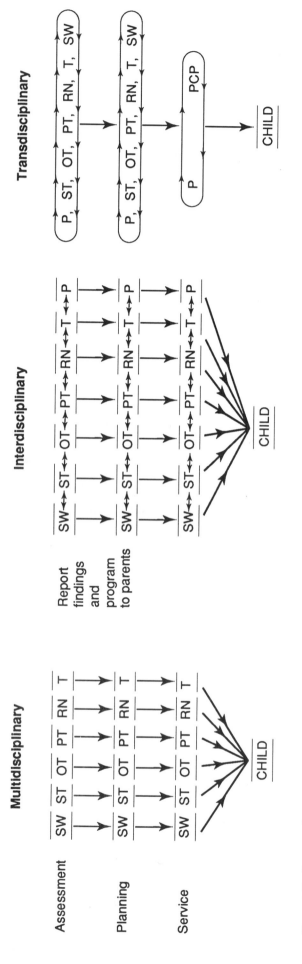

Source: Woodruff, G., and C. Hanson (1987). Project KAI, 77B Warren St., Brighton, MA 02135. Funded by U.S. Department of Education, Special Education Programs, Handicapped Children's Early Education Program. Reprinted from Woodruff, G., and M. J. McGonigel. 1988. Early intervention team approaches: The transdisciplinary model. In *Early childhood special education: Birth to three,* edited by J. B. Jordan, J. J. Gallagher, P. L. Hutinger, and M. B. Karnes. Reston, VA: Council for Exceptional Children. Reprinted by permission.

FIGURE 96

Comparison of Three Models for Early Intervention

	Multidisciplinary	Interdisciplinary	Transdisciplinary
Assessment	Separate assessments by team members	Separate assessments by team members	Team members and family conduct a comprehensive developmental assessment together
Parent Participation	Parents meet with individual team members	Parents meet with team or team representative	Parents are full, active, and participating members of the team
Service Plan Development	Team members develop separate plans for their discipline	Team members share their separate plans with one another	Team members and the parents develop a service plan based upon family priorities, needs, and resources
Service Plan Responsibility	Team members are responsible for implementing their section of the plan	Team members are responsible for sharing information with one another as well as for implementing their section of the plan	Team members are responsible and accountable for how the primary service provider implements the plan
Service Plan Implementation	Team members implement the part of the service plan related to their discipline	Team members implement their section of the plan and incorporate other sections where possible	A primary service provider is assigned to implement the plan with the family
Lines of Communication	Informal lines	Periodic case-specific team meetings	Regular team meetings where continuous transfer of information, knowledge, and skills are shared among team members
Guiding Philosophy	Team members recognize the importance of contributions from other disciplines	Team members are willing and able to develop, share, and be responsible for providing services that are a part of the total service plan	Team members make a commitment to teach, learn, and work together across discipline boundaries to implement unified service plan
Staff Development	Independent and within their discipline	Independent within as well as outside of their discipline	An integral component of team meetings for learning across disciplines and team building

Source: Woodruff, G., and C. Hanson (1987). Project KAI, 77B Warren St., Brighton, MA 02135. Funded by U.S. Department of Education, Special Education Programs, Handicapped Children's Early Education Program. Reprinted from Woodruff, G., and M. J. McGonigel. 1988. Early intervention team approaches: The transdisciplinary model. In *Early childhood special education: Birth to three*, edited by J. B. Jordan, J. J. Gallagher, P. L. Hutinger, and M. B. Karnes. Reston, VA: Council for Exceptional Children. Reprinted by permission.

in the child's program of early intervention to the fullest extent possible. The transdisciplinary model allows for maximal family involvement. Such involvement is also supported and encouraged by the service delivery model presented here, which recognizes that the child's primary caregivers are ultimately responsible for facilitating the child's growth and development and for determining the direction in which the child's education is to proceed.

The transdisciplinary team model has been described, and it is now time to describe the team itself. First, it is important to note that in order for a transdisciplinary team to work effectively, all team members must share a commitment to that model (Fewell 1983b; Woodruff and McGonigel 1988). The transdisciplinary model requires that each member expand his or her "traditional" role to include knowledge about and responsibilities for components of other disciplines as well (Eagen, Petisi, and Toole 1980; Woodruff and McGonigel 1988). At the same time, members must also be willing to release knowledge about and some responsibilities for components of their discipline to other team members, including teachers and parents (Eagen, Petisi, and Toole 1980; Woodruff and McGonigel 1988). These twin concepts of role expansion and role release, integral to the transdisciplinary model, require all team members to be committed to learning, sharing, communicating, and coordinating with others (Woodruff and McGonigel 1988).

Team Members

A child's team consists of the child's caregivers and everyone else who works with the child. Within the early intervention program, professionals on the team may include the teacher, occupational therapist, physical therapist, speech-language pathologist, staff nurse, and social worker. A member of the program administration may sometimes be included on the team as well.

In some cases the child's physician(s) or other professionals from outside the early intervention program may also be considered team members. For children with certain medical conditions, it may be important to include physicians in program planning. For example, the physician should be consulted before changing the feeding program of a child who aspirates during feeding. The physician should also let the intervention team know if the child's activities need to be limited in any way. The team should let the physician know of medical concerns they might have about a child, too. For example, the team might want to talk with the doctor if a child who is taking seizure medication seems too drowsy to participate in activities. Of course, the child's family would be involved in team consultations with the child's physician.

Most likely, doctors and other professionals outside the intervention program would participate only occasionally in program planning and delivery. The rest of the time, the team will consist of the child's therapists, teacher(s), teaching assistant(s), and parents and/or caregivers. There is controversy over how much to involve parents and alternative caregivers in the child's program. On the one hand, professionals want caregivers to be actively involved in carrying out program goals and activities when the child is not at school. On the other hand, professionals are often reluctant to give up much of their control over setting goals and managing behavior. Professionals are used to telling parents what they want them to do. Involving parents as full participants in the child's intervention team requires that professionals give up some of that control and listen more to what parents want. Different families want different levels of involvement, of course, and teams must be flexible and creative in their efforts to accommodate these different needs. Some time does need to be set aside for the intervention team to meet without parents to discuss team issues, general planning issues, and issues of family-team dynamics that cannot appropriately be discussed with family members present.

There is also some controversy over the teaching assistant's role as a team member. In many programs, teaching assistants are assigned the more menial tasks of diaper changing, table wiping, and other cleanup chores. They often carry out the majority of the classroom activities but may not have been involved in planning any of them. They may also be asked to carry out behavioral programs with which they may disagree. Yet intervention activities cannot be effective if they are not carried out from the heart. Another way of saying this is that the adults must believe in what they are doing in order for the program to work well (Morris 1987). Therefore, including teaching assistants in program planning and in discussions of children's progress is a step toward improving the situation just described.

Also, teaching assistants often have valuable observations about children's behavior and interactions that other professionals may overlook because they are too focused on their areas of specialty. Including teaching assistants as full team members provides other professionals with access to these observations and ideas.

It helps team functioning and service delivery if the same therapists work with all of the children in a given classroom. Having three different physical therapists each working with three different children in a classroom of nine is a situation almost guaranteed to drive the teacher crazy, if not the therapists as well. If the classrooms are half-day classrooms and there are two sessions a day, it would be ideal if the same therapists see all of the children in a given teacher's two classes, and that the teaching assistant(s) also be consistent for both sessions. In this way, teams have a better opportunity to develop good working relationships. They can usually make more effective use of meeting time than if, for example, one physical therapist sees half the children in the class and another sees the others. Keeping consistent teams also makes for easier and more effective program planning, since only one set of people is involved.

Services Delivered by the Transdisciplinary Team

Team members are involved with a child's family from the time that a referral is first made to an early intervention program. The usual flow of services proceeds for an initial contact to gather information about the child and family, at which time an initial evaluation is scheduled. The initial evaluation usually involves all, or almost all, of the team members and is conducted in arena fashion. (See the section on assessment in chapter 1 for more details on the initial evaluation.) Following the initial evaluation, representatives from the team meet with parents to discuss the results of the evaluation, including recommendations for participation in an early intervention program.

Once the child is placed in a program, the team meets again with parents to develop the IEP or IFSP. This process is discussed in more detail later in this chapter. Regular staffings are also scheduled throughout the year to discuss the child's progress, modifications to the child's program, suggestions for therapeutic activities, or any other issues related to the child's development. Parents may be invited to attend these meetings. In addition to such staffings, team members are also available to meet with parents at their mutual convenience to discuss any issues of special concern to either the team member or the parent. These sessions can involve teaching parents or other caregivers special techniques that have been successful in the child's intervention program. The team also prepares brief written progress reports at regular intervals throughout the school year, based on observations of performance in the classroom and during therapy sessions.

The team evaluates the child's progress on a formal basis at least once a year. For infants, P.L. 99-457 requires that the IFSP be reevaluated every six months. A formal evaluation facilitates that process. Ideally, in a trandisciplinary model these evaluations are conducted arena style, just as in the initial evaluation. (See the assessment section in chapter 1 for a more complete discussion of this type of evaluation.) In many cases, however, they may be conducted by each team member individually, interdisciplinary style. This often happens because transdisciplinary evaluations are too time consuming in a program that includes center-based programming and ongoing initial evaluations of newly referred children. Also, full evaluations may be more costly to the parents. Again, the chapter on assessment discusses these reevaluations in more detail.

Following the reevaluations, team members confer with each other and write reports of their findings. At this time, another formal parent conference is scheduled to discuss the results of the reevaluations and implications for future program planning. If necessary, a new IEP or IFSP is prepared.

Team Meetings

There are basically two kinds of team meetings. One is held to discuss general program issues, such as planning activities, deciding what equipment is needed, grouping children for placement, and so on. The other is the staffing to discuss individual children's progress in the program. Both kinds of meetings are essential for good service delivery and need to be scheduled on a regular basis (Fewell 1983b; Woodruff and McGonigel 1988).

Planning meetings. In a program based on an integrated service delivery approach, it is important to have regular meetings in which representatives of the different disciplines suggest activities and work out ways to incorporate goals from different developmental areas into each activity planned. In this way, too, team members learn more about development in areas other than their area of specialty. With this expanded knowledge, team members will be better able to incorporate developmentally appropriate activities from other areas into activities planned to facilitate development in their own areas.

During these planning meetings, it is important for team members not only to suggest activities, but also to explain what skills they will help facilitate and how they will do so. It is also important for team members to suggest activities that can be adapted for a whole class as well as for individual children. For example, if several children in a class needed to develop rolling skills, the physical therapist might suggest that gross motor time be devoted to rolling activities two times each week. The occupational therapist might suggest that this would be a good time to incorporate some proprioceptive activities such as rolling up in a mat or rolling a ball over the children. Also, rolling over different textured surfaces such as an egg-crate mattress, vinyl mat, and fuzzy blanket could increase the tactile component of the activity. Rolling might facilitate more vocalizations because of the movement, trunk elongation, and rotation involved. The teacher might also suggest having the children roll up and down an incline to incorporate the concepts *up* and *down.* The idea of movement down an incline could be reinforced afterward by rolling other objects down the incline. Thus, from a single suggestion, a whole morning's activities could be planned to incorporate goals from all developmental areas, involving much interaction among the different areas and among the different interventionists.

Staffings. These meetings should be held at a regularly scheduled time once a week. Also each child's progress should be reviewed at least once every six weeks or more often if necessary. The child's parents and/or caregivers should be invited to participate in these meetings, especially if there are any problems that need to be discussed. All other members of the intervention team should attend, and meetings may need to be rescheduled if more than one significant team member cannot attend. The team members and parents/caregivers will need to make that decision on an individual basis. The child's progress toward IEP or IFSP goals, behavior in the classroom and/or at home, changes in interests or abilities, medical issues, equipment needs, or individual programming within the classroom are all examples of issues that might be discussed at a staffing. Figures 97-99 (pages 81-84) provide sample formats for staffing notes to give further ideas of how and why such meetings are conducted. One team member should make notes on each staffing. These notes become part of the child's permanent record.

In-Services

In-services are presentations or workshops that the team attends as part of its regularly scheduled work time. They are usually held at the intervention center, but sometimes the staff is encouraged to attend an in-service off site, with staff from similar intervention programs attending as well. Usually, no children are scheduled to be in the intervention center during these times.

As with sharing information at team meetings, in-services provide a way for members of each discipline to learn more about intervention in other areas. When planning in-services, it is important to provide a balance between sessions conducted by experts outside the intervention program and sessions in which various staff members have an opportunity to share their expertise or to discuss information from recently attended workshops or classes. Especially when first establishing a transdisciplinary approach, either with a new team or with team members who have previously worked together under a different model, workshops on team building may be very useful. It is also important that in-service topics focus on issues currently relevant to the program staff. The most useful in-services are planned around topics suggested by staff members (Eagen, Petisi, and Toole 1980; United Cerebral Palsy Association's Task Force on Staff Development 1976).

FIGURE 97
Team Meeting Summary

Date _____

Classroom _____

Attending _____

_____

_____

_____

_____

Agenda _____

_____

_____

_____

Discussion _____

_____

_____

_____

_____

_____

Action _____

_____

_____

_____

_____

_____

Source: Developed by Easter Seal Society staff, The Children's Center, 2800 13th St., N.W., Washington, DC 20009. Used by permission.

FIGURE 98

Case Conference Report Summary

Child's Name: _____

Date of Conference: _____ Case Manager: _____

Participants:

_____

_____

_____

_____

Agenda/Concerns:

Behavioral Issues: _____

_____

_____

Positioning: _____

_____

_____

Intervention Plan: _____

_____

_____

Equipment Needs: _____

_____

_____

Transition and Follow-Up: _____

_____

_____

Therapies: _____

_____

_____

Social Work: _____

_____

_____

Evaluation: _____

_____

_____

Discussion: _____

_____

_____

_____

_____

_____

_____

_____

Recommendations/Actions to Be Taken:_____

_____

_____

_____

_____

_____

_____

_____

Source: Developed by Easter Seal Society staff, The Children's Center, 2800 13th St., N.W., Washington, DC 20009. Used by permission.

FIGURE 99

Monthly Staffing Notes

Child's Name:_____ Date: _____

Team Members' Names:_____

_____

Treatment Goals: _____

_____

_____

_____

	Progress Toward Goals	**Problems Noted—Suggested Responses**
O.T.	_____	_____
	_____	_____
	_____	_____
P.T.	_____	_____
	_____	_____
	_____	_____
S.T.	_____	_____
	_____	_____
	_____	_____
Education	_____	_____
	_____	_____
	_____	_____
Social Services	_____	_____
	_____	_____
	_____	_____

Source: Developed by the staff of the Child Development Center of Northern Virginia, 111 N. Cherry St., Falls Church, VA 22046. Used by permission.

In-services can also be used to provide information to new staff members while reviewing information for staff members more familiar with it. For example, an introductory session on NDT, SI, and Piagetian approaches would be useful if several members of the staff are not familiar with these theories. To support the transdisciplinary approach, team members from different disciplines could be asked to present information from another discipline, with assistance from that discipline as needed (Eagen, Petisi, and Toole 1980; United Cerebral Palsy Association's Task Force on Staff Development 1976).

Like children, adults learn best when they are actively participating in the learning experience. This usually means incorporating some type of motor component into the activity, as well as providing opportunities for role playing and other forms of large- and small-group participation.

Incorporating Therapy in the Classroom

One of the most effective ways to provide integrated services for a child is to provide therapy in the child's classroom. In this way, the child does not have to generalize from an isolated setting to one with distractions and ongoing activities. The activities performed during therapy are accepted as a more normal part of the child's existence rather than an isolated activity that occurs once or twice a week only when the physical therapist is present. Furthermore, when therapy sessions are conducted in the classroom, teachers and teaching assistants are able to see what the therapist is doing and will then be better able to incorporate the same goals into classroom activities when the therapist is not present. This provides a natural teaching session for the therapist to instruct other team members on special techniques to use with individual children.

I have talked with many therapists who have remarked that conducting therapy sessions in the classroom also gives them an opportunity to get input and feedback from other team members about treatment sessions. The physical therapist may be able to work with the occupational therapist to resolve a positioning problem. The teacher may be able to help the physical therapist through a behavior problem. Other possibilities for teamwork are opened up in this way.

Therapy sessions conducted in the classroom also can be based on ongoing activities that are of interest to the child. The child is not separated from peers and does not miss out on classroom fun. Rather, therapeutic activities are incorporated into classroom activities so that the child experiences them as part of the activity. Since one goal of the motor therapies is often to improve the child's processing and response patterns in a nonconscious way, incorporating facilitation techniques into classroom activities helps to ensure that the child's conscious attention is with the activity and not with the motor therapist. Language activities are so much a part of cognitive activities that they cannot really be separated in most cases, anyway.

Conducting therapy sessions in the classroom can be effective only if the intervention team is committed to that model, however. Therapists sometimes argue that the child is too distracted in the classroom or that they are too distracted in the classroom. It may be necessary in such cases to start by conducting sessions outside the classroom and then gradually move into the classroom. Some children, too, are difficult to work with and might distract the class if their sessions are conducted completely in the classroom. Again, sessions might begin outside the classroom and be gradually moved into the classroom.

One effective way around some of these problems is to set up a group session centered around a particular child's therapy goals for the session. The therapist can work specifically with that child, and other team members can work with the rest of the class. For example, if one child needs lots of help with motor planning skills, the physical therapist can set up an obstacle course and work with the child in negotiating it. The classroom teacher and teaching assistants can help the rest of the class as needed. Or if the physical therapist wants to work on trunk rotation and mobility, he or she can set up a class "exercise group," done to music. The teacher and teaching assistants can help some of the children with the exercises, while the physical therapist concentrates on the two children who most need his or her specialized skills. Such activities incorporate goals from several developmental areas and can be adapted so that they are appropriate for all the children in the class.

IEP or IFSP Development

P.L. 99-457 calls for an individualized family service plan (IFSP) to be developed for all children served under its auspices. The IFSP differs from the IEP provided for under P.L. 93-147 in several ways. The IEP is a child-focused document, and it is developed with the child's strengths and needs in mind. The IFSP is a family-centered document. It is based on the notion that the child is dependent on the family and that enhancing the family's ability to meet the needs of the child with a developmental disability will enhance the child's development (NEC*TAS and ACCH 1989). Because of its focus on the child in isolation, the IEP tends to be a school-centered document, focusing on the child's behaviors in school. The IFSP focuses on the child in the larger environment of family and community systems, of which the school is but one. The IFSP, then, is concerned with the child's behavior in a network of environments.

IEP goals tend to be developed by the intervention team and discussed with the child's parents/caregivers for approval. IFSP goals are identified by the family, and the steps to achieve these goals may then be developed in consultation with the intervention team. As a consequence, IEP goals are written in behavioral terms, while IFSP goals are written in family terms. Also, in an IEP the professionals usually determine whether the goals have been met, whereas in an IFSP the family may well decide whether goals have been met and how successfully.

Ideally, parents/caregivers will have had several opportunities to meet with all members of the intervention team before the IFSP is developed. The parents/caregivers will have been able to tell team members their concerns and goals for the child. In this situation, the IFSP meeting simply provides all team members with a chance to clarify program goals for the child by putting them in a written form. It can also provide team members with a chance to explain any activities that may be unclear to caregivers and to answer any questions about program goals or philosophy that may have come up.

Since IFSP goals are related to the child's functioning across a variety of settings, a degree of generalization is built in. A transdisciplinary approach is also built in, in that the parents' goals may incorporate skills from a variety of developmental areas. For example, Melvin's parents would like to be able to take him to a restaurant with the family sometimes. In Melvin's case, this goal involves speech therapy to improve feeding and communication skills so that he can manage table foods reasonably well and can express his wants without embarrassing his parents. Physical therapy is also needed to provide appropriate seating and to address issues of normalizing muscle tone and improving head control to the point where Melvin can use adaptive seating in a public place long enough for the family to finish their meal. The teaching staff would be needed to implement program suggestions along with the parents and to help prepare Melvin for restaurant outings by providing practice in the classroom and possibly during field trips. Thus the IFSP produces goals directed toward functional activities, rather than separate therapy goals isolated from function. These integrated goals also help contribute to a program model based on activities in which goals from several developmental areas are integrated and are incorporated into everyday activities. Figure 100 (pages 87-91) provides a sample IFSP form. The reader is referred especially to NEC*TAS and ACCH (1989) for additional sample formats and for a more thorough discussion of the IFSP process.

FIGURE 100

Individualized Family Service Plan

Name_____

Date of Birth _____ CA _____

Parent/Guardian _____

Address _____

Phone No. (H) _____ (W) _____

Diagnosis_____

Special Medications _____

Requires Transportation _____

Case Manager _____

1st Quarter: Date_____ Period of Plan _____ to _____

Signature   **Position**   **Signature**   **Position**

_____   _____

_____   _____

_____   _____

_____   _____

Parent Notification (dates)_____

2nd Quarter: Date _____

_____   _____

_____   _____

_____   _____

_____   _____

Parent Notification (dates)_____

3rd Quarter: Date _____

_____   _____

_____   _____

_____   _____

_____   _____

Parent Notification (dates) _____

4th Quarter: Date _____

_____   _____

_____   _____

_____   _____

_____   _____

Parent Notification (dates) _____

Source: Developed by Easter Seal Society staff, The Children's Center, 2800 13th St., N.W., Washington, DC 20009. Used by permission.

FIGURE 100 (continued)

I. Special Notations

Name _____

Date of Birth _____

Auditory Acuity _____
_____

Visual Acuity _____
_____

Motor Development _____
_____
_____
_____
_____
_____
_____
_____
_____
_____
_____

Adaptive Equipment _____
_____

Precautions _____
_____

Observed Learning Style _____
_____

FIGURE 100 (continued)

Assessment of Functioning Level

Name _____ Date of Birth _____ CA _____

Skill Area	Date	Functioning Level	Date	Functioning Level	Date	Functioning Level	Date	Functioning Level
Social-Emotional								
Gross Motor								
Perceptual/Fine Motor								
Cognition								
Speech/Language								
Self-Help								

FIGURE 100 (continued)

Quarterly Reviews

Name _____

Date of Birth _____ CA _____

Case Manager _____ IEP Dates: _____ to _____

Long-term Goal _____

_____

_____

Short Term Objectives	Date Initiated	Level Score	Quarterly Reviews			
			1st	2nd	3rd	4th

Special materials/equipment needed:

Codes: NA—Not applicable I—Introduced E—Emerging M—Mastered

Progress recorded on attached sheets.

Appendix 1: Resources

Chapter 1:
Assessment

Bagnato, S. J., and J. T. Neisworth. 1981. *Linking developmental assessment and curricula*. Rockville, MD: Aspen Publishers.

Barnes, K. E. 1982. *Preschool screening: The measurement and prediction of children at-risk*. Springfield, IL: Charles C. Thomas.

Black, T., ed. 1979. *Perspectives on measurement: A collection of readings for educators of young handicapped children*. Chapel Hill, NC: Technical Assistance Development System.

Brinker, R. P., and M. Lewis. 1982. Discovering the competent handicapped infant: A process approach to assessment and intervention. *Topics in Early Childhood Special Education* 2(2):1-16.

Brooks-Gunn, J., and M. Lewis. 1981. Assessing young handicapped children: Issues and solutions. *Journal of the Division of Early Childhood* 2:84-95.

Carlson, C. I., M. Scott, and S. J. Eklund. 1980. Ecological theory and method for behavioral assessment. *School Psychology Review* 9:75-82.

Caro, P. N.d. *Educational assessment for the child with little or no fine motor skills*. Charlottesville, VA: Hospital Education Program, Children's Rehabilitation Center.

Copeland, M. E., and J. R. Kimmel. 1989. *Evaluation and management of infants and young children with developmental disabilities*. Baltimore, MD: Paul H. Brookes.

Cross, L., and K. Goin, eds. 1977. *Identifying handicapped children: A guide to casefinding, screening, diagnosis, assessment, and evaluation*. New York: Walker and Co.

Darby, B., and M. J. May. 1979. *Infant assessment: Issues and applications*. Seattle, WA: Western States Technical Assistance Resource.

Dollar, S., and C. Brooks. 1989. Assessment of severely and profoundly handicapped. *Exceptional Educational Quarterly* 1(3):87-101.

DuBose, R. F. 1981. Assessment of severely impaired young children: Problems and recommendations. *Topics in Early Childhood Special Education* 1(2):9-21.

DuBose, R. F., M. B. Langley, and V. Stagg. 1977. Assessing severely handicapped children. *Focus on Exceptional Children* 9(7):1-13.

Dunst, C., C. Trivette, and A. Deal. 1988. *Enabling and empowering families: Principles and guidelines for practice*. Cambridge, MA: Brookline Books.

Erickson, M. L. 1976. *Assessment and management of developmental changes in children*. St. Louis, MO: C. V. Mosby Co.

Fewell, R. 1983. Assessing handicapped infants. In *Educating handicapped infants: Issues in development and intervention*, edited by S. G. Garwood and R. R. Fewell, 257-97. Rockville, MD: Aspen Publishers.

Friedlander, B. Z., G. M. Sterritt, and G. K. Kirk, eds. 1975. *Exceptional infant, Vol. 3: Assessment and intervention*. New York: Brunner/Mazel.

Horowitz, F. 1982. Methods of assessment for high-risk and handicapped infants. In *Finding and educating high-risk and handicapped infants*, edited by C. T. Ramey and P. L. Trohanis, 101-18. Baltimore, MD: University Park Press.

Johnson, K., and C. B. Kopp. 1979. *A bibliography of screening and assessment measures for infants*. Los Angeles: UCLA, Department of Psychology.

Johnson, N. M. 1982. Assessment paradigms and atypical infants: An interventionist's perspective. In *Intervention with at-risk and handicapped infants: From research to application*, edited by D. D. Bricker, 63-76. Baltimore, MD: University Park Press.

Kearsley, R. B., and I. Sigel, eds. 1979. *Infants at risk: Assessment of cognitive functioning*. Hillsdale, NJ: Lawrence Erlbaum Associates Inc.

Meier, J. H. 1975. Screening, assessment, and intervention for young children at developmental risk. In *Issues in the classification of children*, Vol. 2, edited by N. Hobbs. San Francisco: Jossey-Bass, Inc.

Minifie, F. D., and L. L. Lloyd, eds. 1978. *Communicative and cognitive abilities: Early behavioral assessment*. Baltimore, MD: University Park Press.

Mulliken, R. K., and J. J. Buckley. 1983. *Assessment of multihandicapped and developmentally disabled children*. Rockville, MD: Aspen Publishers.

National Early Childhood Technical Assistance System (NEC*TAS). 1989. *Guidelines and recommended practices for the individualized family service plan*. Washington, DC: Association for the Care of Children's Health.

Paget, K. D., and B. A. Bracken. 1983. *The psychoeducational assessment of preschool children*. New York: Grune and Statton.

Parmelee, A. H., C. B. Kopp, and M. Sigal. 1976. Selection of developmental assessment techniques for infants at risk. *Merrill-Palmer Quarterly* 22:177-99.

Powell, M. L. 1981. *Assessment and management of developmental changes and problems in children*. St. Louis, MO: C. V. Mosby Co.

Simeonsson, R. J., G. S. Huntington, and S. A. Parse. 1980. Expanding the developmental assessment of young handicapped children. *New Directions for Exceptional Children* 3:51-74.

Southworth, L. E., R. L. Burr, and A. E. Cox. 1980. *Screening and evaluating the young child: A handbook of instruments to use from infancy to six years.* Springfield, IL: Charles C. Thomas.

Stangler, S. R., C. J. Huber, and D. K. Routh. 1980. *Screening growth and development of preschool children: A guide for test selection.* New York: McGraw-Hill Inc.

Thorum, A. R. 1981. *Language assessment instruments: Infancy through adulthood.* Springfield, IL: Charles C. Thomas.

Yang, R. K. 1979. Early infant assessment: An overview. In *Handbook of infant development,* edited by J. D. Osofsky. New York: Wiley.

Zelazo, P. R. 1982. Alternative assessment procedures for handicapped infants and toddlers: Theoretical and practical issues. In *Intervention with at-risk and handicapped infants: From research to application,* edited by D. D. Bricker, 107-28. Baltimore, MD: University Park Press.

Chapter 1:
Program Evaluation

Garwood, S. G., ed. 1982. Program evaluation. *Topics in Early Childhood Special Education* 1.

Johnson, L. J. 1988. Program evaluation: The key to quality programming. In *Early childhood special education: Birth to three,* edited by J. B. Jordan, J. J. Gallagher, P. L. Hutinger, and M. B. Karnes, 184-212. Reston, VA: Council for Exceptional Children.

Korner, A., J. Pawl, V. Seitz, and J. Shonkoff. 1985. Program evaluation. Panel presentation at the Fourth Biennial National Training Institute of the National Center for Clinical Infant Programs, Washington, DC.

Sheehan, R., and J. Lasky. 1987. Program evaluation. In *The young exceptional child: Early development and education,* edited by J. T. Neisworth and S. J. Bagnato, 443-66. New York: Macmillan.

Sheehan, R., and R. J. Gallagher. 1983. Conducting evaluations of infant intervention programs. In *Educating handicapped infants,* edited by S. G. Garwood and R. R. Fewell, 495-524. Rockville, MD: Aspen Publishers.

Suarez, T. M. 1982. Planning evaluation of programs for high-risk and handicapped infants. In *Finding and educating high-risk and handicapped infants,* edited by C. T. Ramey and P. L. Trohanis, 193-215. Baltimore, MD: University Park Press.

Chapter 2:
Motor Development

Apgar, V., and J. Beck. 1973. *Is my baby all right?* New York: Trident Press.

Barnes, B. S., C. A. Crutchfield, and C. B. Heriza. 1978. *The neurological basis of patient treatment,* Vol. 2: *Reflexes in motor development.* Atlanta, GA: Stokesville.

Bigge, J. L. 1982. *Teaching individuals with physical and multiple disabilities.* 2d ed. Columbus, OH: Charles E. Merrill.

Bly, L. 1983. *The components of normal movement during the first year of life and abnormal motor development.* Birmingham, AL: Pittenger and Associates.

Boehme, R. 1987. *Approach to treatment of the baby.* Milwaukee, WI: Boehme Workshops.

————. 1987. *Developing mid-range control and function in children with fluctuating muscle tone.* Milwaukee, WI: Boehme Workshops.

————. 1987. *The hypotonic child: Treatment for postural control, endurance, strength, and sensory organization.* Milwaukee, WI: Boehme Workshops.

Brinson, C. L. 1982. *The helping hand: A manual describing methods for handling the young child with cerebral palsy.* Charlottesville, VA: Children's Rehabilitation Center, University of Virginia.

Connor, F., G. Williamson, and J. Siepp. 1978. *Program guide for infants and toddlers with neuromotor and other developmental disabilities.* New York: Teachers College Press.

Curtis, S. R. 1982. *The joy of movement in early childhood.* New York: Teachers College Press.

Doyle, P., J. Goodman, J. Grotsky, and L. Mann. 1979. *Helping the severely handicapped child: A guide for parents and teachers.* New York: Thomas Y. Crowell.

Finnie, N. 1975. *Handling the young cerebral palsied child at home.* New York: Dutton.

Fiorentino, M. R. 1972. *Normal and abnormal development.* Springfield, IL: Charles C. Thomas.

————. 1973. *Reflex testing methods for evaluating central nervous system development.* 2d ed. Springfield, IL: Charles C. Thomas.

————. 1981. *A basis for sensorimotor development—normal and abnormal.* Springfield, IL: Charles C. Thomas.

Fraser, B. A., G. Galka, and R. N. Hensinger. 1980. *Gross motor management of severely multiply impaired students,* Vol. 1: *Evaluation guide.* Baltimore, MD: University Park Press.

Fraser, B. A., and R. N. Hensinger. 1983. *Managing physical handicaps: A practical guide for parents, care providers, and educators.* Baltimore, MD: Paul H. Brookes.

Galka, G., B. A. Fraser, and R. N. Hensinger. 1980. *Gross motor management of severely multiply impaired students,* Vol. 2: *Curriculum model.* Baltimore, MD: University Park Press.

Gilfoyle, E. M., A. P. Grady, and J. C. Moore. 1981. *Children adapt.* Thorofare, NJ: Charles B. Slack.

Golbin, A., ed. 1977. *Cerebral palsy and communication: What parents can do.* Washington, DC: George Washington University.

Hackett, L. C., and R. G. Jenson. 1973. *A guide to movement exploration.* Palo Alto, CA: Peek Publications.

Hanson, M. J., and S. R. Harris. 1986. *Teaching the young child with motor delays.* Austin, TX: Pro-Ed.

Haynes, U. 1983. *Holistic health care for children with developmental disabilities.* Baltimore, MD: University Park Press.

Healy, H., and S. B. Stainback. 1980. *The severely motorically impaired student.* Springfield, IL: Charles C. Thomas.

High, E. C. N.d. *A resource guide to habilitative techniques and aids.* Washington, DC: George Washington University.

Jaeger, L. 1987. *Home program instruction sheets for infants and young children.* Tucson, AZ: Therapy Skill Builders.

Kliewer, D., W. Bruce, and J. Trembath. 1977. *The Milani-Comparetti motor development screening test.* Omaha, NE: Meyer Children's Rehabilitation Institute.

Kline, J. 1977. *Children learn to move.* Tucson, AZ: Communication Skill Builders.

Levitt, S., ed. 1984. *Paediatric developmental therapy.* Oxford: Blackwell Scientific Publications.

Lynch-Fraser, D. 1982. *Danceplay: Creative movement for very young children.* New York: Walker and Co.

Marsallo, M., and D. Vacante. 1983. *Adapted games and developmental motor activities for children.* Annadale, VA: authors.

Montgomery, P., and E. Richter. 1979. *Sensorimotor integration for developmentally disabled children: A handbook.* Los Angeles: Western Psychological Services.

Morrison, D., P. Pothier, and K. Horr. 1978. *Sensory-motor dysfunction and therapy in infancy and early childhood.* Springfield, IL: Charles C. Thomas.

Mullins, I., and M. Thompson. 1986. *Teach me!* Intensive Related Services for the Severe/Profoundly Handicapped Project. Wise, VA: Wise County Schools.

Prechtl, H., and D. Beintema. 1984. *The neurological examination of the full-term newborn infant.* London: Spastics Society Medical Education and Information Unit with W. Heinemann Medical Books.

Robinault, I. P. 1973. *Functional aids for the multiply handicapped.* New York: Harper and Row.

Schleichkorn, J. 1983. *Coping with cerebral palsy.* Baltimore, MD: University Park Press.

Sensorimotor activities. 1977. San Rafael, CA: Academic Therapy Publications.

Siegling, L. S., and M. Click. 1984. *At arm's length: Goals for arm and hand function.* Mesa, AZ: EdCorp.

Skinner, L. 1979. *Motor development in the preschool years.* Springfield, IL: Charles C. Thomas.

Smith, J. 1980. *Play environments for movement experience.* Springfield, IL: Charles C. Thomas.

Sontag, E., J. Smith, and N. Certo. 1977. *Educational programming for the severely and profoundly handicapped.* Reston, VA: Council for Exceptional Children.

Strum, T. M., ed. 1980. *Carolina developmental curriculum structured learning activities, ages 3-6; Activities in gross motor, fine motor, visual perception.* New York: Walker and Co.

Wirth, M. J. 1976. *Teacher's handbook of children's games: A guide to developing perceptual-motor skills.* West Nyack, NY: Parker Publishing Co.

Chapter 5:
Speech-Language

Ausberger, C., M. J. Martin, and J. Creighton. 1982. *Learning to talk is child's play: Helping preschoolers develop language.* Tucson, AZ: Communication Skill Builders.

Baker, B. L., A. J. Brightman, N. B. Carroll, B. B. Heifetz, and S. P. Hinshaw. 1978. *Speech and language: Level 1.* Champaign, IL: Research Press.

————. 1978. *Speech and language: Level 2.* Champaign, IL: Research Press.

Blank, M., and M. A. Marquis. 1987. *Directing discourse.* Tucson, AZ: Communication Skill Builders.

Emerick, L. L., and J. T. Hatten. 1979. *Diagnosis and evaluation in speech pathology.* 2d ed. Englewood Cliffs, NJ: Prentice Hall.

Heasley, B. E. 1980. *Auditory processing disorders and remediation.* 2d ed. Springfield, IL: Charles C. Thomas.

Horstmeier, D. S., and J. D. MacDonald. 1978. *Ready, set, go: Talk to me.* Columbus, OH: Charles E. Merrill.

Johnston, E. B., and A. V. Johnston. 1984. *The Piagetian nursery: An intensive group language intervention program for preschoolers.* Rockville, MD: Aspen Publishers.

Johnston, E. B., B. D. Weinrich, and A. R. Johnson. 1984. *A sourcebook of pragmatic activities.* Tucson, AZ: Communication Skill Builders.

Makohon, L., H. D. B. Fredericks, and the staff of the Teaching Research Infant and Child Center. 1985. *Teaching expressive and receptive language to students with moderate and severe handicaps.* Austin, TX: Pro-Ed.

Marquardt, T. P., and H. A. Peterson. 1981. *Appraisal and diagnosis of speech and language disorders.* Englewood Cliffs, NJ: Prentice Hall.

McClowry, D. P., A. M. Guilford, and S. O. Richardson. 1982. *Infant communication: Development, assessment, and intervention.* New York: Grune and Stratton.

McLean, J. E., and L. K. Snyder-McLean. 1978. *A transactional approach to early language training.* Columbus, OH: Charles E. Merrill.

Miller, E., and J. Cooper. 1976. *Experiences: Our world, our words.* Nashville, TN: Language Development Programs.

Morris, S. E. 1982. *The normal acquisition of oral feeding skills.* Central Islip, NY: Therapeutic Media Inc.

————. 1982. *The pre-speech assessment scale.* Clifton, NJ: J. A. Preston.

————. 1987. *Prefeeding skills.* Tucson, AZ: Therapy Skill Builders.

————. 1987. Therapy for the child with cerebral palsy: Interacting frameworks. *Seminars in Speech and Language* 8:71-86.

Mullins, I., and M. Thompson. 1986. *Teach me! Language: Participant's training handbook for teachers of the severe/profoundly handicapped.* Wise, VA: Intensive Related Services for the Severe/Profoundly Handicapped Project, Wise County Schools.

Musselwhite, C. R., and K. W. St. Louis. 1988. *Communication programming for persons with severe handicaps: Vocal and augmentative strategies.* Boston: College-Hill.

Peyton, J. L. 1986. *Puppetools.* Richmond, VA: Prescott, Durrell and Co.

Reidlich, C. E., and M. E. Herzfeld. 1983. *Zero to three years: An early language curriculum.* Moline, IL: LinguiSystems.

Richman, L. G. 1987. *Listen to this! An auditory processing program.* Solano Beach, CA: Mayer-Johnson Co.

Shea, V., and M. Mount. 1982. *How to arrange the environment to stimulate and teach pre-language skills in the severely handicapped.* Lawrence, KS: H and H Enterprises.

Spade, M., M. Connar, and M. Gordon. 1985. *Language and concept development.* Baltimore, MD: Maryland State Department of Education.

Sperry, V. B. 1973. *Of course I can: Sourcebook of language activities.* Palo Alto, CA: Consulting Psychologists Press.

Strong, J. M. C. 1983. *Language facilitation: A complete cognitive therapy program.* Austin, TX: Pro-Ed.

Strum, T. M., ed. 1980. *Activities in reasoning,* Vol. 2: *Receptive language, expressive language.* New York: Walker and Co.

Worthley, W. J. 1978. *Sourcebook of language learning activities.* Boston, MA: Little, Brown, and Company.

Chapter 5:
Cooking and Snack Ideas

Barrett, I. 1974. *Cooking is easy when you know how.* New York: Arco.

Burdick, A. 1972. *Look! I can cook.* New York: Crescent Books.

Christenberry, M. A., and B. Stevens. 1984. *Can Piaget cook?* Atlanta, GA: Humanics.

Cobb, V. 1973. *Science experiments you can eat.* Philadelphia, PA: J. B. Lippincott Co.

Goldberg, P. Z. 1980. *So what if you can't chew, eat hearty! Recipes and a guide for the healthy and happy eating of soft and pureed foods.* Springfield, IL: Charles C. Thomas.

Goodwin, M. T., and G. Pollen. 1974. *Creative food experiences for children.* Washington, DC: Center for Science in the Public Interest.

Johnson, B., and B. Plemons. 1978. *Cup cooking: Individual child portion picture recipes.* Lake Alfred, FL: Early Educators Press.

Kahan, E. H. 1974. *Cooking activities for the retarded child.* New York: Abingdon Press.

Lansky, V. 1974. *Feed me! I'm yours.* New York: Bantam.

Levine, L. 1968. *The kids in the kitchen.* New York: Macmillan.

Marcus, E. F., and R. F. Granovetter. 1986. *Making it easy: Crafts and cooking activities skill building for handicapped learners.* Palo Alto, CA: VORT Corp.

Parents Nursery School. 1972. *Kids are natural cooks: Child-tested recipes for home and school using natural foods.* Boston: Houghton Mifflin.

Paul, A. 1975. *Kids cooking without a stove: A cookbook for young children.* Garden City, NY: Doubleday.

Steed, F. R. 1977. *A special picture cookbook.* Lawrence, KS: H and H Enterprises.

Technical Assistance Center II. N.d. *Cooking with kids.* Harrisonburg, VA: TAC II, Early, Middle, and Special Education, James Madison University.

Chapter 5:
Augmentative Communication

Behrmann, M. M., J. K. Jones, and M. L. Wilds. 1989. Technology intervention for very young children with disabilities. *Infants and Young Children.* 1:66-77.

Blackstone, S. W. 1986. *Augmentative communication: An introduction.* Rockville, MD: American Speech-Language-Hearing Association.

Brandenburg, S. A., D. A. Bengston, and G. C. Vanderheiden. 1987. *The rehab/education technology resourcebook series: Book 1, Communication aids.* Madison, WI: Trace Research and Development Center.

Burkhart, L. J. 1987. *Using computers and speech synthesis to facilitate communicative interaction with young and/or severely handicapped children.* College Park, MD: author.

Carlson, F. 1982. *Prattle and play: Equipment recipes for nonspeech communication.* Omaha, NE: Meyer Children's Rehabilitation Institute.

Charlebois-Marois, C. 1985. *Everybody's technology: A sharing of ideas in augmentative communication.* Montreal: Charlescoms.

First annual Minspeak conference proceedings. Wooster, OH: Prentke Romich Company.

Fishman, I. 1986. *Electronic communication aids: Selection and use.* Boston: College-Hill.

Goossens, C., and S. Crain. 1986. *Augmentative communication intervention resource.* Lake Zurich, IL: Don Johnson Developmental Equipment.

Hutinger, P. L. 1986. *Activating children through technology: Starter kit.* Macomb, IL: Project ACTT, Western Illinois University.

Johnson, R. M. 1981. *The picture communication symbols.* Stillwater, MN: Mayer-Johnson Co.

Montgomery, J. 1980. *Non-oral speech: A training guide for the child without speech.* Fountain Valley, CA: West Orange County Consortium for Special Education.

Musselwhite, C., and K. W. St. Louis. 1988. *Communication programming for persons with severe handicaps: Vocal and augmentative strategies.* Boston: College-Hill.

Oakander, S. M. N.d. *Language board instruction kit.* Fountain Valley, CA: West Orange County Consortium for Special Education.

Schiefelbusch, R. L., ed. 1980. *Nonspeech language and communication: Analysis and intervention.* Baltimore, MD: University Park Press.

Shane, H. C., and A. S. Bashir. 1980. Election criteria for the adoption of an augmentative communication system: Preliminary considerations. *Journal of Speech and Hearing Disorders* XLV:408-14.

Vanderheiden, G. C., and K. Grilley. 1975. *Non-vocal communication techniques and aids for the severely physically handicapped.* Baltimore, MD: University Park Press.

Wright, C., and M. Nomura. 1985. *From toys to computers: Access for the physically disabled child.* San Jose, CA: Christine Wright.

Yoder, D. E., and A. Kraat. 1983. *Intervention issues in nonspeech communication.* Rockville, MD: American Speech-Language-Hearing Association.

Chapter 5:
Augmentative Communication
Organizations

ACTT (Activating Children Through Technology)
Macomb Projects
27 Horrabin Hall
Western Illinois University
Macomb, IL 61455

Closing the Gap
P. O. Box 68
Henderson, MN 56044

HEECP (Handicapped Children's Early Education Project)
Technical Assistance Development System
North Carolina University
Chapel Hill, NC 27514

Innotek
Division of National Lekotek Center
2100 Ridge Ave.
Evanston, IL 60201

ISAAC (The International Society for Augmentative
and Alternative Communication)

Membership:

NY State Association for the Help of Retarded Children
2900 Veterans Memorial Highway
Bohemia, NY 11716

Publications:

Artificial Language Laboratory
Michigan State University
East Lansing, MI 48824

Pennsylvania Special Education Assistive Device Center
Elizabethtown Hospital and Rehabilitation Center
Elizabethtown, PA 17022

Preschool Technical Assistance Center
George Mason University
Fairfax, VA 22030

Trace Research and Development Center on Communication,
Control, and Computer Access for Handicapped Individuals
S-151 Waisman Center
1500 Highland Ave.
Madison, WI 53705

Chapter 5:
Sign Language

Bornstein, H., and I. K. Jordan. 1984. *Functional signs*. Baltimore, MD: University Park Press.

Bornstein, H., L. B. Hamilton, K. L. Saulnier, and H. L. Roy, eds. 1975. *The signed English dictionary for preschool and elementary levels*. Washington, DC: Gallaudet College Press.

Bornstein, H., and K. L. Saulnier. 1984. *The signed English starter: A beginning book in the signed English system*. Washington, DC: Kendall Green Publications.

Bove, L. 1980. *Sign language fun*. New York: Random House.

Carr, E. G. 1982. *How to teach sign language to developmentally disabled children*. Lawrence, KS: H and H Enterprises.

Greenberg, J. C., M. Vernon, J. H. DuBois, and J. C. McKnight. 1982. *The language arts handbook: A total communication approach*. Baltimore, MD: University Park Press.

Riekehof, L. L. 1978. *The joy of signing*. Springfield, MO: Gospel Publishing House.

Sanders, J. I., ed. 1968. *The ABC's of sign language*. Tulsa, OK: Modern Education Corp.

Schaeffer, B., A. Musil, and G. Kollinzas. 1980. *Total communication: A signed speech program for nonverbal children*. Champaign, IL: Research Press.

The signed English series. 1973. Washington, DC: Gallaudet College Press.

Chapter 6:
Working with Families

Bell, C. 1981. *Helping parents grow*. Machias, ME: Washington County Children's Program.

————. 1982. *Helping families grow*. Machias, ME: Washington County Children's Program.

Bromwich, R. 1981. *Working with parents and infants: An interactional approach*. Baltimore, MD: University Park Press.

Cansler, D. P., G. H. Martin, and M. C. Valand. 1975. *Working with families: A manual for early childhood programs serving the handicapped*. Winston-Salem, NC: Kaplan Press.

Cliff, S., J. Gray, and C. Nymann. 1974. *Mothers can help: A therapist's guide for formulating a developmental text for parents of special children*. El Paso, TX: El Paso Rehabilitation Center.

Coletta, A. J. 1977. *Working together: A guide to parent involvement*. Atlanta, GA: Humanics.

D'Audney, W., ed. 1978. *Giving a head start to parents of the handicapped*. Omaha, NE: Meyer Children's Rehabilitation Institute.

Dunst, C., C. Trivette, and A. Deal. 1988. *Enabling and empowering families: Principles and guidelines for practice*. Cambridge, MA: Brookline Books.

Lillie, D. L., and P. L. Trohanis, eds. 1976. *Teaching parents to teach*. New York: Walker and Co.

Rotherberg, B. A., S. Hitchcock, M. L. Harrison, and M. Graham. 1981. *Parentmaking: A practical handbook for teaching parent classes about babies and toddlers*. Menlo Park, CA: Banster Press.

Chapter 6:
Books for Parents

Abraham, W. 1976. *Living with preschoolers from the terrible twos to the fascinating fives!* Phoenix, AZ: O'Sullivan, Woodside and Co.

Becker, W. C. 1971. *Parents are teachers: A child management program*. Champaign, IL: Research Press.

Bishop, M., and T. Compernolle. 1981. *Your child can do it alone*. Englewood Cliffs, NJ: Prentice Hall.

Brazelton, T. B. 1978. *Infants and mothers: Differences in development*. New York: Pantheon.

Burtt, K. G., and K. Kalkstein. 1981. *Smart toys for babies from birth to two*. New York: Harper Colophon.

Cansler, D. P., ed. 1978. *Programs for parents of preschoolers*. Winston-Salem, NC: Kaplan Press.

Caplan, F. 1973. *The first twelve months of life*. New York: Grosset and Dunlap.

————. 1977. *The second twelve months of life*. New York: Grosset and Dunlap.

Cook, S. 1977. *Helping children grow*. Machias, ME: Washington County Children's Program.

Cunningham, C., and P. Sloper. 1978. *Helping your exceptional baby*. New York: Pantheon.

Darling, R. B., and J. Darling. 1982. *Children who are different: Meeting the challenges of birth defects in society.* St. Louis, MO: C. V. Mosby Co.

Dickman, I., and S. Gordon, 1986. *One miracle at a time.* New York: Simon and Schuster.

Evans, J., and E. Ilfeld. 1982. *Good beginnings: Parenting in the early years.* Ypsilanti, MI: High/Scope Press.

Fantini, M. D., and R. Cardenas. 1980. *Parenting in a multi-cultural society.* New York: Longman.

Featherstone, H. 1980. *A difference in the family: Living with a disabled child.* New York: Basic Books.

Fewell, R. R., and P. F. Vadasy. 1983. *Learning through play.* Hingham, MA: Teaching Resources.

Frank, A., and C. W. Garland, eds. 1982. *Teaching activities for parents.* Lightfoot, VA: Williamsburg Area Child Development Resources, Inc.

Goldberg, S. 1981. *Teaching with toys.* Ann Arbor, MI: University of Michigan Press.

Goldberg, S., and B. DeVitto. 1983. *Born too soon.* San Francisco: W. H. Freeman.

Gordon, I. J. 1970. *Baby learning through baby play: A parent's guide for the first two years.* New York: St. Martin's Press.

Gordon, I. J., B. Guinagh, and J. E. Jester. 1972. *Child learning through child play: Learning activities for two- and three-year-olds.* New York: St. Martin's Press.

Gotts, E. E., ed. 1977. *Home visitor's kit.* New York: Human Sciences Press.

Hagstrom, J., and J. Morrill. 1979. *Games babies play.* New York: A and W.

Hale, G., ed. 1979. *A source book for the disabled.* New York: Paddington.

Harrison, H. 1983. *The premature baby book: A parent's guide to coping and caring in the first years.* New York: St. Martin's Press.

Henig, R. M., and A. B. Fletcher. 1983. *Your premature baby.* New York: Ballantine.

Honig, A. 1982. *Playtime learning games.* Syracuse, NY: Syracuse University Press.

Kannenberg, G. D. 1981. *From birth to twelve: How to be a successful parent to infants and children.* Saratoga, CA: Century Twenty-One Publishing.

Klein, M. D., S. P. Myers, B. Hogue, L. J. Waldo, A. M. Marshall, and M. K. Hall. 1981. *Parent's guide: Classroom involvement, communication training, resources.* Lawrence, KS: Comprehensive Communication Curriculum, Early Childhood Institute, Document Reprint Service, University of Kansas.

Leach, P. 1978. *Your baby and child.* New York: Knopf.

Lerman, S. 1980. *Parent awareness: Positive parenting for the 1980s.* Minneapolis, MN: Winston Press.

Levy, J. 1975. *The baby exercise book.* New York: Pantheon.

Maryland State Department of Education. 1981. *Parent helper: Handicapped children birth to five.* Baltimore, MD: Maryland State Department of Education.

————. 1982. *Parent helper: Handicapped children birth to five: Communication.* Baltimore, MD: Maryland State Department of Education.

————. 1982. *Parent helper: Handicapped children birth to five: Socialization.* Baltimore, MD: Maryland State Department of Education.

————. 1983. *Parent helper: Handicapped children birth to five: Cognition.* Baltimore, MD: Maryland State Department of Education.

————. 1984. *Parent helper: Handicapped children birth to five: Motor Development.* Baltimore, MD: Maryland State Department of Education.

McCall, R. B. 1979. *Infants.* New York: Vintage.

McNamara, J., and B. McNamara. 1977. *The special child handbook.* New York: Hawthorn.

Nance, S. 1982. *Premature babies.* New York: Pridon.

Norrohin, M., and J. Ryders. 1975. *To give an edge.* Minneapolis, MN: Caldwell.

Painter, G. 1971. *Teach your baby.* New York: Simon and Schuster.

Parks, S. 1986. *Make every step count: Birth to one year developmental parenting guide.* Palo Alto, CA: VORT Corp.

Patterson, G. R. 1971. *Families.* Champaign, IL: Research Press.

————. 1976. *Living with children.* Champaign, IL: Research Press.

Powell, T. H., and P. A. Ogle. 1985. *Brothers and sisters: A special part of exceptional families.* Baltimore, MD: Paul H. Brookes.

Pueschel, S. M., J. C. Bernier, and L. E. Weidenman. 1988. *The special child: A source book for parents of children with developmental disabilities.* Baltimore, MD: Paul H. Brookes.

Ross, B. M. 1981. *Our special child: A guide to successful parenting of handicapped children.* New York: Walker and Co.

Schrank, R. 1984. *Toddlers learn by doing.* Atlanta, GA: Humanics.

Sears, W. 1982. *Creative parenting.* New York: Everest House.

Segal, M. 1983. *Your child at play: Birth to one year.* New York: Newmarket Press.

————. 1988. *In time and with love: Caring for the special needs baby.* New York: Newmarket Press.

Segal, M., and D. Adcock. 1983. *Your child at play: One to two years.* New York: Newmarket Press.

————. 1983. *Your child at play: Two to three years.* New York: Newmarket Press.

Sparling, J., and I. Lewis. 1979. *Learning games for the first three years.* New York: Walker and Co.

Spock, B. 1965. *Caring for your disabled child.* New York: Macmillan.

Turnbull, A. P., and H. R. Turnbull III. 1978. *Parents speak out.* Columbus, OH: Charles E. Merrill.

Weiner, F. 1973. *Help for the handicapped child.* New York: McGraw-Hill.

Wilson, G. B., and B. Wingate. N.d. *Parents and teachers: Humanistic educational techniques to facilitate communication between parents and staff of educational programs.* Atlanta, GA: Humanics.

Chapter 6:
Journals and Related Services for Parents and Professionals

Especially Grandparents
King County ARC
2230 Eighth Avenue
Seattle, WA 98121

The Exceptional Parent
Psy-Ed Corporation
605 Commonwealth Avenue
Boston, MA 02115

The Growing Child and The Growing Parent
Dunn and Hargitt, Inc.
22 North Second Street
Lafayette, IN 47902

Infant Development Program
Johnson and Johnson
6 Commercial Street
Hicksville, NJ 11801

Infants and Young Children
Aspen Publishers, Inc.
7201 McKinney Circle
Frederick, MD 21701

The National Newspatch
Oregon School for the Blind
700 Church Street, S.E.
Salem, OR 97310

Special Care: For Families of Preterm and High Risk Infants
1011 Caminito Zar
San Diego, CA 92126

Special Parent, Special Child
P.O. Box 462
South Salem, NY 10590

Support Lines
Published by Parents of Premature and High Risk Infants
International, Inc.
c/o Self-Help Clearinghouse
33 West 42nd St., Room 1227
New York, NY 10036

Topics in Early Childhood Special Education
Pro-Ed
8700 Shoal Creek Boulevard
Austin, TX 78758

Zero to Three
National Center for Clinical Infant Programs
733 15th Street, N.W., Suite 912
Washington, DC 20005

Chapter 6:
Organizations

Advocacy Center for Children's Education and Parent Training
P.O. Box 10565
Raleigh, NC 27605
(919) 762-3451

Alexander Graham Bell Association for the Deaf
3417 Volta Place, N.W.
Washington, DC 20007

American Academy for Cerebral Palsy and
Developmental Medicine
2315 Westwood Avenue, P.O. Box 11083
Richmond, VA 23230
(804) 355-0147

American Academy of Pediatrics
1801 Hinman Avenue
Evanston, IL 60204

American Association on Mental Deficiency
5201 Connecticut Avenue, N.W.
Washington, DC 20015
(202) 686-5400

American Brittle Bone Society
1256 Merrill Drive
West Chester, PA 19380

American Council of the Blind
1211 Connecticut Avenue, N.W.
Washington, DC 20036

American Foundation for the Blind, Inc.
15 W. 16th Street
New York, NY 10011
(212) 924-0420

American Occupational Therapy Association (AOTA)
1383 Piccard Drive
Rockville, MD 20850
(301) 948-9626

American Physical Therapy Association (APTA)
1111 N. Fairfax Street
Alexandria, VA 22314
(703) 684-2782

American Printing House for the Blind
P.O. Box 6085
Louisville, KY 40206-0085

American Speech, Hearing, and Language Association (ASHA)
10801 Rockville Pike
Rockville, MD 20852
(301) 897-5700

American Tuberous Sclerosis Association
339 Union Street
P.O. Box 44
Rockland, MA 02370
(617) 878-5528; (800) 446-1211

Association for Childhood Education International (ACEI)
3615 Wisconsin Avenue, N.W.
Washington, DC 20016

Association for Children with Down Syndrome
2616 Martin Avenue
Bellmore, NY 11710
(516) 221-4700

Association for Children with Learning Disabilities
5225 Grace Street
Pittsburg, PA 15236

Association for Education of the Visually Handicapped
919 Walnut Street, 7th Floor
Philadelphia, PA 19107

Association for Neurologically Impaired/Brain
Injured Children
217 Lark Street
Albany, NY 12210

Association for Persons with Severe Handicaps
7010 Roosevelt Way, N.E.
Seattle, WA 98115
(206) 523-8446

Association of Birth Defect Children
3526 Emerywood Lane
Orlando, FL 32806
(305) 859-2821

Asthma and Allergy Foundation
1302 18th Street, N.W., Suite 203
Washington, DC 20036
(202) 293-2950

Children in Hospitals (CIH)
31 Wilshire Park
Needham, MA 02192

Children's Brain Diseases Foundation for Research
350 Parnassus, Suite 900
San Francisco, CA 94117
(415) 566-5402, 566-6259

Children's Defense Fund
1520 New Hampshire Avenue, N.W.
Washington, DC 20036
(202) 483-1470

Children's Hearing Foundation
220 South 16th Street
Philadelphia, PA 19102

Closer Look
National Information Center for the Handicapped
Box 1492
Washington, DC 20013

Compassionate Friends, Inc.
Box 3696
Oak Brook, IL 60522-3696
(312) 323-1510

Congress of Organizations for the Physically Handicapped
16630 Beverly Avenue
Tinley Park, IL 60477-1904
(312) 523-3566

Cornelia de Lange Syndrome Foundation
60 Dyer Avenue
Collinsville, CT 06022
(203) 693-0159; (800) 223-8355

Council for Exceptional Children
1920 Association Drive
Reston, VA 22091
(703) 620-3660

Cystic Fibrosis Foundation
Suite 510
6000 Executive Boulevard
Rockville, MD 20852
(301) 881-9130; (800) 638-8815

Dental Guidance Council for Cerebral Palsy
122 E. 23rd Street
New York, NY 10010
(212) 677-7400

Down Syndrome Congress
1640 W. Roosevelt Road
Room 156-E
Chicago, IL 60608

(Membership Committee
P.O. Box 1527
Brownwood, TX 76801
(312) 226-0416)

Down Syndrome—Papers and Abstracts for Professionals
P.O. Box 620
2525 Belmont Road, N.W.
Washington, DC 20008
(Subscription:
10404 Leslie Court
Silver Springs, MD 20902)

Dystonia Medical Research Foundation
8383 Wilshire Boulevard, Suite 800
Beverly Hills, CA 90211
(213) 852-1630

Epilepsy Foundation of America
1828 L Street, N.W., Suite 405
Washington, DC 20036
(202) 293-2930

Friedreich's Ataxia Group in America, Inc.
P.O. Box 11116
Oakland, CA 94611
(415) 655-9833

Gallaudet College Press
Gallaudet College
Washington, DC 20002

Gesell Institute of Child Development
310 Prospect Street
New Haven, CT 06511

Guardians of Hydrocephalus Research Foundation
2618 Avenue Z
Brooklyn, NY 11235
(718) 743-4473

Handicapped Children's Early Education Program (HCEEP)
Office of Special Education (OSE)
Donohue Bldg., Room 3117
400 Maryland avenue, S.W.
Washington, DC 20202

Head Start
Administration for Children, Youth, and Families
Office of Human Development Services
U.S. Department of Health and Human Services
P.O. Box 1182
Washington, DC 20013

Hydrocephalus Support Group
225 Dickinson Street, H-893
San Diego, CA 92103
(619) 695-3139, 726-0507

International Association of Lions' Clubs
(assistance for the visually impaired)
300 22nd Street
Oak Brook, IL 60521

International Association of Parents of the Deaf
814 Thayer Avenue
Silver Spring, MD 20910

International Institute for Visually Impaired 0-7, Inc.
Rutgers Circle
East Lansing, MI 48823

International Rett Syndrome
8511 Rose Marie Drive
Fort Washington, MD 20744
(301) 248-7031

Intraventricular Hemorrhage Parents
P.O. Box 56-111
Miami, FL 33156
(305) 232-0381

Juvenile Diabetes Foundation International
60 Madison Avenue
New York, NY 10010
(212) 998-7575; (800) 223-1138

John F. Kennedy Institute
707 North Broadway
Baltimore, MD 21205

Laurence-Moon-Boedl Syndrome Network
122 Rolling Road
Lexington Park, MD 20653
(301) 863-5658

Little People of America, Inc.
P.O. Box 633
San Bruno, CA 94066
(415) 589-0695

Lowe's Syndrome Association
222 Lincoln Street
West Lafayette, IN 47906
(317) 743-3634

Maple Syrup Urine Disease Support Group
24806 SR 119
Goshen, IN 46526
(219) 862-2922

Metabolic Illness Foundation
210 South Fourth Street
Monroe, LA 71202
(318) 343-0416

Muscular Dystrophy Association
810 Seventh Avenue
New York, NY 10019
(212) 586-0808

National Association for Down Syndrome
Box 63
Oak Park, IL 60303

National Association for the Education of Young Children
(NAEYC)
1834 Connecticut Avenue, N.W.
Washington, DC 20009

National Association for the Parents of the
Visually Impaired, Inc.
P.O. Box 180806
Austin, TX 78718

National Association for Retarded Citizens (NARC)
2501 Avenue J, P.O. Box 6109
Arlington, TX
(817) 261-4961

National Association for Sickle Cell Disease
4221 Wilshire Boulevard, Suite 360
Los Angeles, CA 90010-3503
(213) 936-7205; (800) 421-8453

National Association of the Deaf
814 Thayer avenue
Silver Spring, MD 20910

National Association of the Physically Handicapped
76 Elm Street
London, OH 43130
(614) 852-1664

National Autism Hotline
Autism Services Center
Douglass Education Building
Tenth Avenue and Bruce
Huntington, WV 25701
(304) 525-8014

National Center for Clinical Infant Programs
Suite 912
733 15th Street, N.W.
Washington, DC 20005

National Center for Law and the Handicapped
P.O. Box 477
University of Notre Dame
Notre Dame, IN 46556
(219) 283-4536

National Cleft Palate Association
906 Hillside Lane
Flower Mound, TX 57028
(316) 543-6623

National Committee for Prevention of Child Abuse (NCPCA)
332 S. Michigan Avenue
Chicago, IL 60612

National Down Syndrome Society
141 Fifth Avenue
New York, NY 10010
(212) 460-9330; (800) 221-4602

National Easter Seal Society for Crippled Children and Adults
2023 West Ogden Avenue
Chicago, IL 60612
(312) 243-8400

National Federation of the Blind
1800 Johnson Street
Baltimore, MD 21230

National Foundation for Asthma, Inc.
P.O. Box 30069
Tucson, AZ 85751-0069
(602) 323-6046

National Foundation—March of Dimes
1275 Mamaroneck Avenue
White Plains, NY 10605
(914) 428-7100

National Genetics Foundation, Inc.
555 West 57th Street
New York, NY 10019
(212) 586-5800

National Health Information Clearinghouse
P.O. Box 1133
Washington, DC 20013
(800) 336-4797

National Hydrocephalus Foundation
Route 1, River Road
Box 210A
Joliet, IL 60436

National Information Center on Deafness
Gallaudet College
Washington, DC 20002

National Institute for Autistic Children (NIAC)
Suite 1017
1234 Massachusetts Avenue, N.W.
Washington, DC 20005

National Institute of Child Health and Human Development
National Institutes of Health
Public Health Service
Department of Health and Human Services
Bethesda, MD 20014
(301) 496-5133

National Institute of Handicapped Research (NIHR)
Office of Special Education and Rehabilitative Services
U.S. Department of Education
Washington, DC 20202
(202) 732-1134

National Mucopolysaccharidoses Society
17 Kraemer Street
Hicksville, NY 11801
(516) 931-6338

National Neurofibromatosis Foundation, Inc.
141 Fifth Avenue, Suite 7-S
New York, NY 10019
(212) 460-8980

National Organization for Albinism and Hypopigmentation
919 Walnut street, Room 400
Philadelphia, PA 19107
(215) 627-0600

National Organization for Rare Disorders
P.O. Box 8923
New Fairfield, CT 06812
(203) 746-6518

National Society for Prevention of Blindness, Inc.
79 Madison Avenue
New York, NY 10016

National Special Education Information Center
P.O. Box 1492
Washington, DC 20013

National Tay-Sachs and Allied Diseases Association
385 Elliot street
Newton, MA 02164
(617) 964-5508

National Tuberous Sclerosis Association, Inc.
P.O. Box 612
Winfield, IL 60190
(312) 668-0787

Office of Human Development Services
Department of Health and Human Services
309F Hubert H. Humphrey Building
200 Independence Avenue, S.W.
Washington, DC 20201
(202) 245-7246

Organization for Parents of Cleft Children
10 Carlsbad Street
Kenner, LA 70065

Osteogenesis Imperfecta Foundation, Inc.
P.O. Box 245
Eastport, NY 11941

Parents of Dwarfed Children
11524 Colt Terrace
Silver Spring, MD 20902
(301) 649-3275

Parents of Twins with Disabilities
2129 Clinton Avenue, #E
Alameda, CA 94501

Prader-Willi Syndrome Association
5515 Malibu Drive
Edina, MN 55436
(612) 933-0113

Prescription Parents, Inc.
P.O. Box 426
Quincy, MA 02269
(617) 479-2463

President's Committee on Mental Retardation
Regional Office Building (ROB) 3
7th and D Streets, S.W.
Washington, DC 20201
(202) 245-7520

Retinitis Pigmentosa Association International
23241 Ventura Boulevard
Woodland Hills, CA 91364
(800) 344-4877

Retinitis Pigmentosa Foundation Fighting Blindness
1401 Mt. Royal Avenue, Fourth Floor
Baltimore, MD 21217
(301) 225-9400; (800) 638-2300

Sibling Information Network
Department of Educational Psychology
Box U-64
University of Connecticut
Storrs, CT 06268

Siblings for Significant Change
823 United Nations Plaza, Room 808
New York, NY 10017

Siblings Understanding Needs (SUN)
Department of Pediatrics
University of Texas, Medical Branch
Galveston, TX 77550

Sick Kids Need Involved People (SKIP)
216 Newport Drive
Severna Park, MD 21146
(301) 647-0164

Spina Bifida Association of America
343 South Dearborn, Room 317
Chicago, IL 60604
(312) 662-1562

Support Organization for Trisomy 18/13
c/o Kris and Hal Halladay
478 Terrace Lane
Tooele, UT 84074
(810) 882-6635

Turner's Syndrome Society
Administrative Studies #006
4700 Keele Street, York University
Downsview, Ontario
Canada M3J 1P3
(416) 3773

United Cerebral Palsy Association, Inc. (UCPA)
66 East 34th Street
New York, NY 10016
(212) 481-6300

Williams Syndrome Association
P.O. Box 178373
San Diego, CA 92117-0910
(619) 275-6628

Appendix 2:
Initial Evaluation

Name:_____

Date of Birth: _____ Parent's Name: _____

Address:_____

_____ Telephone: _____

Referred by:_____

Date Seen: _____

Seen by: _____

_____

Diagnosis: _____

Special Precautions: _____

Medical History: _____

_____

_____

_____

_____

_____

_____

_____

_____

_____

_____

_____

_____

_____

_____

_____

Hearing: _____

_____

_____

_____

_____

_____

_____

Vision: _____

_____

_____

_____

_____

_____

_____

_____

Social: _____

_____

_____

_____

_____

_____

_____

_____

Cognitive: _____

_____

_____

_____

_____

_____

_____

_____

Language (including feeding): _____

_____

_____

_____

_____

_____

_____

_____

Self-Help: _____

_____

_____

_____

_____

_____

_____

_____

Gross Motor: _____

_____

_____

_____

_____

_____

_____

_____

Fine Motor: _____

_____

_____

_____

_____

_____

_____

_____

Summary:_____

_____

_____

_____

_____

_____

_____

_____

_____

_____

_____

Recommendations:_____

_____

_____

_____

_____

_____

_____

_____

_____

_____

_____

_____

Source: Developed by Easter Seal Society staff, The Children's Center, 2800 13th St., N.W., Washington, DC 20009. Used by permission.

Appendix 3: Assessments

Commonly Used Screening Tests

Name and Source	Ages	Comments
California Preschool Social Competency Scale Palo Alto, CA: Consulting Psychologists Press, 1969	2½ to 5½ years	ED, autistic. Social/emotional test.
Circus Reading, MA: Addison-Wesley Testing Service, 1976	Preschool to grade 1	LD, MR, PH, hearing and speech impaired. Language, motor, cognitive, perceptual tests.
Comprehensive Identification Process Bensenville, IL: Scholastic Testing Services, 1975	2½ to 5½ year	Screens children in eight areas, one of which is cognitive-verbal. Uses professionals and paraprofessionals.
Denver Developmental Screening Test (Frankenburg, Dodds, and Fandal) Denver: Ladoca Project and Publishing Foundation, Inc., 1975 East 51st Street and Lincoln Denver, CO 80216	6 weeks to 6 years	Screens four areas: gross motor, language, fine motor, and adaptive personal-social. Assists in early detection of developmentally delayed young children. Norm-referenced.
Denver Prescreening Developmental Questionnaire (PDQ) Denver: Ladoca Project and Publishing Foundation, Inc., 1975	3 months to 6 years	All disabilities. Language, motor, perceptual, social/emotional tests.
Developmental Activities Screening Inventory (DASI) Boston: Teaching Resources Corporation, 1977	6 to 60 months	Provides information on communication, cognitive, and motor abilities. Adapted for use with blind children. Teacher administered.
Developmental Indicators for Assessment of Learning (DIAL) (C. Mardell and D. Goldenberg) Highland Park, IL: DIAL, Inc., 1972	2½ to 5½ years	Screens four areas: gross motor, fine motor, concepts, and communication. Administered by professional-paraprofessional team.
Developmental Screening Philadelphia: J. P. Lippincott Co., 1969	Birth to 5 years	Presents guide for rapid successive screenings by physician.
Preschool Attainment Record (PAR) Circle Pines, MN: American Guidance Service, Inc., 1966	6 months to 7 years	All disabilities. Language, motor, cognitive, social/emotional tests.
Pupil Rating Scale: Screening for Learning Disabilities Myklebust, H., 1971	No age specified	All disabilities. Language, motor, cognitive, social/emotional tests.

Source: Adapted from *Evaluation and Management of Infants and Young Children with Developmental Disabilities*, by M. E. Copeland and J. R. Kimmel (Baltimore, MD: Paul H. Brookes, 1989), and *Assessment of Multihandicapped and Developmentally Disabled Children*, by R. K. Mulliken and J. J. Buckley (Austin, TX: Pro-Ed, Inc., 1983). Used by permission.

Neonatal Assessments

Name and Source	Ages	Comments
Apgar Scoring System (Apgar, 1960)	Birth	Scores pulse, grimace, respiration, activity, appearance. Administered at 1, 5, and/or 15 minutes after birth. Each item is scored as 0, 1, or 2. Normal range is between 7 and 10. Assesses current status; not predictive. Criterion-referenced measure.
Graham-Rosenblith Behavioral Assessment of the Neonate Providence: Brown University Press, 1961	1 to 14 days	Measures pain threshold, maturational level, visual response, ratings of irritability, and muscle tension. Motor and tactile adaptive scales.
Neonatal Behavioral Assessment Scale (Brazelton, 1984)	Birth to 1 month	Assesses reflexes and movements, habituation, orientation, motor maturity, variation, self-quieting abilities, social behavior. Rated on best performance in neurological items (4-point scale) and behavioral items (9-point scale). Assesses current status; not predictive.

Infant Developmental Scales

Name and Source	Ages	Comments
Bayley Scales of Infant Development (Bayley, 1969) The Psychological Corp. 1372 Peachtree St. N.E. Atlanta, GA 30309	2 to 30 months	Three parts—mental, motor, and infant behavior record. Scored as a pass or fail and results give a developmental index score with 100 as the mean performance at any given age. Norm-referenced measure.
Behavioral Developmental Profile Marshalltown, IA: Marshalltown Project, 1975 (Available from ERIC Document Reproduction Service, P. O. Box 190, Arlington, VA 22210, ED 79 917)	Birth to 6 years	Measures development in areas of social, communication, and motor skills.
Brigance Diagnostic Inventory of Early Development (Brigance, 1978) Curriculum Associates, Inc. 5 Esquire Rd. North Billerica, MA 01862	Birth to 72 months	Assesses psychomotor, self-help, speech and language, general knowledge and comprehension, early academic skills. Determines developmental or performance level, identifies areas of strengths and weaknesses, identifies instructional objectives. Contributes data for referral or diagnosis. Criterion- and domain-referenced measure.
The Carolina Curriculum for Handicapped Infants and Infants At Risk (Johnson-Martin, Jens, and Attermeier, 1986)	Birth to 24 months	Developed in response to the need for curricular materials for severely handicapped, deaf-blind infants and toddlers. Criterion- and curriculum-based measure. Includes twenty-four content areas: tactile integration, auditory localization, object permanence, reach and grasp, object manipulation, bilateral hand activity, space localization, functional use of objects, control of physical environment, gestural communication, gestural imitation, feeding, dressing, grooming, vocal imitation, vocal communication, responses to communication from others, social, gross motor—prone, gross motor—supine, gross motor—upright, auditory localization, readiness concepts, self-directed.
Cornell Infant Intelligence Scale New York: The Psychological Corporation, 1940	1 to 30 months	Tests at levels 1 month apart from 1 to 12 months, 2-month intervals from 12 to 24 months; 3-month intervals from 24 to 30 months. Downward extension of Stanford-Binet (Form L-M). Relatively large number of items at each age, with alternate items.
Developmental Profile II (rev. ed.) (Alpern, Boll, Shearer, 1980) Western Psychological Services 12031 Wilshire Blvd. Los Angeles, CA 90025	Birth to 9.6 years	186-item inventory designed to assess a child's functional, developmental age level in the areas of physical, self-help, social, academic, and communication. Can be given as an interview or as a direct test. Provides an overall profile. Criterion-referenced measure.
Early Intervention Developmental Profile and Developmental Screening of Handicapped Infants (D'Eugenio and Rogers, 1975) The University of Michigan Publications Distribution Service 615 East University Ann Arbor, MI 48109	Birth to 36 months	Assesses language, social, self-care, cognition, perceptual-fine motor, gross motor. Helps in screening a child's skills, selecting appropriate objectives for treatment of developmental delays, and designing an appropriate individual curriculum. Given 4 times a year; reflects the child's highest levels.
Early Learning Accomplishment Profile for Developmentally Young Children (E-LAP) (Glover and Preminger, 1978) Kaplan School Supply Corp. 600 Jonestown Rd. Winston Salem, NC 27103	Birth to 36 months	Assesses gross motor, cognitive, fine motor, language, self-help, social-emotional. Determines an appropriate developmental age; designed to generate developmental-appropriate instructional objectives and task analysis programming. Domain- and norm-referenced measure.

Infant Developmental Scales (continued)

Name and Source	Ages	Comments
Gesell Developmental Scale (Revised by Knoblock and Pasamanick) New York: Harper and Row Publishers, Inc., 1974	4 to 60 months	Examines five areas: gross motor, fine motor, adaptive, language, and personal-social. For 4-week-old infants there are nine gross motor items, two fine motor, four adaptive, three language, and three personal-social.
Griffiths Mental Developmental Scale New York: McGraw Hill Book Company, 1954	1 to 24 months	Presents five sections: locomotor, personal-social, hearing and speech, eye and hand, and performance. Explores abilities of both handicapped and normal children.
Hawaii Early Learning Profile (HELP) (rev. ed.) (Furuno et al., 1985) VORT Corporation P. O. Box 60880 Palo Alto, CA 94306	Birth to 36 months	Assesses cognitive, expressive language, gross motor, fine motor, social-emotional, self-help. Results provide developmental sequence in small incremental steps and suggestions for activities to teach developmental skills. Curriculum-based measure.
Koontz Child Developmental Program (Koontz, 1974) Western Psychological Services 12031 Wilshire Blvd. Los Angeles, CA 90025	Birth to 48 months	Assesses gross motor, fine motor, social, language—receptive, language—expressive. Provides a method for assessing, for plotting progress, and for planning suitable activities.
Lexington Developmental Scale Lexington, KY: United Cerebral Palsy of the Bluegrass, Inc., Child Developmental Centers, 1974	Birth to 2 years; 2 to 6 years	Assesses five areas, one of which is personal-social. Both long and short forms. Designed to be used by teacher.
Memphis Comprehensive Developmental Scale Belmont, CA: Fearon Publishers, Inc., 1974	Birth to 5 years	Covers five developmental areas, one of which is personal-social. Material helpful in planning Individualized Education Programs for developmentally delayed children.
Portage Guide to Early Education (Bluma, Shearer, Frohman, and Hilliard, 1976) CESA 12 Portage Project Box 564 Portage, WI 53901	Birth to 6 years	Assesses socialization, motor, language, self-help, cognitive. Includes a checklist and a card file to aid in assessing present behavior, targeting emerging behavior, and providing suggested techniques to teach each behavior. Domain- and curriculum-referenced measure.
Rockford Infant Developmental Evaluation Scales (RIDES) Bensenville, IL: Scholastic Testing Services, Inc., 1979	Birth to 4 years	Permits teachers to assess the range within which children are functioning in areas of personal-social and self-help skills. Motor and language skills also measured.
Social-Emotional Developmental Profile (SEED) Denver: SEED Program, Seawall Rehabilitation Center, 1975	Birth to 48 months	Covers seven developmental areas, including social-emotional, feeding, dressing, and simple hygiene.
Uzgiris-Hunt Scales of Infant Psychological Development (Uzgiris and Hunt, 1978) University of Illinois Press Urbana, IL 61801	Birth to 24 months	Evaluates seven sensorimotor domains using six stages of development based on Piagetian theory of development. Norm-referenced measure. Assesses cognitive development.
Vineland Social Maturity Scale Circle Pines, MN: American Guidance Service, 1947	Birth to 30 months	Measures self-help, self-direction, and social relations. Items are arranged in order of increasing difficulty. Social age and social quotient given.
Vulpe Assessment Battery Toronto: National Institute on Mental Retardation, 1977	Birth to 6 years	Assesses development in detail. Two of areas measured are self-help skills and organizational behavior.

Preschool Developmental Scales

Name and Source	Ages	Comments
AAMD Adaptive Behavior Scales (Nihira, Foster, Shellaas, and Leland, 1974) American Association on Mental Deficiency 1719 Kalorama Rd. N.W. Washington, DC 20009	3 to 16 years	Assesses independent functioning, physical and language development, socialization, antisocial behavior, time and number concepts, domestic activity, self-direction, maladaptive behaviors, unacceptable vocal habits, use of medication. Measures some of the ways individuals act in a number of different situations. It is a measure of how a person is able to adapt to his/her surroundings and is not an intellectual measure.
Balthazar Scales of Adaptive Behavior (I and II) (Balthazar, 1971) Consulting Psychologists Press, Inc. 577 College Ave. Palo Alto, CA 94306	3 to 57 years	Measures functional independence (eating, dressing, toileting), play activities, verbal communication, unadaptive self-directed behaviors, unadaptive interpersonal behavior, response to instructors. Derived from direct observation; then performance levels can be determined and remedial programs can be developed.
Basic Concepts Inventory Chicago: Follett Educational Corp., 1967	3 to 10 years	Provides information on specific instructional deficits. Designed for slow learners and mentally retarded children.
Burks Behavior Rating Scale, Preschool and Kindergarten Los Angeles: Western Psychological Services, 1977	3 to 6 years	Presents a rating scale. Parent or teacher of child can be respondent. Includes 105 items.
Lakeland Village Adaptive Behavior Grid Medical Lake, WA: Lakeland Village	3 months to 16 years	Evaluates developmental levels for areas such as eating, dressing, toileting, grooming, socialization, and behavior control.
Learning Accomplishment Profile (LAP) (rev. ed.) (Sanford and Zelman, 1981) Kaplan School Supply 600 Jamestown Rd. Winston Salem, NC 27103	12 to 36 months	Gives behavior-oriented evaluation of skills of handicapped preschoolers. Developmental tasks arranged hierarchically. Leads to specific criteria levels for gross motor, fine motor, self-help, language, cognitive skills, prewriting.
Learning Accomplishment Profile—Diagnostic Winston Salem, NC: The Kaplan Press, 1977	Birth to 6 years	Provides standardized criterion-referenced instrument for assessment. Trained paraprofessionals can administer.
McCarthy Scales of Children's Abilities New York: The Psychological Corporation, 1972	2½ to 8½ years	Tests fine and gross motor skills and eye-hand coordination.
Merrill-Palmer Scale of Mental Development New York: Harcourt, Brace and Company, 1931 (rev. 1978)	3 to 5 years	Consists predominantly of performance tests; some verbal items useful with hearing impaired preschoolers and children with language delay. Widely used.
Minnesota Child Development Inventory H. Dreton and E. Thwing, *Clinical Pediatrics*, 1976, 15(10):875-82	1 to 6 years	Covers several areas, two of which are self-help and personal-social. To be completed by primary caregivers. Norms based on suburban white children.
Minnesota Preschool Scale Circle Pines, MN: American Guidance Service, Inc., 1940	6 months to 5 years	Assesses development of mental ability; verbal, nonverbal, and total scores for children 3 to 5, total score for 6 months to 3 years.
TARC Assessment System Lawrence, KS: H and H Enterprises, 1975	3 to 16 years	Offers checklist that is filled in from direct observations. Self-help and social skills are two of areas measured. Can be used for older severely and profoundly handicapped.
TMR Performance Profile for Moderately and Severely Retarded Ridgefield, NJ: Educational Performance Associates, 1973	No age specified	Measures social behavior and self-care skills.
Wachs Analysis of Cognitive Structures Los Angeles: Western Psychological Services, 1977	3 to 6 years	Presents nonverbal culture-free, Piagetian-based test.

Tests for Special Populations*

Name and Source	Ages	Comments
Behavior Developmental Profile Marshalltown, IA: Marshalltown Project, 1975	Birth through 6 years	Measures development of the handicapped and culturally deprived and facilitates individualized teaching of children in home setting. Criterion referenced.
Callier-Azuza Scale (Stillman, 1978) Callier Center for Communication Disorders University of Texas/Dallas 1966 Inwood Road Dallas, TX 75235	Birth to 9 years	Completed by observation in structured or unstructured environments. Provides a rough developmental age profile. Criterion-referenced measure. Designed for deaf-blind and severely handicapped. Includes assessment of gross motor, fine motor, cognitive, language, social, self-help.
Columbia Mental Maturity Scale New York: The Psychological Corporation, 1972	3 to 9 years	For use with children who have both manual and verbal difficulties. Requires no verbalization and limited motor response.
Developmental Checklist Boston: Boston Center for Blind Children, 1978	1 to 8 years	Visually impaired, severely/profoundly MR. Language, motor, social/emotional, self-help tests.
French's Pictorial Test of Intelligence Boston: Houghton Mifflin Company, 1964	3 to 8 years	Requires only a pointing response. Assesses children's abilities in a number of areas: picture vocabulary concepts, similarities, recall and comprehension, and memory of visual stimuli.
Haeussermann's Developmental Potential for Preschool Children New York: Grune and Stratton, Inc., 1958	2 to 6 years	Screens functioning vision and visual perceptual skills as they relate to cognitive development. Designed for cerebral palsied children but can be used with other handicapping conditions.
Hiskey-Nebraska Test of Learning Aptitude Lincoln, NE: Union College Press, 1966	3 to 16 years	Consists of standardized test for deaf and hard-of-hearing; also includes norms for the normal hearing.
Leiter International Performance Scale Chicago: C. J. Stoelting Co., 1979	2 to 18 years	Presents noncultural, nonverbal test of intelligence. Can be used for children with sensory motor defects who have difficulty speaking or reading.
Maxfield-Buchholz Scale of Social Maturity New York: American Foundation for the Blind, 1957	Birth to 6 years	Blind. Language, motor, social/emotional, self-help tests.
Peabody Intellectual Performance Scale—Experimental Edition Nashville: Peabody Child Study Center, 1974	6 to 53 months	Assesses children with significant auditory and visual problems. Some usable vision is needed; hearing is not necessary.
Pennsylvania Training Model (Somerton, Fair, and Turner, 1979)	Birth to 36 months	Curriculum assessment guide, competency checklists, individual prescriptive planning, and data sheet. Intended for persons with physical impairments.
Prescriptive Behavior Checklist for the Severely and Profoundly Retarded (Popovich, 1977)	All ages	Not standardized but reliability was taken on all but motor development and physical eating problems. Information also given on parent training and writing behavior objectives and task analysis in the areas of motor development (head and trunk control, sitting, hand-knee position, standing), eye-hand coordination, language development (attending, physical imitation, auditory training, object discrimination, concept development, sound imitation), physical eating problems.
Topeka Association for Retarded Children (TARC) Assessment System Lawrence, KS: H and H Enterprises, Inc., 1975	No age specified	Offers a short-form behavioral assessment of capabilities of severely handicapped children. Rater uses checklist from observation of data.

*Most of these tests have been designed with handicapped children included in the standardization samples, or the format is particularly suitable for use with disabled children.

Tests Used to Assess Motor Development in Children with Cerebral Palsy

Name (reference)	Age range	Content	Description
A Cerebral Palsy Assessment Chart (Semans, Phillips, Romanoli, Miller, and Skillea, 1965)	No age specified	Assesses gross motor control in the supine, prone, sitting, kneeling, squatting, and standing positions. All of these positions are considered necessary for various functional activities.	First the child is placed in various test positions. Second, the child is asked to maintain the positions. Finally, the child is asked to move into the test positions independently.
Development Hand Dysfunction (Erhardt, 1982)	Newborn to 15 months and 1 to 6 years	Assesses hand function, including involuntary arm-hand patterns, cognitively directed voluntary movements, and prewriting skills.	Specific stimuli are presented to the child and the child's responses are recorded on the protocol sheets.
Milani-Comparetti Motor Development Screening Test (Kliewer, Bruce, and Trembath, 1977)	Birth to 12 months	Assesses the status of head control, primitive reflexes, and higher level reactions, which include equilibrium reactions.	A specific stimulus is presented or the child is placed in a specific position. The child's response is recorded on the scoring chart.
Norton's Basic Motor Evaluation (Norton 1972)	No age specified	Assesses movement and posture in supine, prone, sitting, kneeling, crawling, standing, and components of walking. This assessment is based on the cerebral palsy assessment by Semans et al. (1965) and is for less severely involved children.	The child assumes and holds specific positions after a verbal command is given. Demonstration is given only if the child has difficulty following directions.
Reflex Evaluation (Barnes, Crutchfield, and Heriza, 1977)	No age specified	Assesses the status of the primitive reflexes, prehensile reactions, righting reactions, and equilibrium reactions.	A specific stimulus is presented or the child is placed in a specific position. The child's responses are observed and the responses are recorded on the recording form.
Reflex Testing Methods for Evaluating CNS Dysfunction (2d ed.) (Fiorentino, 1973)	No age specified	Assesses the status of the spinal brainstem and midbrain reflexes; automatic reactions and equilibrium reactions, and the effect of different positions on the status of movements and arm and hand development.	Specific stimuli are presented and the child's responses are recorded on the recording form.

Tests of Motor Skills and Motor Development

Name and Source	Ages	Comments
Basic Motor Fitness Philadelphia: Temple University Press, 1970	All	Tests fundamental and gross motor skills and balance.
Bayley Scales of Infant Development—Motor Scale (N. Bayley) New York: The Psychological Corporation, 1969	3 days to 30 months	Assesses fine and gross motor skills in 81 items.
Developmental Test of Visual-Motor Integration (Beery and Berktencia, 1967)	Form A: 2 to 8 years; Form B: 2 to 15 years	Tests child's integration of visual and motor ability when asked to copy different shapes and designs. Becomes more complex with each succeeding design.
Gross Motor Management of Severely Multiply Impaired Students (Fraser, Galka, and Hensinger, 1980)	All	Can be administered by therapist or a special education teacher. Provides information on normal range-of-motion positions for neophyte staff member. Also has numerous pictures and descriptions of equipment used by severely multiply handicapped persons. Volume 2 includes treatment techniques. Assesses range of motion, reflexes, gross motor.
Milani-Comparetti Motor Development Screening Test (Pearson, 1973)	Birth to 24 months	Identifies reflexes that remain beyond normal age and identifies those that have not emerged. Can be used to identify problems such as cerebral palsy or motor delays.
Miller Assessment for Preschoolers Littleton, CO: Foundation for Knowledge in Development	Preschool	Includes sensory, motor, and cognitive abilities, with emphasis on sensory and motor. Also includes behavioral observation.
Move-Grow-Learn Movement Skills Survey Chicago: Follett Publishing Co., 1971	All	Tests gross, fine, and fundamental skills.
Peabody Developmental Motor Scales (Folio and Fewell, 1983) Teaching Resources Corp. 50 Pond Park Rd. Hingham, MA 02043	Birth to 83 months	Assesses—*Gross motor:* Reflexes, balance, nonlocomotion, locomotion, receipt, and propulsion of objects. *Fine motor:* Grasping, hand use, eye-hand coordination, manual dexterity. Identifies motor skills that are delayed or abnormal. Gives a comparison between gross and fine motor. Provides assessment and programming information. Criterion-referenced measure.
A Prescriptive Behavioral Checklist for the Severely and Profoundly Retarded Baltimore: University Park Press, 1977	All	Assesses body movement and posture through four motor development checklists; designed with task analyses of skills.
The Teaching Research Motor Development Scale for Moderately and Severely Retarded Children Springfield, IL: Teaching Research, Inc., 1972	All	Tests fine and gross motor coordination, visual-motor skills, balance, and body perception.

Screening Instruments

Name and Source	Ages	Comments
Communicative Evaluative Chart Cambridge, MA: Educators Publishing Service, Inc., 1963	Infancy to 5 years	Provides checklist categorized by age. Half of the items deal with development and comprehension of language as a communicative tool.
Del Rio Language Screening Test Austin, TX: National Educational Laboratory Publishers, Inc., 1975	3 to 6 years	Identifies children whose language skills are inappropriate for their age and background. Both Spanish and English editions. Reliability and validity established.
Developmental Activities Screening Inventory Boston: Teaching Resources Corporation, 1977	6 to 60 months	Presents nonverbal instrument that does not penalize multihandicapped children.
Fluharty Preschool Language Screening Test Boulder, CO: INREAL Project University of Colorado, 1975	3 to 6 years	Assesses language skill in rapid screening. Should be administered by speech pathologist.

Batteries with Strong Language Components

Name and Source	Ages	Comments
Brigance Diagnostic Inventory of Early Development Woburn, MA: Curriculum Associates, Inc., 1978	Birth to 6 years	Assesses children's functional and academic development. Criterion referenced.
EMI Assessment Scale Charlottesville, VA: University of Virginia Hospital, Education for Multihandicapped Infants, 1975	Birth to 30 months	Evaluates gross and fine motor, socialization, cognition, and language. Checklist derived from standardized test items.
Lexington-Developmental Scale Lexington, KY: United Cerebral Palsy of the Bluegrass, Inc. Child Developmental Centers, Inc., 1974	Birth to 2 years; 2 to 6 years	Assesses abilities of children and can be used as basis for curriculum planning. To be administered by teacher. The original scale has 452 items; there also is a shortened form.
Teaching Research Placement Test, in *Teaching Research Curriculum for Moderately and Severely Handicapped* Springfield, IL: Charles C. Thomas, Publisher, 1976	Birth to 8 years	Provides material for educational programming for handicapped children. Criterion referenced.
Test of Early Learning Skills (TELS) Bensenville, IL: Scholastic Testing Service, Inc., 1979	Preschool and Kindergarten	Covers areas of thinking and language. Teacher administered.
Vulpe Assessment Battery Toronto: Canadian Association for the Mentally Retarded, 1977	Birth to 6 years	Covers many areas of development. Assessment ties in directly to curriculum planning.
Yellow Brick Road Austin, TX: Learning Concepts, Inc., 1975	4¾ months to 6¾ months	Offers test that is more of a screening battery, used in game atmosphere. Team administered by professionals, paraprofessionals, and volunteers. Can be administered individually or in groups.

Language Development

Name and Source	Ages	Comments
Birth to Three Developmental Scales Boston: Teaching Resources Corporation, 1979	Birth to 3 years	Provides for early identification of developmental delay. Can be administered by teacher or paraprofessional.
Bzoch-League Receptive/Expressive Emergent Scales (REEL) (L. Bzoch and R. League) Tallahassee, FL: Anhinga Press, 1971	Birth to 4 years	Contains interview scale plus directed observation. A language quotient can be obtained. Can be used to assess multiply handicapped blind children.
Environmental Prelanguage Battery Columbus, OH: The Charles E. Merrill Publishing Co., Inc., 1969	12 to 18 months	Assesses child's comprehension, verbal, and gestural imitative ability. Can be used by parents, teachers, and paraprofessionals.
Houston Test for Language Development Houston: Houston Test Company, 1963	Part I: 6 months; Part II: 36 months	Consists of two segments: Part I is primarily an observational measure; Part II contains 18 subtests to evaluate the language status of the child. Observation may be helpful. Handicapped children were not included in sample.
Illinois Children's Language Assessment Test Danville, IL: Interstate Printers and Publishers, Inc., 1977	For children who already exhibit a language delay	Evaluates language performance and the acquisition of speech.
Illinois Test of Psycholinguistic Abilities Urbana, IL: University of Illinois Press, 1968	2½ to 9½ years	Assesses children's psycholinguistic abilities. Tests abilities to use language processes both receptively and expressively.
Infant Scale of Communicative Intent *Update Pediatrics*, 7, 1982	Birth to 18 months	Assesses intent to communicate in several modes. Assesses attempt at social interaction. Tests comprehension and expression. Appropriate for infants with motor limitations.
Inner Language Scale Nashville, TN: Vanderbilt-Peabody University, Child Study Center, 1980	Birth to 24 months	Uses Piagetian scale to assess children's responses to objects and environmental stimuli.

Developmental Levels

Name and Source	Ages	Comments
Language Assessment Aid and Scoring Procedure for the Classroom Teacher Seattle: University of Washington Experimental Education Unit, 1975	4 months to 4½ years	Provides tool for teachers to measure receptive and expressive language.
Preschool Language Scale (rev. ed.) Columbus, OH: The Charles E. Merrill Publishing Co., Inc., 1979	1½ to 7 years	Presents informal inventory to evaluate auditory comprehension and verbal ability with reference to normal stages of development. Only nonverbal responses required. Quotients derived are not particularly useful. No special preparation required of examiner.
Receptive Expressive Language Assessment for the Visually Impaired Mason, MI: Ingham Intermediate School District, 1972	Birth to 6 years	Assesses receptive and expressive language. Auditory and tactual modalities used for administering items.
Scales of Early Communication Skills for Hearing Impaired Children St. Louis: Central Institute for the Deaf, 1975	2 to 8 years	Produces information from its four scales that can be used in curriculum planning. Scales include expressive language, receptive language, nonverbal receptive, and nonverbal expressive communication. Teacher administered.
SRC Language Development Scale Commack, NY: Suffolk Rehabilitation Center, 1975	Birth to 6 years	Speech pathologist can administer scale in about one-half hour.
Utah Test of Language Development Salt Lake City: Communication Research Associates, Inc., 1967	9 months through 16 years	Measures expressive and receptive language skills. Test requires a skilled examiner.
Verbal Language Development Scale Circle Pines, MN: American Guidance Service, Inc., 1971	1 month to 15 years	Consists of an extension of the Vineland Social Maturity Scale. Uses interview format. Items use names of familiar objects and sounds.

Auditory Language Assessment

Name and Source	Ages	Comments
Goldman-Fristoe Test of Articulation Circle Pines, MN: American Guidance Service, Inc., 1967	2 through 16 years	Uses familiar pictures of objects. An articulatory profile can be drawn from the results. Speech pathologist or someone trained in the field should administer this test.
Goldman-Fristoe-Woodcock Test of Auditory Discrimination Circle Pines, MN: American Guidance Service, Inc., 1970	3.8 years to adult	Uses tape-recorded stimulus. Test includes a training procedure, a quiet subtest, and a noise subtest.
Language-Structured Auditory Extension Span Test Novato, CA: Academic Therapy Publications, 1973	Mental age of 3 to 7 years	Presents sentence recall test to measure the child's ability to recall sentences.
Preschool Language Scale (rev. ed.) Columbus, OH: Charles E. Merrill Publishing Co., Inc., 1979		This is described in "developmental levels" section above.
Search: A Scanning Instrument for the Identification of Potential Learning Disability New York: Walker Educational Book Corp., 1975	Preschool	Identifies children who have not yet achieved adequate neurophysiological maturation in skills basic to academic achievement. Articulation and auditory discrimination included.
Smith-Johnson Nonverbal Performance Scale Los Angeles: Western Psychological Services, 1977	2 to 4 years	Assesses functioning of children suspected of hearing loss or language difficulty.
Test for Auditory Comprehension of Language (Carrow) Boston: Teaching Resources Corporation, 1973	3 to 6 years	Requires examiner familiar with psycholinguistics. English/Spanish editions measure receptive language.
Test of Auditory Comprehension North Hollywood, CA: Los Angeles Public Schools, 1976	Preschool and school	Provides a profile of children's auditory abilities and progress. Begins with simple discrimination tasks.

Language Structure

Name and Source	Ages	Comments
Carrow Elicited Language Inventory Boston: Teaching Resources Corporation, 1974	3 to 8 years	Provides method for obtaining information on children's grammatical structure. Speech pathologist usually administers.
Developmental Sentence Analysis, in *Developmental Sentence Analysis,* by L. L. Lee Evanston, IL: Northwestern University Press, 1974	2 to 8 years	Analyzes spontaneous speech to assess syntactic development. Can be used to assess multiply handicapped blind children. May not be appropriate for children from bilingual homes.
Environmental Language Inventory Columbus, OH: The Charles E. Merrill Publishing Co., Inc.	Whenever child can make one- and two-word utterances	Assesses application of semantical grammatical rules in two- and three-word sentences. Uses imitation, conversation, and play.
Expressive One-Word Picture Vocabulary Test Novato, CA: Academic Therapy Publications, 1979	2 to 12 years	Provides information about speech defects, auditory processing, and possible learning difficulties. Standardized.
Full Range Vocabulary Test Missoula, MT: Psychological Test Specialists, 1948	2 years to adult	Provides an index of vocabulary comprehension. Since a pointing response can be made, it is helpful for physically disabled children.
Northwestern Syntax Screening Test Evanston, IL: Northwestern University Press, 1971	3 to 9 years	Consists of a structured screening test for expressive and receptive defects in using syntax. In wide use.
Peabody Picture Vocabulary Test Circle Pines, MN: American Guidance Service, Inc., 1980 ed.	2 to 18 years	Measures receptive vocabulary. Can be given by teacher, paraprofessional. Pointing response useful for multiply or physically handicapped children. Should not be used as a measure of intelligence.

Communication Development

Name and Source	Ages	Comments
Assessment of Expressive Language: Assessment of Children's Language Comprehension Palo Alto, CA: Consulting Psychologists Press, Inc., 1973	3 to 7 years	Assesses children's ability to identify words in syntactical sequence. Standardized sample information presents mean scores for neurologically or educationally handicapped children.
Communication Assessment for the Nonverbal Pupil Seattle: University of Washington, Experimental Education Unit, 1975	4 to 24 months	Measures early development of responses to spoken language.
GATE: General Approval to Thought and Expression Nashville, TN: Vanderbilt-Peabody University, Child Study Center, 1976	Birth to 3 years	Uses nonverbal scale to assess manual and gestural communication attempts by multihandicapped children and necessary skills for signing.
Porch Index of Communicative Ability in Children Palo Alto, CA: Consulting Psychologists Press, Inc., 1974	Part I: Preschool to 5 years: Part II: First grade to age 12	Assesses general communication ability as well as verbal, gestural, and graphic skills. Trained examiner should administer. Materials in subtests are common household objects. Child responds verbally, graphically, and with gestures.
Sequenced Inventory of Communication Development Seattle: University of Washington Press	4 to 48 months	Measures awareness, understanding, imitation, responsiveness, and spontaneous speech. Adaptable for blind children, including the totally blind.

Appendix 4: Music Resources*

Introducing Music into a Learning Environment

Music can play a very significant role in creating an environment in which both the child and the adult are open to learning from each other and from the activities or materials that are presented. Music supports what is being taught and learned. When combined with systematic introduction, careful observation, and responsiveness to the child's nonverbal communication signals, music can assist the process of change.

THE INITIAL DECISION TO USE MUSIC

In deciding whether music or specific musical selections are appropriate to use at home, during therapy, or in the classroom you want to answer the following questions:

- Does the music make a difference for the child?
- Does the music make a difference for the therapist (or teacher)?
- Does the music make a difference for the parent (or family)?
- What kinds of differences are observed when specific types of music or specific pieces of music are played?

SELECTING THE TYPE OF MUSIC

Music can be described or categorized according to its structure (i.e., tempo, rhythm, frequencies, tonal qualities), origin (folk music, rock, opera), or its effect on the listener (dance music, "superlearning music," calming music). Several specific types of music have been used successfully to support learning and change in the areas of movement, feeding, sensory organization, language, and communication.

Types of music that have been utilized in the therapy, classroom, and home environments include:

Quiet, Centering Music—To develop quieting and relaxation of the mind and emotions in order to enhance communication and learning (for example, during meals, rest periods, bedtime, quiet times with an adult).

Superlearning Music—To enhance receptivity to learning through a 60-beat-per-minute tempo. To provide a clear rhythmical structure similar to the rhythms of the heartbeat, sucking, and walking gait. To assist mental and physical relaxation.

Hemi-Sync Metamusic—To create a sustained focus of attention for learning. To facilitate a balanced activation of the information processing capabilities of both the right and left hemispheres of the brain. To increase the organization and integration of sensory information. To provide physical relaxation with simultaneous mental alertness. To reduce fearfulness and negativity, which interfere with learning.

Folk Music—To provide a clear, rhythmical structure and tempo as a basis for facilitation of coordinated body movement. To provide the opportunity for exploration of vocalization, sound play patterns, gestures, and other forms of communication. To provide rhythmical opportunities for the stimulation of the face and mouth. To provide an environment of mutual enjoyment and shared rhythms for the child and adult.

It is helpful to have two or three selections of music from each general category of music. There is a wide range of personal preferences in the children and adults you are working with. It is important to find the type of music that is appropriate to use with the child and to have enough variety within that type that you don't have to consistently use the same taped selection.

---

*Developed by and printed with permission of Suzanne Evans Morris.

Hemi-sync metamusic can assist children in experiencing some very profound differences in the way they physically feel and process information. Sudden changes can be frightening and can create added resistance. It may be important to introduce changes involving relaxation and focus of attention gradually. Superlearning music with a 50- to 70-beat-per-minute tempo has a similar effect for many children and is very gentle. You may wish to begin with this type of music and gradually introduce music containing the hemi-sync signals into the environment. Hemi-sync also produces a more gradual effect when played over open speakers. Listeners report a much stronger effect when they listen to hemi-sync metamusic tapes through headphones. Thus, a continuum of experiential intensity can be created according to the type of music or sound selected and according to the way it is presented to the listener.

OBSERVING THE EFFECTS OF MUSIC ON THE INDIVIDUAL

- Identify the child's characteristic patterns of sensorimotor, emotional, and learning behaviors that might be influenced by a musical background. These could include factors such as muscle tone, movement coordination, attending behaviors, activity level, acceptance of touch, acceptance of movement, acceptance of unfamiliar activities, and imitation abilities.

- Identify changes or directions in these specific areas that would benefit the child. What changes would you like to see happen more easily (e.g., more frequent eye contact, reduction in hypertonicity, acceptance of touch to the face, greater trust and willingness to try new activities, regular sucking rhythm)?

- Identify the general type of music or characteristics of a specific piece of music that would support the changes you would like to facilitate. For example, a very rhythmical piece of music might support greater rhythm in walking or sucking; hemi-sync sounds on a tape would support greater attending and sensory organization.

- Within the category of music you have selected, choose a tape that you (i.e., the therapist, teacher, or parent) like and respond to positively. If you select music that is unpleasant for you or that you dislike, you automatically communicate your discomfort to the child. This can influence children's responses in a negative direction so that their reaction is more a response to you than a response to the music.

- It is helpful to listen to the tape selections ahead of time and become familiar with your general response to the tape. This can assist you in choosing the tape(s) you will use with the child.

- Observe your response to the musical background as you use it with the child. Some of the changes that you may notice include: more flowing rhythms in moving with a child with folk music; enhanced intuitive knowledge of when to continue or alter an activity; stronger focus of attention in the shared activity (i.e., less mind wandering or mind chatter); easier awareness of the child's nonverbal communication; increased intuition; increased creativity.

- Identify the child's verbal or nonverbal patterns of communication. How does the child express likes, dislikes, or preferences in other situations (e.g., turning away, increasing the level of hyperactivity, reducing eye contact, arching, crying or fussing, looking toward the object, reaching, smiling)?

- Introduce the music you have selected to accompany the therapy or home activity you have selected.

- Observe the child's reactions for any signs that the music is aversive. If the music appears to be aversive in any way, turn it off for that period of time. Explore another tape in the same general category of music (i.e., folk music, superlearning music, hemi-sync metamusic) at several other sessions, and observe the child's response. Decide whether the child's aversive response is to a particular piece of music or to an entire category of music.

- Observe the child's reactions for signs that the music is pleasant or enjoyed. This may take the form of increased relaxation, smiling, fuller participation in the activity, looking with interest toward the tape player, etc.

- If the music you have selected appears to be positive or helpful for at least one person in the therapy, classroom, or family setting (i.e., child, therapist, teacher, caregiver), it may be used, providing it is not aversive to the others in the environment.

- Keep a journal describing the child's behavior and responses during sessions or time periods in which you are using the music you have selected. You may wish to select a specific area or behavior to measure during the periods in which you use the music. If you have taken the same measurements for a number of sessions before you introduce the music, you will have established a baseline for comparison. The journal and any measurements you make will allow you to decide how valuable the music background has been for the child.

- Keep a journal describing your own reactions to the music background and changes in your response to the child and the time you spend together. This will enable you to decide whether the musical background to your therapy, play, or learning session enhances your own learning interaction.

- The speed with which change occurs will vary with each individual. For some children and adults there is an immediate awareness of change. For others, there may be acceptance of the music and a slower or more subtle change in behavior or learning. Be aware of small changes that can occur, and resist the temptation to eliminate the music because large shifts do not occur quickly. For example, a child may engage in a familiar activity such as working a puzzle in the same way with or without the music. However, when the music is on, the child shares the activity with the mother and even leans against her. When the child works the puzzle without the musical background, he or she moves slightly away and prefers to play alone. If changes in working the puzzle were the sole measure of effectiveness, the more subtle interpersonal change might go unobserved.

- The frequency with which the music is used will depend upon the child's response and the desirability of using the music in different settings. Some children profit from using music throughout the day; others benefit more from brief (30- to 45-minute) periods once a day. Some music seems to create an effect primarily while it is being played (i.e., folk music). Hemi-sync metamusic appears to create a long-term learning or carryover effect. Because of the carryover effect it is not necessary to use hemi-sync tapes throughout the day for them to be effective. The tapes may be used frequently during the day, however, if both the children and adults in the environment find them pleasant.

- If the tapes are used frequently each day, it is helpful to use breaks during which no music is played. This creates a contrast for the child and provides an opportunity to continue the behaviors facilitated by the music. Hemi-sync tapes are essentially training wheels for the mind that assist the brain with a new way of organizing and integrating sensorimotor experiences. Once this has been learned, the training wheels are no longer necessary.

EQUIPMENT

- Hemi-sync tapes are designed to be played on a stereo tape playback unit. The hemi-sync effect is created by different frequencies on the two channels of a stereo tape. This will not occur if the tapes are played on a monaural tape player.

- A tape player with an auto-reverse feature eliminates the distraction that may occur when a tape reaches the end and must be turned over in the middle of an activity.

- A stereo tape player (i.e., "boom box") with detachable speakers is helpful in creating a headphonelike effect when the speakers are placed on either side of the child's head. This may be desirable if you wish to use headphones with infants or young children who cannot tolerate anything directly touching the ears or head. If lying supine is appropriate for the child and the activity selected, the speakers can be placed within two inches of each ear. Small individual speakers can also be purchased to use with a small personal cassette player. Since these players are small and often have an auto-reverse feature, this combination may offer many advantages in flexibility and price not found in the larger tape players.

- Headphones may provide an advantage for specific children or environments. Headphones enable the child to listen to music at a low volume in an environment where an open-speaker system is unavailable or undesirable. Music through headphones would enable a child to listen to quiet music while being driven in the car, in a classroom, or while taking a school examination when music is not desired for others in the same room. Since the effect of hemi-sync metamusic is more intense with headphones, listening through headphones may become important for some children.

- Commercial headphones are made for adult head sizes. They often slip and are uncomfortable for small children. Several alternatives exist in customizing headphones for infants and toddlers.

Purchase inexpensive headphones with a metal band. Most metal headbands of this type have a bump or metal hump toward the end to prevent extreme movement of the earphones as the band is adjusted for different head sizes. Use a metal file to remove this bump, giving a full range of movement of the individual earphones on the metal band. Adjust the metal band to fit the size of the child's head. Secure the band size with masking tape. Use metal cutters to remove the extra length of the band so that it doesn't poke into the child. Since these headphones are relatively inexpensive (i.e., $6 to $12), several could be constructed, either for different children or for different ranges of head size.

Or

Purchase inexpensive headphones. Use metal cutters to remove the earphones from the band. Alternatively, purchase the type of earphones designed to be inserted directly into the ear canal. Adapt an infant/child's cap or hat, sewing in a flap or pocket that can be closed with Velcro® or a snap. When the child wears the cap, these new pockets will be on the inside, directly at ear level. The separate earphones are inserted into the pockets on each side. The child simply wears this music hat to receive the music. This works particularly well with infants or toddlers who generally do not adapt well to headphones. This should be used with caution with children who do not like hats or having anything touch the head or ears.

LOCATION

Music can be utilized during individual therapy sessions (speech and language therapy, occupational therapy, physical therapy, counseling, or psychotherapy), at home, and in the classroom to assist with relaxation and learning. Somewhat different considerations and guidelines may be used in each setting.

Music during Individual Therapy

- It is ideal for music to be introduced initially in therapy sessions, where the child's responses to the music and to learning can be carefully observed. If the music is used in the background for therapy activities that are familiar, differences in the child's responses can be observed with greater ease.

- Therapy sessions can be utilized to identify individual areas of change that could then become generalized through using music in other environments. Therapists can work with an interested teacher to identify individual children in the classroom who might benefit from the group use of music.

Music in the Home

- When music is introduced into the home setting, the therapist (or teacher) should develop a plan with the family. This plan would include an agreement on the tapes to be used, the times or activities during which they will be used, and the frequency of use. A journal can be kept by the parents to note any changes in the child's behavior that they observe.

- It is helpful to develop a tape library that can be loaned to the family for a period of several weeks. This will enable them to listen to tapes with the child and decide which ones work well at home. When the family has identified tapes that are liked by the child and adults, these can be purchased.

- Quiet music (e.g., centering music, superlearning music, hemi-sync metamusic) can be used in a home or family environment at meals, bedtime, or in specific play or learning activities that would be supported by physical relaxation, mental alertness, or openness to communication.

- Music can be used during an activity or prior to it. For example, the child might spend a quiet time with soft music playing for 30 minutes before the dinner meal; or the music might be used during the meal itself.

- Folk music tapes can be used with all of the children in the family. When siblings are involved with dancing together, singing, turn taking, and sharing with music, the disabled child is no longer the center of attention. It is important to involve the other children in a family during activities that are fun and therapeutic for the child who needs therapy carryover activities.

Music in the Classroom

- Select quiet, organizing music to use in the background as children enter the classroom. This creates a nonverbal message of intention to become more quiet and organized for the school day.

- Accompany specific types of activity with a specific piece of music. Children will gradually associate the music with the activity and will learn to carry over the effects experienced with the music when it is not playing. For example, one piece of music might be played during lunch while another might be used during rest time or table activities.

- Place the tape player so that the speakers are directed toward the children in the classroom. To receive the benefit of the stereo presentation of hemi-sync sound, the speakers should be directed toward the children.

- If hemi-sync metamusic is to be used in the classroom with children with neurological or emotional dysfunction, it is particularly important to observe each child's reaction individually before presenting this music to the entire classroom. A small number of these children may show a disorganized or aversive response to the hemi-sync signals. It is helpful to identify children who appear to benefit and those who may indicate that they do not like the sounds. If there are children in the classroom who are clearly irritated by hemi-sync metamusic tapes, these tapes should not be used while the sensitive children are in the room. The tapes, however, might be used with other children while the sensitive child is involved in a pull-out activity or if the speakers are directed so that they are not facing children who might be irritated by the sounds.

Selection of Music for the Development of Movement

1. Music selections should be clear and rhythmical. They should not contain a great deal of fancy elaboration and instrumentation. They should be performed as straightforwardly as possible, emphasizing a basic rhythm and melody that are strong and uncluttered. Many variations in tempo are appropriate. Syncopation and irregularity in the underlying rhythm pattern should be avoided. We are striving for a clearer rhythm pattern in the child's movement. The structure of the music should mirror the type of movement being worked on.

2. Music should have a rhythmical structure and tempo that meet the needs of the individual child. A tape with slower songs and rhythms might be developed for a child who needs a slower response time for postural reactions. Baroque music or folk dance music could be used in place of songs with lyrics. Instrumental music is less distracting for some children and is more appropriate if you wish to incorporate visual and movement imagery with the movement. It is generally easier to create custom-made tapes for a child or group of children than to find a commercial tape or record that is totally appropriate.

3. Music should be conducive to health and growth. Despite its popularity with today's children and adolescents, rock music should be avoided during treatment sessions. There is data to show that the irregular rhythm of rock music has a negative effect on growth (in plant research), that it weakens muscle responses, and that it reduces the amount of coordinated activity

of the hemispheres of the brain. The precise structure of baroque music, on the other hand, has been associated with greater growth and health (in plants), and with accelerated learning. This type of music can be used as an initial background for movement awareness or to provide a background for sensory integration activities that create the foundation for movement facilitation.

4. Folk music can be extremely effective. It contains many themes of interest to children (animals, people, humor) and utilizes a simple melody structure with a great deal of rhythmical repetition of melodic and lyric phrases. Folk music should be selected that contains a sincere feeling tone and an underlying honesty and respect for children. This is often identified intuitively rather than through a logical sequential analysis of the song. Most traditional folk songs have withstood time and many generations of children and adults who have loved them and played with them. Many of these songs are already familiar to the adult who is working/playing with the child. Contemporary songs composed in a folk style are also appropriate. It is important to sense whether the song was written as an expression of childhood and a knowledge and appreciation of children, or whether the underlying theme is simply to teach something with music. Many of the songs written for straight educational purposes lack the spark and feeling tone of pleasure and playfulness that is carried in the more traditional folk song. Some music written directly for children is patronizing or overly "cute." An emotional tone of respect for the child and the sheer enjoyment of the music is crucial.

5. If you wish to develop tape materials for your program the following suggestions and observations will be helpful:

   a. Determine the kind of music that is appropriate for one or more of the children with whom you work. Assess the initial needs of your program. It is not necessary to create a full program immediately.

   b. Begin listening to different types of music that would be appropriate. Listen first at an intuitive, feeling level for what the specific piece has to offer. Move with the music and let it create images for you. Imagine yourself moving with children to the music. Listen again to the music with a more analytical ear. What does it have to offer a specific child or family in your program? What is the tempo? the rhythm? the theme of the song?

   c. Broaden your exposure to music that is available in your community. Check listings of specific com-

positions, records, and artists in books or articles on the therapeutic use of music (i.e., see the discography). Begin to listen to selections on records borrowed from your library or school or in your own tape or record collection. Include music from the cultural traditions of the children and families with whom you are working.

   d. Create several custom tapes for your program. These may include songs or instrumental pieces from a single record or artist, or they may include a mixture of artists and recordings. Consider your purposes for creating the tape as you decide whether a given song or composition belongs on the tape. For example, you may wish to begin a tape with slow to moderately paced music that has a clear, steady rhythm. The slow tempo and steady rhythm lend themselves well to activities that build postural tone and stability. Add songs that create an appropriate background for more complex movement and coordination. These songs may be interspersed with slower tempos and with songs that are specifically appropriate for building and steadying postural tone. As overall movement control improves throughout the first half of the tape, songs can be added that include active vocalization, play with the mouth, gestures, use of a communication miniboard, etc.

   e. Explore the use of the new tape with specific children. You will gain a clearer sense of which materials work for you and for the child. Look for an overall pleasurable response from the child. The child may become more playful and willing to work/play with you as the tape is playing. The child may become more alert to a specific song. There may be smiling, vocalization, increased relaxation, or increased body movement with the music. Watch for an increase in endurance and tolerance in treatment. The child may be able to focus on activities for longer periods and not tire as readily. Touch and movement may be accepted more readily with the music. You may observe a child become more interactive and communicative when the tape or specific songs are used during the session.

   f. As you use the tape, make written notes of the types of activity that seem particularly appropriate with each song. This written listing can be typed and given to parents, teachers, or other therapists who are using a copy of your tape with the child.

Music for the Development of Learning, Communication, and Movement

QUIET, CENTERING MUSIC

Purpose: To develop quieting and relaxation of the mind and emotions in order to enhance communication and learning (e.g., during meals, rest periods, bedtime, quiet times with an adult).

*Comfort Zone
Steven Halpern
Halpern Sounds

Spectrum Suite
Steven Halpern
Halpern Sounds

Ancient Echoes
Steven Halpern
Halpern Sounds

Dawn
Steven Halpern
Halpern Sounds

Eventide
Steven Halpern
Halpern Sounds

Birds of Paradise
Georgia Kelly
Heru Records

Tarashanti
Georgia Kelly
Heru Records

Seapeace
Georgia Kelly
Heru Records

Harp and Soul
Georgia Kelly
Heru Records

Silk Road
Kitaro
Canyon Records

*Fairy Ring
Mike Rowland
Music Design

*Golden Voyage: Vol. 1
Bearns & Dexter
Awakening
Productions

Golden Voyage: Vol.4
Bearns & Dexter
Awakening Productions

Gregorian Chant from
Hungary:
Medieval Christmas

Hungaroton Melodies

Christopher Parkening
Plays J. S. Bach
Christopher Parkening
Angel

The Pachelbel
Canon in D
Jean-Francois Paillard
Chamber Orchestra
RCA

Mother Earth's Lullaby
Synchestra
Synchestra

Silver Ships
Synchestra
Synchestra

December
George Winston
Windom Hill
Productions

Autumn
George Winston
Windom Hill
Productions

Winter into Spring
George Winston
Windom Hill
Productions

Childhood and Memory
Will Ackerman
Windom Hill
Productions

*Transitions
Burt Wolff and
Joe Wolff
Placenta Music

Lullabies from Around
the World
Steven Bergman
Steven Bergman

Sweet Baby Dreams
Steven Bergman
Steven Bergman

Dream Passage
Daniel Kobialka
LiSem Enterprises

Fragrances of a Dream
Daniel Kobialka
LiSem Enterprises

*Going Home
Daniel Kobialka
LiSem Enterprises

Timeless Motion
Daniel Kobialka
LiSem Enterprises

When You Wish
upon a Star
Daniel Kobialka
LiSem Enterprises

Miracles
Rob Whitesides-Woo
Serenity Music

Chistofori's Dream
David Lanz
Narada Music

SUPERLEARNING MUSIC

Purpose: To enhance receptivity to learning through a 60-beat-per-minute tempo. To provide a clear rhythmical structure similar to the rhythms of the heartbeat, sucking, and walking gait.

*Comfort Zone
Steven Halpern
Halpern Sounds

Superlearning Music
(baroque classical
music)
Superlearning Inc.

*Relax with the
Classics: Vol. #1,
Largos (baroque
classical music)
LIND Institute

*Relax with the
Classics: Vol. #2,
Adagios (baroque
classical music)
LIND Institute

*Relax with the
Classics: Vol. #3,
Pastorale (baroque
classical music)
LIND Institute

*Relax with the
Classics: Vol. #4,
Andante (baroque
classical music)
LIND Institute

Music for Mellow Minds
Janalea Hoffman
Mellow Minds

Mind-Body Tempo
Janalea Hoffman
Mellow Minds

*Alleluia
Robert Gass and
On Wings of Song
Spring Hill Music

*Om Namaha Shivaya
Robert Gass and
On Wings of Song
Spring Hill Music

HEMI-SYNC MUSIC

Purpose: To create a more sustained focus of attention for learning. To facilitate a more balanced activation of the information processing capabilities of both the right and left hemispheres of the brain. To reduce fearfulness and negativity, which interfere with the learning of new skills.

Metamusic Back Room
Robert Monroe,
Alan Phillips
The Monroe Institute

Metamusic Blue
Robert Monroe
The Monroe Institute

*Metamusic Converse
Robert Monroe,
Alan Phillips
The Monroe Institute

*Metamusic
  Downstream
Robert Monroe,
Alan Phillips
The Monroe Institute

*Metamusic Eddys
Robert Monroe,
Alan Phillips
The Monroe Institute

Metamusic Green
Robert Monroe
The Monroe Institute

Metamusic Highland
  Ring
Robert Monroe,
Alan Phillips
The Monroe Institute

Metamusic Limbic
Robert Monroe,
Alan Phillips
The Monroe Institute

*Metamusic
  Midsummer Night
Robert Monroe,
Alan Phillips
The Monroe Institute

*Metamusic Modem
Robert Monroe,
Alan Phillips
The Monroe Institute

Metamusic Nostalgia
Robert Monroe,
Alan Phillips
The Monroe Institute

Metamusic Outreach
Robert Monroe,
Alan Phillips
The Monroe Institute

Metamusic Random
  Access
Robert Monroe,
Alan Phillips
The Monroe Institute

Metamusic Sam &
  George
Robert Monroe,
Alan Phillips
The Monroe Institute

Soft and Still
Robert Monroe
The Monroe Institute

Metamusic Sunset
Robert Monroe,
Alan Phillips
The Monroe Institute

*Metamusic
  Trailing Edge
Robert Monroe,
Alan Phillips
The Monroe Institute

FOLK MUSIC

Purpose: To provide a clear, rhythmical structure and tempo as a basis for facilitation of coordinated body movement. To provide the opportunity for exploration of vocalization, sound play patterns, gestures, and other forms of communication. To provide an environment of mutual enjoyment and shared rhythms for the child and the adult.

*I've Got a Song
Sandy and
Carolyn Paton
Folk-Legacy Records

*When the Spirit
Says Sing
Sandy and
Carolyn Paton
Folk-Legacy Records

*Teaching Peace
Red Grammer
Smilin' Atcha Music

Birds, Beasts, Bugs
and Little Fishes
Pete Seeger
Folkways

Birds, Beasts, Bugs
and Bigger Fishes
Pete Seeger
Folkways

Song and Playtime
with Pete Seeger
Pete Seeger
Folkways

American Game and
Activity Songs for
Children
Pete Seeger
Folkways

American Folk Songs
for Children
Pete Seeger
Folkways

Marching Across the
Green Grass and
Other American
Children's Game
Songs
Jean Ritchie
Folkways

14 Numbers, Letters
and Animals Songs
Alan Mills
Folkways

I'll Sing You a Story
Sam Hinton
Folkways

Woody Guthrie's
Children's Songs
Logan English
Folkways

Songs to Grow On
Woody Guthrie
Folkways

Animal Folksongs
for Children
Peggy Seeger
Folkways

*Lullabies and Other
Children's Songs
Nancy Raven
Pacific Cascades

*People and Animal
Songs
Nancy Raven
Pacific Cascades

Songs for the
Holiday Season
Nancy Raven
Pacific Cascades

Singing, Prancing,
and Dancing
Nancy Raven
Pacific Cascades

*Many Blessings
On Wings of Song
Spring Hill Music

Lets Sing Fingerplays
Tom Glazer
CMS Records

Rhythms of Childhood
Ella Jenkins
Scholastic

My Street Begins at
  My House
Ella Jenkins
Folkways

Growing Up with
  Ella Jenkins
Ella Jenkins
Folkways

You'll Sing a Song and
  I'll Sing a Song
Ella Jenkins
Folkways

Howjadoo
John McCutcheon
Rounder Records

Grandma Slid Down
  the Mountain
Cathy Fink & Friends
Rounder Records

Monsters in the Closet
Gerri Gribi and
Tom Pease
Makin' Jam Etc.

My Rhinoceros and
  Other Friends
Guy Carawan
A Gentle Wind

A Home in Tennessee
Sparky Rucker
A Gentle Wind

A Song or Two for You
Nick Seeger
A Gentle Wind

Sing a Song, Sing Along
Faith Petric
A Gentle Wind

Down in the Valley
Robin and Linda
Williams
A Gentle Wind

Camels, Cats, and
  Rainbows
Paul Strausman
A Gentle Wind

*The Dildine Family
The Dildine Family
A Gentle Wind

Hello Everybody
Rachel Buchman
A Gentle Wind

Singable Songs for the
  Very Young
Raffi
A & M Records

More Singable Songs
Raffi
A & M Records

ADDRESSES OF DISTRIBUTING COMPANIES

Folk Lagacy Records
Sharon, CT 06069

A Gentle Wind
Box 3103
Albany, New York
12203

The Monroe Institute
Route 1, Box 175
Faber, VA 22938

Music Design
207 East Buffalo
Milwaukee, WI 53202

New Leaf Distributing
Company
5425 Tulane Dr. S.W.
Atlanta, GA 30336

New Visions
Route 1, Box 175-S
Faber, VA 22938

Rounder Records
One Camp Street
Cambridge, MA 02140

Silo
P.O. Box 429
Waterbury, VT 05676

Superlearning Inc.
450 Seventh Ave
New York, NY 10123

(*Items available through New Visions)

Glossary

accommodation—adapting one's familiar responses to fit the demands of a new stimulus

active—having to do with the individual's conscious involvement and participation

adaptive equipment—devices used for positioning or to assist with active movement that help to normalize tone and facilitate normal patterns of movement or response

adaptive response—an appropriate or effective reaction in response to a stimulus or environmental demand

adaptive transactive—having to do with each individual's modification of behaviors in response to the behaviors of another

agent—the entity responsible for the action or state described

AIDS (acquired immune deficiency syndrome)—a viral illness in which the body's immune system is repressed, leaving the individual vulnerable to a variety of other infections; usually fatal

ARC (AIDS-related complex)—a less acute form of AIDS

articulation—the clarity with which speech is produced

aspirate—inhale liquid or solid materials into the lungs

assessment—a process for determining appropriate intervention services and activities that involves systematic observation and standardized testing of the individual

assimilation—giving the same response to a new stimulus that one has in the past given to similar (but different) stimuli

asymmetrical tonic neck reflex (ATNR)—a primitive reflex in which the head turning from midline to one side activates extension (or increase in extensor tone) in the arm and leg on the face side and flexion (or increase in flexor tone) in the arm and leg on the opposite side

attribute—characteristic

atypical movement patterns—movement patterns that are unusual or different from those normally used

auditory—having to do with sound

augmentative communication—a formal system of nonspeech communication used as an alternative or supplement to spoken language when the individual's ability to use spoken language is impaired

automatic responses—movements or responses performed without conscious thought or control, to realign body parts or maintain balance against gravity

balance—stability of the body against gravity; equilibrium

balance reaction—one of a set of automatic movement patterns that occurs in response to changes in the relationship of the body's center of gravity to the force of gravity that allows the individual to maintain balance

base of support—the center of stability from which the individual moves (often derived from those body parts in contact with a solid surface such as the ground)

behavioral observations—objective descriptions of the individual's behavior in specific circumstances, for example, during free play in the classroom

body awareness—body schema

body image—the conscious awareness and perception of one's own body, including values and feelings about one's bodily function and appearance

body schema—the unconscious awareness of one's own body both in terms of its individual parts and how they are related to make up the whole

breath capacity—the amount of air taken into the lungs in a single breath

cause-effect behaviors—responses related to bringing about a repetition of a desired event or behavior and to understanding what causes the event or behavior to recur

center-based program—an intervention program in which services are delivered in a school, day-care, or clinic setting rather than in the home

central nervous system (CNS)—the brain and spinal cord, where incoming sensory impulses are received and from which outgoing motor impulses are sent. The CNS supervises and coordinates the activity of the entire nervous system.

cerebral palsy—a condition producing abnormalities in the motor functions (tone, control, and/or strength) due to nonprogressive central nervous system damage or defect during the developmental years

clinical observations—objective descriptions of the individual's behavior made by a trained professional and based on a comparison with typical behavior under similar circumstances

CMV (cytomegalic virus)—a common virus, causing mild to no symptoms in adults, that can cause severe damage to the developing fetus if contracted during pregnancy

cocktail speech—speech that consists of words and sentences in which appropriate inflections are used but that lacks meaning in the situational context

co-contraction—the balanced activation of muscle groups on both sides of a body part, providing stability for movement against gravity and for the maintenance of antigravity postures

cognitive—having to do with thinking and problem solving; relating to knowledge

compensation—atypical posture or pattern of movement used instead of a normal posture or pattern to accomplish a functional goal

conscious—marked by thought or awareness

contingency games—activities, usually between adult and child, in which the adult's action is dependent on the child's producing a specific behavior

contracture—permanent shortening of muscles or tendons, resulting in reduced range of motion around the affected joint

criterion-referenced assessment—a type of assessment in which the individual's behavior is compared to a standardized behavioral description rather than to the performance of other individuals

developmental delay—an indication during infancy or early childhood that a skill or set of skills has not been achieved or mastered within the normal age range expected

diagnosis—a process for identifying and/or describing an individual's medical condition

direct treatment—intervention treatment provided by a trained professional on an individual basis

discrimination—the ability to perceive and respond to differences between or among stimuli

dissociation—the ability to move different body parts or muscle groups separately from one another as appropriate

Down syndrome—a genetic syndrome resulting from a disorder of chromosome 21 and associated with low muscle tone and some degree of mental retardation

dysfunction—impaired or abnormal functioning

echolalia—speech in which individuals repeat whatever is said to them

ecological approach—an approach to early intervention based on the idea that skills taught must be functional in the individual's daily environment (home and community) and during daily activities in order to be considered appropriate for teaching

encephalitis—an inflammation of the brain

equilibrium—balance

equilibrium reaction—one of a set of automatic patterns of body movements that enable the individual to adapt in response to change in the position of the body's center of gravity

evaluation—a process for gathering and analyzing information, especially information related to progress, over time

exhale—breathe out

extension—straightening; a movement that causes an increase in the angle between two adjoining bones

extensors—those muscles that, when contracted, produce extension

facilitate—to make easier; to guide toward an appropriate response

fixing—using abnormal bodily mechanisms (e.g., increased muscle tone, atypical posturing) to increase postural stability. Fixing increases stability but decreases mobility.

flexion—bending; a movement that causes a decrease in the angle between two adjoining bones

flexors—those muscles that, when contracted, produce flexion

generalization—the ability to use skills learned in one situation appropriately in other situations

genetic syndrome—any one of a number of sets of abnormal characteristics resulting from chromosomal disorders at conception

graded response—a degree of response appropriate to the level of stimulus; a response from the midrange of possible responses rather than an extreme (all-or-nothing) response

grasp reflex—a primitive response to tactile stimulation on the palm of the hand characterized by grasping the source of stimulation

handling—therapeutic ways of moving an individual that help to normalize tone and facilitate normal movement patterns

head control—the ability to bring the head upright using smooth, graded movements when tilted in any direction; the ability to maintain the head upright against gravity without using abnormal patterns or postures

head-righting reaction—one of a set of automatic patterns of body movements that enables the individual to maintain the head in a vertical position against gravity

high tone—increased tone in the muscles above normal limits; hypertonia

HIV—the virus that causes AIDS in humans

hyperactive—excessively active, usually also with disorganized behavior

hypersensitive—overly sensitive or overly responsive to stimuli

hypertonia—increased tension in the muscles that results in reduced mobility and limited range of motion

hypotonia—decreased tension in the muscles that results in lack of postural stability and excessive range of motion

IEP—individualized education program

IFSP—individualized family service plan

imitation—copying or mimicking behavior that another has been observed to have produced

inhibition—techniques to decrease or prevent the use of atypical postures or movement patterns

inhibitive casts—casts, often removable, designed to hold the foot and ankle in proper alignment, thereby helping to reduce high tone

in-service—presentations or workshops designed to expand or enhance job-related skills that team members attend as part of their regularly scheduled work time

intentionality—having to do with the ability to plan actions in advance to achieve a goal

interactive—having to do with an individual's responses to another individual, and especially with an exchange of responses

interdisciplinary model—an approach to early intervention in which professionals from various disciplines provide direct services independently but in consultation with one another

internalize—to incorporate into one's spontaneous thinking and/or responding

interpretive meeting—a meeting to discuss and explain assessment results to parents and other interested and involved persons

jaw control—techniques to facilitate more normal movement patterns for eating and/or drinking

joint—the place where two or more bones are joined

joint approximation (also called *joint compression*)—the use of pressure to bring the articulating surfaces closer together

kinesthetic system—the sensory system that responds to (sends information to the brain about) the movement of individual body parts

language—an organized, conventionally agreed upon system for communication

learning disability—difficulty in learning to process language, read, write, compute, or do other school work that cannot be attributed to impaired sight or hearing, mental retardation, or emotional disturbance

localization—the ability to identify the source of a stimulus

low tone—reduced tone in the muscles below normal limits; hypotonia

means-ends behaviors—responses relating to the purposeful or intentional achieving of a goal (solving a problem)

midline—an imaginary line running down the center of the body from head to toe

modeling—a technique for teaching a new behavior in which the target behavior is demonstrated, often repeatedly, by another

motor planning—the ability to plan an appropriate sequence of movements in order to efficiently accomplish a goal

multidisciplinary model—an approach to early intervention in which a variety of professionals from different disciplines provide services independently of one another

muscle tone—amount of tension in the muscles

neural pathway—the route in the nervous system along which a particular type of information is carried

neurological system—the nervous system, which consists of the brain, spinal cord, nerve cells, and nerve fibers running throughout the body

neutral—a position from which the individual has many movement options rather than one that prepares the individual to make a specific response or that limits the possible movement options

normalize—to make more nearly normal through the use of specialized techniques and/or environmental adaptations

norm-referenced assessment—a type of assessment in which an individual's performance is compared to the average performance of a large group of comparable individuals

object—the entity on which the action operates

object permanence—the ability to remember and mentally represent an object when it is not providing direct sensory stimulation or when it is not physically present; the idea that objects have an independent reality

oral—having to do with the mouth

oral-motor—having to do with the muscles and movement patterns of the neck, lips, tongue, cheeks, mouth, and jaw

ordinal scale—a type of assessment that measures where on a developmental continuum an individual's abilities lie. In an ordinal system, all individuals learn the behaviors measured in the same sequence, and the development of higher level behaviors is dependent on the development of all preceding behaviors on the continuum.

passive—acted upon by others or by external forces

pattern of movement—the set of various muscle contractions combined and sequenced so as to move a body part or parts

perception—the process by which the brain organizes, integrates, and makes sense of incoming stimuli and sensations

person permanence—the ability to remember and mentally represent a person when the person is not providing stimulation, is not visible, or is not physically present

pharynx—throat

phenylketonuria (PKU)—a genetic disorder affecting the body's ability to metabolize phenylalanine, a protein contained in many common foods. PKU can be effectively treated with a special diet in most cases. If untreated, severe disabilities, including brain damage and mental retardation, can result.

physical guidance—a technique for teaching a new behavior in which the individual is physically guided through the movements required of the target behavior

physiological—having to do with the body's physical and chemical functioning

positioning—therapeutic ways of placing an individual that help normalize tone and facilitate normal movement patterns

postural stability—the ability to maintain posture against gravity using normal patterns of movement

postural tone—the degree of tension in the muscles

posture—the position from which an individual starts a movement

pragmatics—having to do with the function or use of language and communication

precursor—that which comes before and indicates the approach of another

premature—infants born at or before 38 weeks gestational age

prerequisite—that which must occur before a particular other can occur

primary caregiver—the person who provides the largest percentage of an infant or child's care

primary circular reaction—response characterized by the ability to coordinate two different bodily schemes at the same time, such as looking and listening

primitive reflex—a reflex present at birth or in utero in a normal infant born at full term, which is normally integrated into more mature movement patterns during the first year or two of life

prone—lying on the stomach

proprioceptive system—the sensory system that responds to (sends information to the brain about) sensations from the joints, muscles, and tendons

psychomotor retardation—a diagnostic category used to describe delayed motor development resulting from mental retardation

reciprocity—an exchange of mutually corresponding behaviors

referent—the entity to which a word refers

reflex—a stereotyped movement or posture produced in response to a specific stimulus

reliability—having to do with the consistency of observations or with how accurately an assessment measures reality

responsiveness—the individual's ability to change behavior when environmental stimuli change

restrictive environment—a setting that provides more limits for the individual's experiences and behaviors than would typically be the case

retraction—abnormal pulling back of a body part to increase stability

role expansion—in a transdisciplinary model, the growth of a professional's knowledge and expertise in other related disciplines

role release—in a transdisciplinary model, the ability of a professional in one discipline to give up some responsibilities to a professional from another discipline when appropriate

rooting reflex—a primitive response to tactile stimulation on the lips or cheeks characterized by the mouth opening and the head turning in the direction of the stimulus

rotation—movement around the long axis of the body part

schemes—sets of behaviors; behavioral patterns

screening—a process that involves individual testing to determine whether or not an individual may have a particular condition or disability that requires further assessment

secondary circular reactions—responses characterized by the use of a behavioral scheme to bring about a repetition of an external event or phenomena

seizure disorder—a disorder in which sudden abnormal excessive discharges of electrical impulses occur in localized areas of the brain, resulting in temporary loss of awareness and/or control of function on a recurrent basis

sensation—the awareness of a stimulus

sensory affective disorder—proposed alternative term for tactile defensiveness

sensory integration—the ability of the brain to organize sensory input for use

sensory integration dysfunction—an irregularity in central nervous system function that makes it difficult to process, organize, and/or use sensory input effectively

sensory receptors—nerve cells that receive information to be sent to the central nervous system

shaping—a technique for teaching new behaviors in which the individual is selectively reinforced for responses that are progressively closer to the target behavior

sidelying—lying on one's side; often recommended as a therapeutic positioning

skill—the learned ability to perform a task competently; the tasks referred to are usually developmental milestones

spatial relations—relating to information about the position of objects in space and their relationship to other objects in space

speech—communication through the use of spoken words

spinal tracts—nerves connecting to the spinal cord

staffings—meetings at which an individual's intervention program, progress, and other issues of concern are discussed

standardized test—an assessment instrument that is designed to be administered in a specified way and that provides normative data with which individual scores may be compared

state—short for state of consciousness; relating to the individual's level and type of arousal and alertness

subluxed—partially dislocated

sucking reflex—a primitive response to tactile stimulation on the roof of the mouth used primarily to obtain liquid and characterized by small, rhythmical up-and-down movements of the tongue and jaw with the lips closed

supine—lying on the back

symbolic representation—the ability to let one thing stand for another; especially the ability to let an abstraction, such as a word, stand for (or represent) something more concrete, such as an object, action, or concept

symmetrical—the same on both sides of the body

syntax—having to do with the structure or rules of language

synthesized speech—speech sounds produced by a computer

tactile—having to do with touch

tactile defensiveness—a sensory integrative dysfunction in which the individual is excessively sensitive to touch sensations and responds with negative emotional and/or physical reactions to touch sensations

tactile system—the sensory system that responds to touch sensations

tendon—tough connective tissue joining a muscle with some other body part

tertiary circular reactions—responses characterized by actions modified by differentiated feedback

total communication—a communication system that uses both sign and spoken language simultaneously

total support—external support for all body parts to maintain an antigravity position

toxoplasmosis—a condition resulting from infection by a parasitic organism during pregnancy. While adults experience mild to no symptoms, the infection can cause severe damage to the developing fetus.

traction—the technique of pulling on a joint to increase the distance between the articulating surfaces

transdisciplinary model—an approach to early intervention in which a primary service provider is responsible for implementing the intervention plan based on input from all relevant disciplines, with support services provided by members of other disciplines where indicated

triadic interactions—interactions involving a child, an object, and another person in which the child indicates appreciation of the unique response capabilities of the other as opposed to the capabilities of the object

trunk—the body, excluding the extremities (head, arms, legs)

trunk control—the ability to bring the trunk into an upright position when tilted in any position; the ability to maintain the trunk in an upright position against gravity without using abnormal postures or patterns

vestibular system—the sensory system (whose receptors are located in the semicircular canals of the inner ears) that responds to the position of the head in space and in relation to gravity, and to changes in direction and speed of movement

visual—having to do with sight

vocal—having to do with the use of the voice

weight bearing—supporting some or all of the body's weight

References

Anisfeld, M. 1984. *Language development from birth to three*. Hillsdale, NJ: Lawrence Erlbaum Associates.

Apgar, V. 1953. A proposal for a new method of evaluation of the newborn infant. *Current Researches in Anesthesia and Analgesia* 32:260-67.

Ayres, A. J. 1979. *Sensory integration and the child*. Los Angeles, CA: Western Psychological Services.

Bagnato, S. J., and J. T. Neisworth. 1981. *Linking developmental assessment and curricula*. Rockville, MD: Aspen Publishers.

————. 1987. *Developmental diagnosis of the young exceptional child*. New York: Macmillan.

Barnard, K. 1979. *Nursing child assessment teaching manual*. Seattle, WA: Department of Parent and Child Nursing, NCAST, University of Washington.

Bates, E., L. Benigni, I. Bretherton, L. Camaioni, and V. Volterra. 1977. From gesture to the first word: On cognitive and social prerequisites. In *Interaction, conversation, and the development of language*, edited by M. Lewis and L. A. Rosenblum. New York: John Wiley and Sons.

————. 1979. *The emergence of symbols: Cognition and communication in infancy*. New York: Academic Press.

Bates, E., L. Camaioni, and V. Volterra. 1975. The acquisition of performatives prior to speech. *Merrill-Palmer Quarterly* 21:205-26.

Bayley, N. 1969. *Bayley scales of infant development*. New York: Psychological Corporation.

Behrmann, M. M., J. K. Jones, and M. L. Wilds. 1989. Technology intervention for very young children with disabilities. *Infants and Young Children*. 1:66-77.

Bell, S. M. 1970. The development of the concept of object as related to infant-mother attachment. *Child Development* 41:291-311.

Bender, M., and R. K. Bender. 1979. *Disadvantaged preschool children: A source book for teachers*. Baltimore, MD: Paul H. Brookes.

Bertenthal, B. I., and K. W. Fischer. 1978. The development of self-recognition in the infant. *Developmental Psychology* 14:44-50.

Bly, L. 1983. *The components of normal movement during the first year and abnormal motor development*. Monograph. Oak Park, IL: NDT Association.

Bobath, B. 1975. Sensori-motor development. *NDT Newsletter* 7:1-5.

Bobath, K. 1980. *Neurophysiological basis for treatment of cerebral palsy*. London: William Heinemann Medical Books.

Bobath, K., and B. Bobath. 1952. The treatment of cerebral palsy based on the analysis of the patient's motor behavior. *British Journal of Physical Medicine* 15:107.

Brazelton, T. B. 1973. *Neonatal behavior assessment scale*. London: William Heinemann Medical Books.

Bricker, D. D. 1982. Introduction: From research to application. In *Intervention with at-risk and handicapped infants: From research to application*, edited by D. D. Bricker, 1-9. Baltimore, MD: University Park Press.

Bricker, D. D., and L. Dennison. 1978. Training prerequisites to verbal behavior. In *Systematic instruction of the moderately and severely handicapped*, edited by M. E. Snell, 157-78. Columbus, OH: Charles E. Merrill.

Brigance, A. H. 1978. *Brigance diagnostic inventory of early development*. North Billerica, MA: Curriculum Associates, Inc.

Brossard, M. D. 1974. The infant's conception of object permanence and his reactions to strangers. In *The infant's reaction to strangers*, edited by T. G. Decarie. London: Methuen.

Burkhart, L. J. 1987. *Using computers and speech synthesis to facilitate communicative interaction with young and/or severely handicapped children*. College Park, MD: author.

Butler, C. 1988. High tech tots: Technology for mobility, manipulation, communication, and learning in early childhood. *Infants and Young Children* 1:66-73.

Campbell, P. 1982. *Introduction to neurodevelopmental treatment*. Akron, OH: Children's Hospital Medical Center of Akron.

————. 1983. *Neurodevelopmental treatment intervention procedures*. Akron, OH: Children's Hospital Medical Center of Akron.

————. 1984. Introduction to neurodevelopmental treatment. Workshop held at College Park, MD.

Carey, W. B., and S. C. McDevitt. 1977. *The Carey infant temperament questionnaire*. Media, PA: William B. Carey, M.D.

————. 1978. Ability and change in individual temperament diagnoses from infancy to early childhood. *Journal of Childhood Psychiatry* 17:331-37.

Carter, A. L. 1978. From sensori-motor vocalizations to words. In *Action, gesture, and symbol: The emergence of language,* edited by A. Lock, 309-49. New York: Academic Press.

Cicchetti, D., and L. A. Sroufe. 1978. An organizational view of affect: Illustration from the study of Down's syndrome infants. In *The development of affect,* edited by M. Lewis and L. A. Rosenblum, 309-60. New York: Plenum Press.

Coling, M. C. 1979. Stages of language development during the sensorimotor period: A Piagetian framework. Unpublished manuscript.

————. 1987. Social-emotional development in infancy. Unpublished manuscript.

Connor, F. P., G. G. Williamson, and J. M. Siepp. 1978. *Program guide for infants and toddlers with neuromotor and other developmental disabilities.* New York: Teacher's College Press.

Copeland, M. E., and J. R. Kimmel. 1989. *Evaluation and management of infants and young children with developmental disabilities.* Baltimore, MD: Paul H. Brookes.

Decarie, T. G. 1978. Affective development and cognition in a Piagetian context. In *The development of affect,* edited by M. Lewis and L. A. Rosenblum, 183-204. New York: Plenum Press.

Dougherty, J. M., and J. D. Moran III. 1983. The relationship of Piagetian stages to mental retardation. *Education and Training of the Mentally Retarded* 18:260-65.

Dubowitz, L. M. S., V. Dubowitz, and C. Goldberg. 1970. Clinical assessment of gestational age in the newborn infant. *Journal of Pediatrics* 77:1.

Dunst, C. J. 1978. A cognitive-social approach for assessment of early nonverbal communicative behavior. *Journal of Childhood Communication Disorders* 2:110-23.

————. 1980. *A clinical and educational manual for use with the Uzgiris and Hunt scales of infant psychological development.* Baltimore, MD: University Park Press.

————. 1981. *Infant learning: A cognitive-linguistic intervention strategy.* Allen, TX: DLM Teaching Resources.

Dunst, C. J., and R. M. Rheingrover. 1981. The stage concept revisited: Methodological considerations and strategies. Paper presented at the biennial meeting of the Society for Research in Child Development, Boston.

Dunst, C. J., and R. A. McWilliam. In preparation. Cognitive assessment of multiply handicapped young children. In *Assessment of developmentally disabled children,* edited by T. Wachs and R. Sheehan. New York: Plenum Press.

Eagen, C. S., K. Petisi, and A. L. Toole. 1980. *The transdisciplinary training, assessment, and consultation model.* Yorktown Heights, NY: Board of Cooperative Educational Services.

Edwards, D. 1973. Sensory-motor intelligence and semantic relations in early child grammar. *Cognition* 2:395-434.

Farber, S. D. N.d. *Sensorimotor evaluation and treatment procedures for allied health professionals.* N.p.

Fewell, R. R. 1983a. Assessing handicapped infants. In *Educating handicapped infants: Issues in development and intervention,* edited by S. G. Garwood and R. R. Fewell, 257-97. Rockville, MD: Aspen Publishers.

————. 1983b. The team approach to infant education. In *Educating handicapped infants: Issues in development and intervention,* edited by S. G. Garwood and R. R. Fewell, 299-322. Rockville, MD: Aspen Publishers.

Finnie, N. R. 1975. *Handling the young cerebral palsied child at home.* New York: Dutton.

Foltz, L., and D. Lewis. 1985. Management of the child with neuromotor and prespeech dysfunction. Workshop held at Columbia, MD.

Frankenburg, W. K. 1978. *Denver developmental screening test.* Denver, CO: Ladoca Publishing Foundation.

Furuno, S., K. A. O'Reilly, C. M. Hosaka, T. T. Inatsuka, T. L. Allman, and B. Zeisloft. 1985. *Hawaii early learning profile,* rev. ed. Palo Alto, CA: VORT Corp.

Gardner, H. 1982. *Art, mind, and brain.* New York: Basic Books.

Golbin, A. 1977. Breathing and speech. In *Cerebral palsy and communication: What parents can do,* edited by A. Golbin, 63-74. Washington, DC: George Washington University, Job Development Laboratory.

Gratch, G. 1982. Piaget, the notion of action, and assessing intelligence in handicapped infants. In *Intervention with at-risk and handicapped infants,* edited by D. Bricker, 91-104. Baltimore, MD: University Park Press.

Greenfield, P. M. 1978. Structural parallels between language and action in development. In *Action, gesture and symbol: The emergence of language,* edited by A. Lock, 413-45. New York: Academic Press.

Hanson, M. J., and S. R. Harris. 1986. *Teaching the young child with motor delays.* Austin, TX: Pro-Ed.

High, E. C. 1977. Positioning for speech. In *Cerebral palsy and communication: What parents can do,* edited by A. Golbin, 11-26. Washington, DC: George Washington University, Job Development Laboratory.

Hohmann, M., B. Banet, and D. P. Weikart. 1979. *Young children in action.* Ypsilanti, MI: High/Scope Press.

Holden, R. H. 1972. Prediction of mental retardation in infancy. *Mental Retardation* 10:28-30.

Horowitz, F. 1982. Methods of assessment for high-risk and handicapped infants. In *Finding and educating high-risk and handicapped infants,* edited by C. T. Ramey and P. L. Trohanis, 101-18. Baltimore, MD: University Park Press.

Hupp, S. C., H. Able, and M. Conroy. 1983a. The applicability of stage theory to sensorimotor development of severely retarded children. Paper presented to the Sixteenth Annual Gatlinburg Conference on Research in Mental Retardation and Developmental Disabilities, Gatlinburg, TN.

————. 1983b. Sensorimotor development of severely retarded children and its application to curriculum development in early childhood. Paper presented at the HCEEP/DEC Annual Early Childhood Conference, Washington, DC.

Hutinger, P. L. 1988. Linking screening, identification, and assessment with curriculum. In *Early childhood special education: Birth to three,* edited by J. B. Jordan, J. J. Gallagher, P. L. Hutinger, and M. B. Karnes, 30-66. Reston, VA: Council for Exceptional Children.

Ingram, D. 1978. Sensori-motor intelligence and language development. In *Action, gesture, and symbol: The emergence of language,* edited by A. Lock, 261-90. New York: Academic Press.

Jaeger, L. 1981. *Home program instruction sheets: Infants and young children.* Lexington, KY: Pediatric Publications.

Johnson, L. J. 1988. Program evaluation: The key to quality programming. In *Early childhood special education: Birth to three,* edited by J. B. Jordan, J. J. Gallagher, P. L. Hutinger, and M. B. Karnes, 184-212. Reston, VA: Council for Exceptional Children.

Kahn, J. V. 1983. Sensorimotor period and adaptive behavior development of severely and profoundly mentally retarded children. *American Journal of Mental Deficiency* 88:69-75.

Kaye, K. 1977. Toward the origin of dialogue. In *Studies in mother-infant interaction,* edited by H. R. Schaffer, 89-117. New York: Academic Press.

Kent-Udolf, L. 1984. Programming Language. In *Language handicaps in children,* edited by W. H. Perkins, 15-25. New York: Thieme-Stratton Inc.

Knobloch, H., and B. Pasamanick, eds. 1974. *Gesell and Armatruda's developmental diagnosis: The evaluation and management of normal and abnormal neuropsychologic development in infancy and early childhood,* 3d ed. Hagerstown, MD: Harper and Row.

Kong, E. 1966. The very early treatment of cerebral palsy. *Developmental Medicine and Child Neurology* 8:198-202.

Korner, A., J. Pawl, V. Seitz, and J. Shonkoff. 1985. Program evaluation. Panel presentation at the Fourth Biennial National Training Institute of the National Center for Clinical Infant Programs, Washington, DC.

Lewis, M., and J. Brooks-Gunn. 1979. *Social cognition and the acquisition of self.* New York: Plenum Press.

MacDonald, J., and Y. Gillette. 1985. Taking turns: Teaching communication to your child. *Exceptional Parent* September:49-52.

Mahoney, G. 1982. Early communicative behaviors in handicapped infants. Workshop held at Annapolis, MD.

Mahoney, G., and A. Powell. 1984. *Transactional intervention program: Preliminary teacher's guide.* Ann Arbor, MI: University of Michigan School of Education.

————. 1986. *Transactional intervention program: Teacher's guide.* Farmington, CT: Pediatric Research and Training Center.

McCall, R. B., P. S. Hogarty, and N. Hurlburt. 1972. Transitions in infant sensorimotor development and the prediction of childhood IQ. *American Psychologist* 27:728-48.

McDonough, S. C. 1984. Concept formation in motorically impaired infants. Paper presented at the Fourth Meeting of the International Conference for Infant Studies, New York.

Montgomery, P., and E. Richter. *Sensorimotor integration for developmentally disabled children: A handbook.* Los Angeles: Western Psychological Services.

Morehead, D. M., and A. Morehead. 1974. From signal to sign: A Piagetian view of thought and language during the first two years. In *Language perspectives: Acquisition, retardation, and intervention,* edited by R. L. Schiefelbusch and L. L. Lloyd, 153-90. Baltimore, MD: University Park Press.

Morris, S. E. 1977. *Program guidelines for children with feeding problems.* Edison, NJ: Childcraft Education Corp.

————. 1981. Communication/interaction development at mealtimes for the multiply handicapped child: Implications for the use of augmentative communication systems. *Language, Speech, and Hearing Services in Schools* XII:216-32.

————. 1985. Music for the development of communication and movement. Workshop held at Bethesda, MD.

————. 1987. Communication/interaction at mealtimes: The gateway to augmentative communication. Workshop held at Philadelphia, PA.

————. September 29, 1989. Personal communication.

Mulliken, R. K., and J. J. Buckley. 1983. *Assessment of multihandicapped and developmentally disabled children.* Austin, TX: Pro-Ed, Inc.

National Early Childhood Technical Assistance System (NEC*TAS) and Association for the Care of Children's Health (ACCH). *Guidelines and recommended practices for the individualized family service plan.* Washington, DC: Association for the Care of Children's Health.

Piaget, J. 1952. *The origins of intelligence in children.* New York: International Universities Press.

———. 1954. *The construction of reality in the child.* New York: Ballantine Books.

———. 1962. *Play, dreams, and imitation in childhood.* New York: W. W. Norton and Company.

Robinson, C. C. 1982. *Questions regarding the effects of neuromotor problems on sensorimotor development.* Baltimore, MD: University Park Press.

Robinson, C. C., and J. H. Robinson. 1978. Sensorimotor functions and cognitive development. In *Systemative instruction of the moderately and severely handicapped,* edited by M. E. Snell, 102-53. Columbus, OH: Charles E. Merrill.

Rossetti, L. 1986. *High-risk infants: Identification, assessment, and intervention.* Boston: College-Hill.

Sandall, S. N.d. *Turn taking: Strategies for enhancing adult-child interaction.*

Saudek, C. A. E. 1985. The hip. In *Orthopedic and sports physical therapy,* Vol. 2, edited by J. A. Gould III, and G. J. Davies. St. Louis, MO: C. V. Mosby Co.

Scardina, V. 1986. Sensory integration: Its relationship to development and performance. Workshop sponsored by the Sensory Integration Symposium, Towson, MD.

Sinclair, H. 1971. Sensorimotor action patterns as a condition for the acquisition of syntax. In *Language acquisition: Models and methods,* edited by E. Ingram and R. Huxley, 121-30. New York: Academic Press.

Trevarthen, C., and P. Hubley. 1978. Secondary intersubjectivity: Confidence, confiding and acts of meaning in the first year. In *Action, gesture, and symbol: The emergence of language,* edited by A. Lock, 181-229. New York: Academic Press.

United Cerebral Palsy Association's Task Force on Staff Development. 1976. *Staff development handbook: A resource for the transdisciplinary process.* New York: United Cerebral Palsy Associations, Inc.

Uzgiris, I. C. 1976. Organization of sensorimotor intelligence. In *Origins of intelligence: Infancy and early childhood,* edited by M. Lewis, 123-63. New York: Plenum Press.

Uzgiris, I. C., and J. M. V. Hunt. 1975. *Assessment in infancy.* Urbana, IL: University of Illinois Press.

Vanderheiden, G. C., and K. Grilley. 1975. *Nonvocal communication techniques and aids for the severely handicapped.* Baltimore, MD: University Park Press.

White, O., E. Edgar, N. Haring, J. A. Affleck, and M. Bendersky. 1981. *Uniform performance assessment system.* Columbus, OH: Charles E. Merrill.

Wilbarger, P. September 30, 1989. Personal communication.

———. 1989. *Sensory defensiveness: A parent's guide.* Alameda, CA: Anyk Press.

Wilbarger, P., and C. B. Royeen. 1987. Tactile defensiveness: Theory, research, and treatment of sensory affective disorders. Workshop sponsored by the Sensory Integration Special Interest Group of the District of Columbia Occupational Therapy Association, Bethesda, MD.

Wilbarger, P., and J. Wilbarger. 1988. One year later: An update for therapists who attended the November 1987 conference on tactile defensiveness. Seminar held at Rockville, MD.

Wilson, J. M. N.d. *Helpful hints for feeding children with oral-motor dysfunction.*

Wood, K. 1989. Technology assisted curricula. Workshop held at Washington, DC.

Woodruff, G., and M. J. McGonigel. 1988. Early intervention team approaches: The trandisciplinary model. In *Early childhood special education: Birth to three,* edited by J. B. Jordan, J. J. Gallagher, P. L. Hutinger, and M. B. Karnes, 164-81. Reston, VA: Council for Exceptional Children.

Wright, C., and M. Nomura. 1985. *From toys to computers: Access for the physically disabled child.* San Jose, CA: Christine Wright.

Zachry, W. 1979. The relation of language development to sensorimotor level in second-year infants. *Child Development.* N.p.

Zelazo, P. R. 1982. Alternative assessment procedures for handicapped infants and toddlers: Theoretical and practical issues. In *Intervention with at-risk and handicapped infants: From research to application,* edited by D. D. Bricker, 107-28. Baltimore, MD: University Park Press.